T-Shirt Treas

Creating Heirloom Hooked Rugs from the Humble T-Shirt

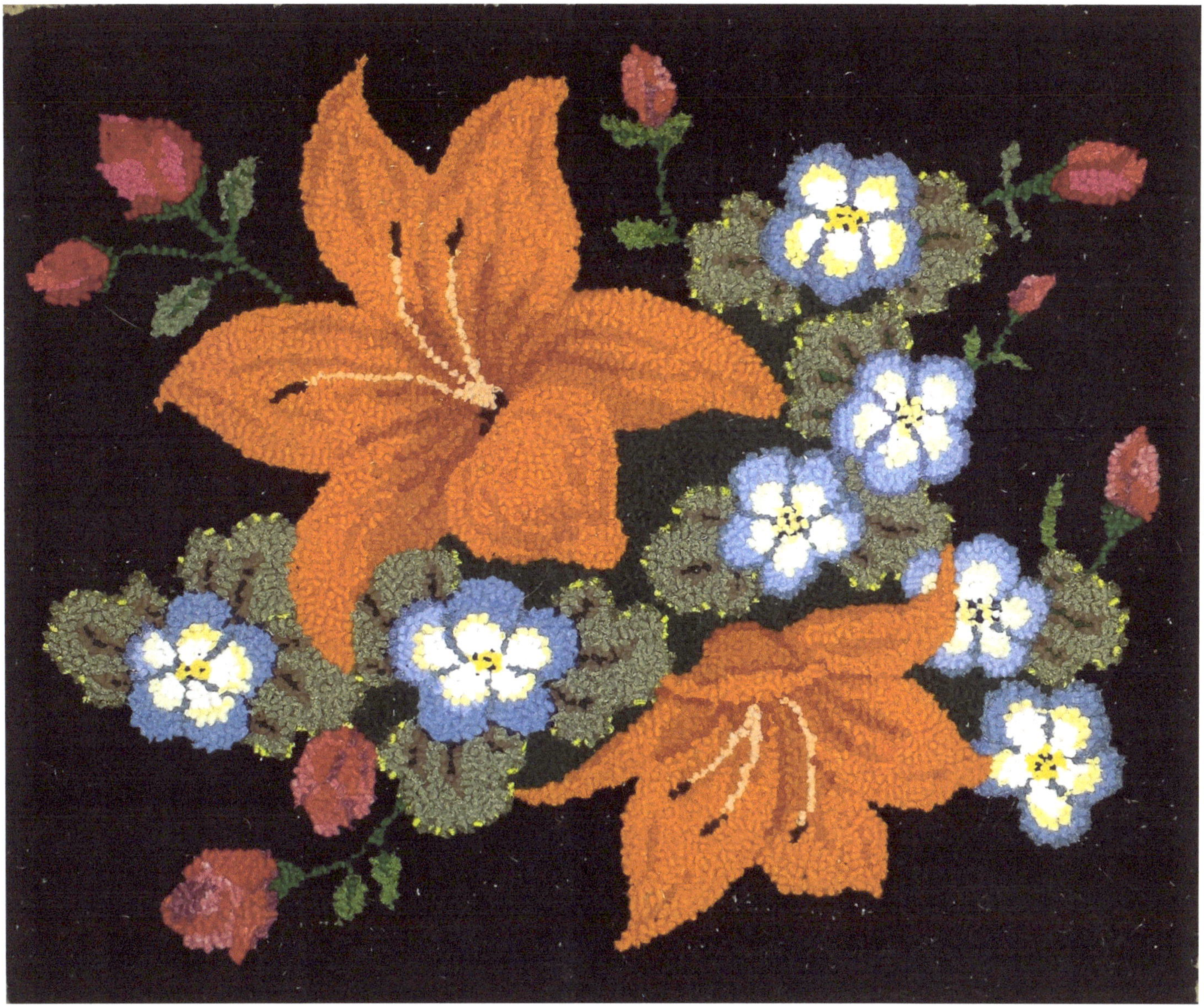

Ma Jolie Fleur 13"x16" Designed and hooked with T-shirts by Judy Taylor
You can find the pattern and instructions for hooking this piece in the Sept/Oct 2019 issue of Rug Hooking Magazine

By Judy Taylor

With thanks to these generous contributors. I hope their work inspires you as much as it did me!

Mary Anne Wise
Cheryl Conway-Daly
Jody Slocum
Karen Brock
Cheryl Walsh Bellville
Joe Coca
Multicolores
Thrums Books
Cultural Cloth
Honey Bee Hive Designs
Paula Laverty
McGill-Queen's U. Press
Graham Leslie McCallum
Connie Hughes

Renate Kirkpatrick
Catherine Kelly
Donna Culp
Gail Nichols
Jane Sittnick
Jo Franco
Nancy Huntington
Judi Tompkins
Laura Salamy
Linda DeVillers
Stephanie Krasney
Wanda Kerr
Miriam Miller
Karla Gerard

María Estela Az Tamayac
Hilda Raquel García Tzunun
Irma Raquel Churunel
Carmen Maldonado
Micaela Churunel Ajú
Rosmery Elizabeth Pacheco
Rosario Gutiérrez Pacheco
Ramona Tzunun
Nicolasa Pacay Baran
Yolanda Sebastiana Calgua Morales
Yolanda Churunel Ajú
Zoila Calgua Morales
María Sacalxot
Aura Perez Can

Judy Taylor has been hooking rugs and teaching rug hooking since 1992. Her rugs have been featured in *Rug Hooking Magazine, ATHA, SpinOff Magazine* and the *Black Sheep Newsletter*. Her rug hooking books, *Joy of Hooking (With Yarn!)*, and *Rug Hooker's Guide to the YARNIVERSE!* both won the eLit Book Awards. Her rug hooking DVD won the Gold Award for Excellence at the ITVA Emerald City Awards (on Youtube, search for "hooking rugs with yarn"). This very book which you hold in your hands also won the eLit Book Awards, and was a finalist in the Foreword Indies Book Awards. Judy raises Jacob sheep, Angora goats and cashmere goats on their farm in the Upper Green River Valley in Washington State. Judy is amazed at the unlimited creativity that rug hooking provides, from hooking with yarn, wool fabric strips and lately, T-shirt strips. She is excited to share this new passion with her readers. It has been a fun journey writing this book, and she couldn't have done it without the support, creativity and patience of all the folks listed above.

For more information, check out her website (https://www.littlehouse-rugs.com), her monthly blog, Hooking With Yarn (judytaylor2013.word-pres,com) and join the online rug hooking community, Rug Hooking Daily (rughookingdaily.ning.com).

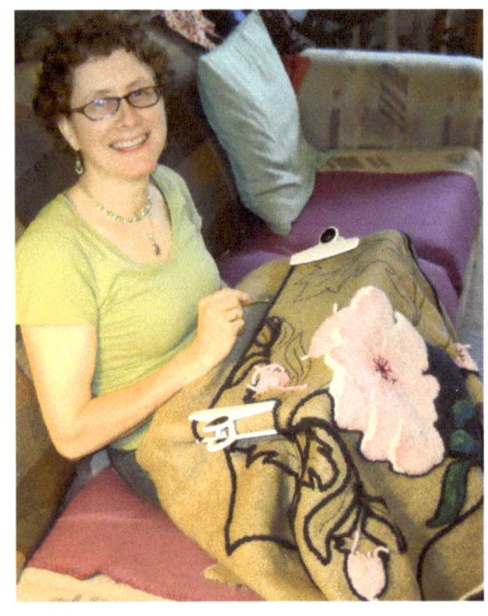

Watch "Rug Hooking With T-Shirts" on YouTube!
https://www.youtube.com/watch?v=ExEbox_Hpns

Published by Little House Rugs
PO Box 2003
Auburn, WA 98071

ISBN: 978-0-9976712-0-9
https://www.littlehouserugs.com
judytaylor2013.wordpress.com
rughookingdaily.ning.com

Cover art designed by Graham Leslie McCallum from *4000 Flower and Plant Motifs Sourcebook*, Batsford Press, London, and Sterling Publishing Company. Hooked by Judy Taylor.

Table of Contents

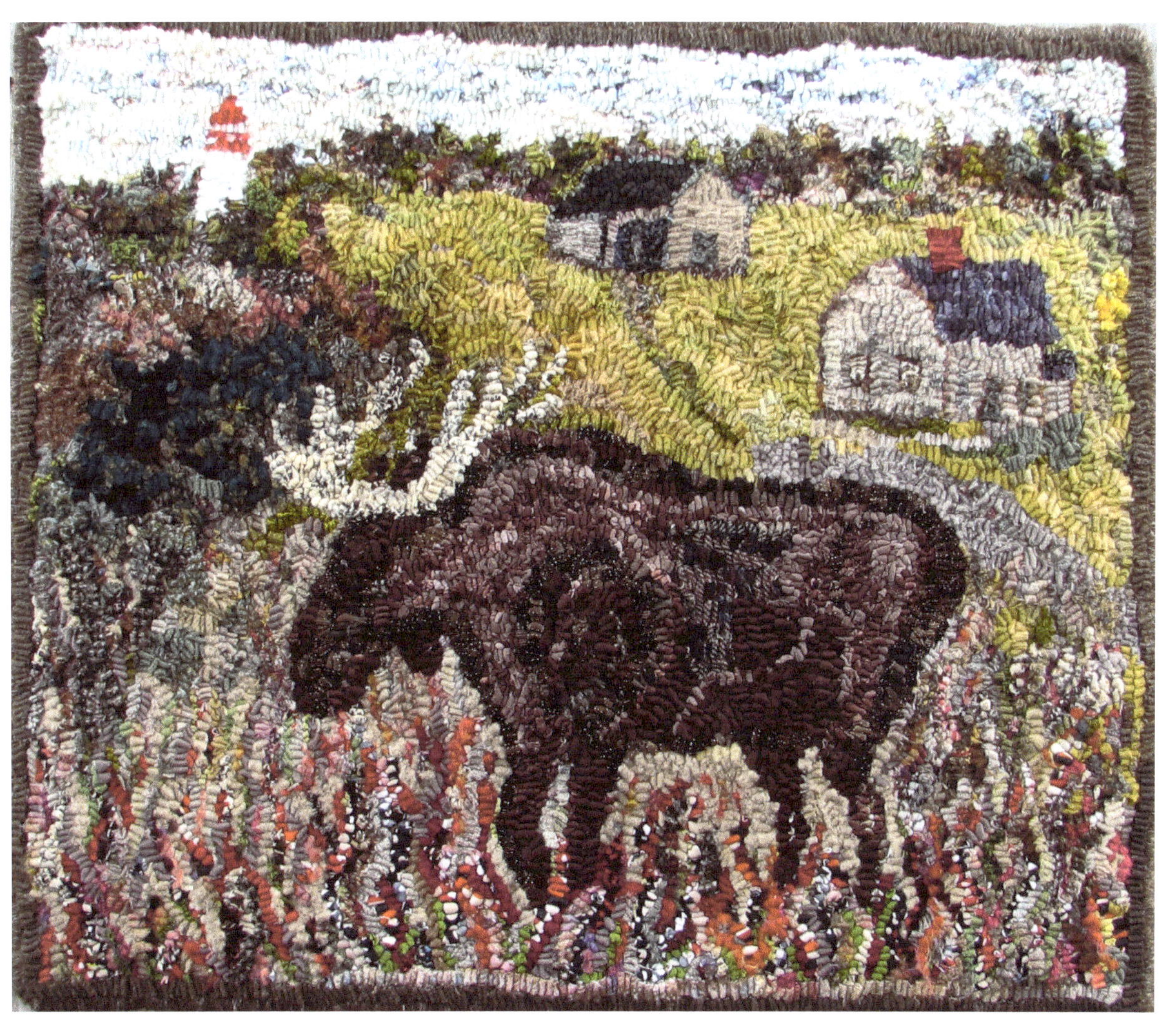

Miscou Moose, 20"x17" Designed and hooked by Jane Sittnick, hooked using a variety of wool, synthetics knits, nylons, woven silk, velvet and yarns. Photo by Jane Sittnick.

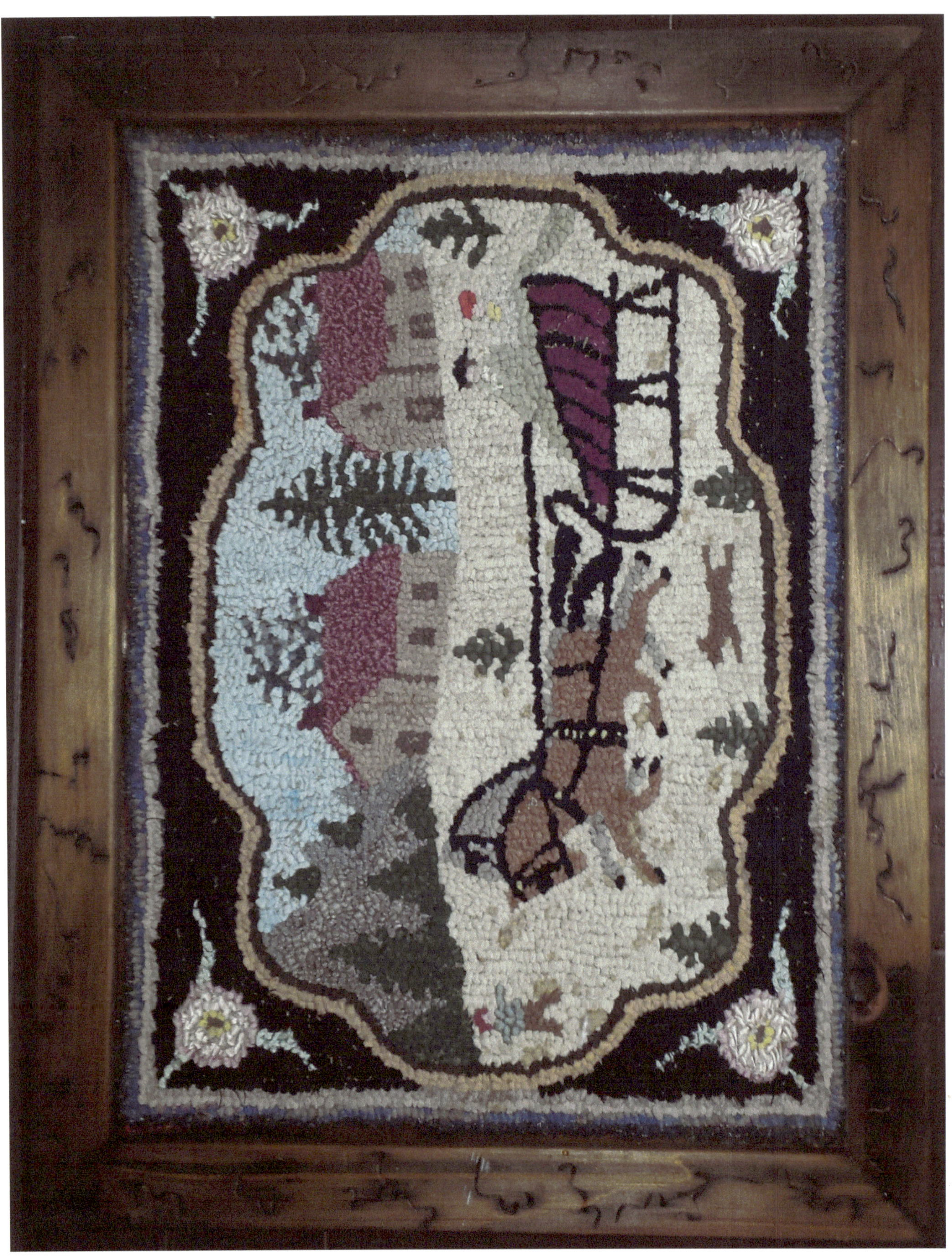

Early 20th century rug hooked with wool stockings, 22.75"x16.75" (not including the frame).

Introduction

Rug hooking has been around for centuries. Of course, it has changed over the years, due to fashion and the availability of materials, but the creativity and versatility of the craft has kept it strong through many generations. It excels as a craft that is unique to its creator; no two people will hook a rug in the same way. It's a blank canvas, packed with possibility, just waiting to be filled with design and color to suit that individual rug hooker.

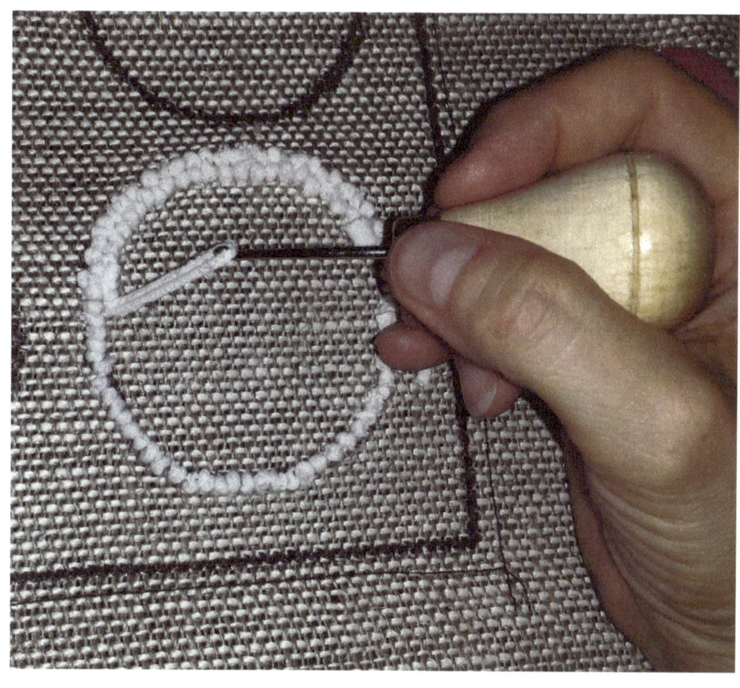

But beyond the creative side, rug hooking has always been about what's practical. Hook with *what you've got* to create useful, durable rugs for the home. And do it with a simple, hand-held tool. Handcrafts may come and go; many crafts that our elders enjoyed like *naalbinding* and bobbin lace are all but lost to us today, but rug hooking has survived and thrived because at its core, it's all about practicality.

Nobody really knows where rug hooking got started. Art historian William Winthrop Kent (*The Hooked Rug*, 1930) figured that European weavers in the 18th century probably came up with the idea, wanting to find something they could do with the leftover warp threads cut off the loom after the cloth was woven. In those days, woolen cloth was far too valuable to cut up into tiny strips for rug hooking (like we do today), but once the pattern pieces were cut out, you can bet those fabric remnants didn't go to waste. They were hooked right alongside the yarn. They hooked with what they had, to make useful, beautiful items for the home.

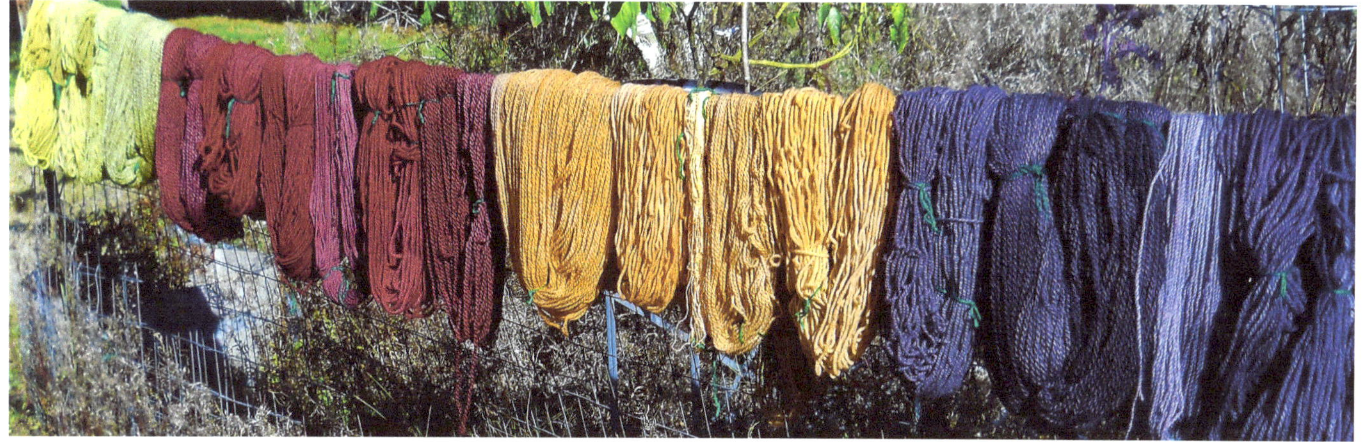

Rug hooking got a big boost when European migrants began to settle in North America. When you have to carry your worldly belongings on a ship or a wagon, space is a premium. People needed crafts that were portable and could be made with common materials. A hand-held hook won out over a large and bulky loom for those long journeys. There were whole homes to be built and furnished from scratch, and if you couldn't make it yourself, you went without.

I like to think that those pioneers were a pretty creative bunch. They were problem-solvers. They had big ideas, and they poured that sense of innovation into the rugs they hooked.

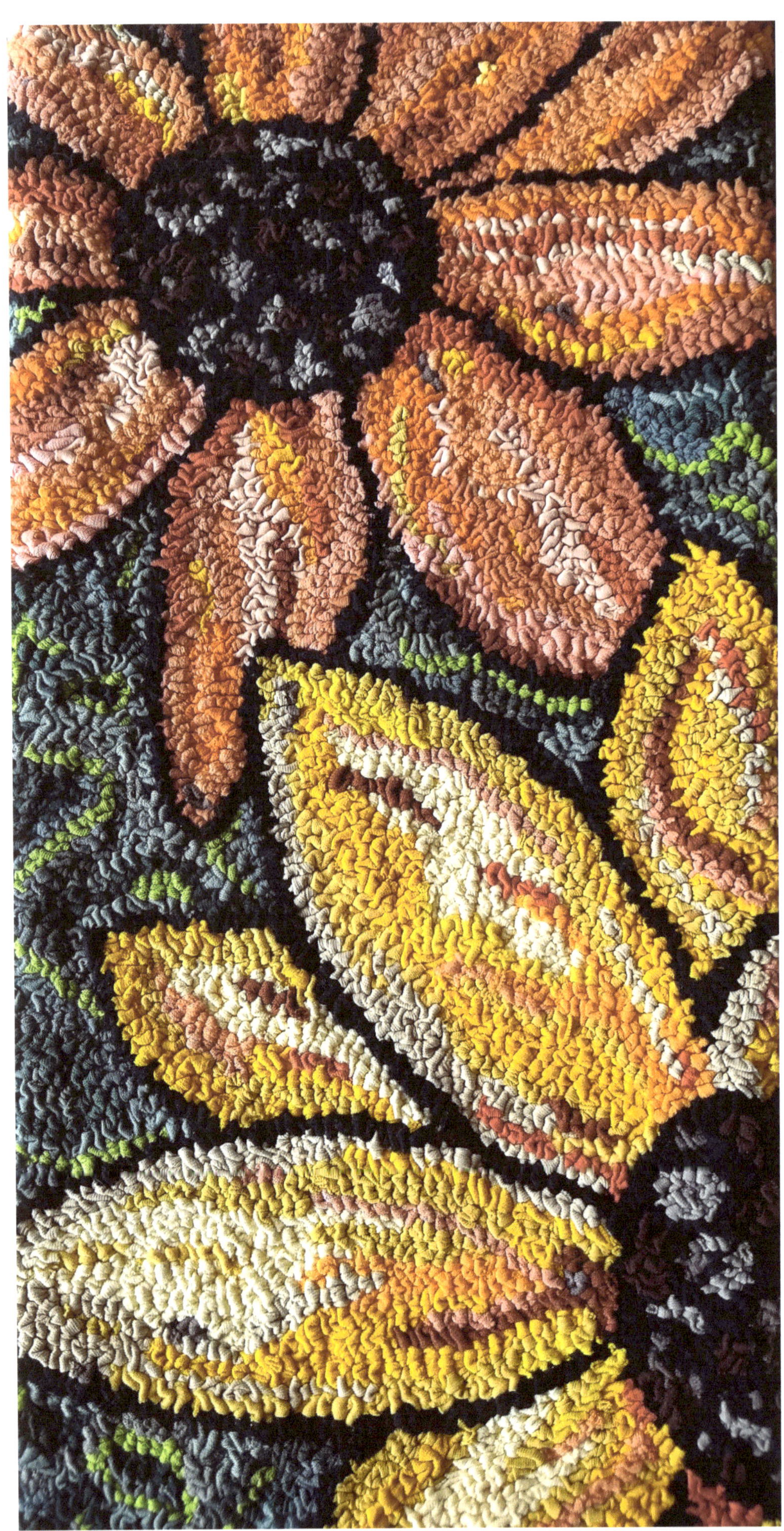

Late Summer Sunflowers, 22"x10"
Designed and hooked with T-shirts by Laura Salamy.

Photo by Laura Salamy

The Future of T-Shirt Rugs

How many T-shirts do you figure are produced worldwide these days? 100 million? 500 million? How about two billion? Every. Single. Year. My friends, we live in a T-shirt glut.

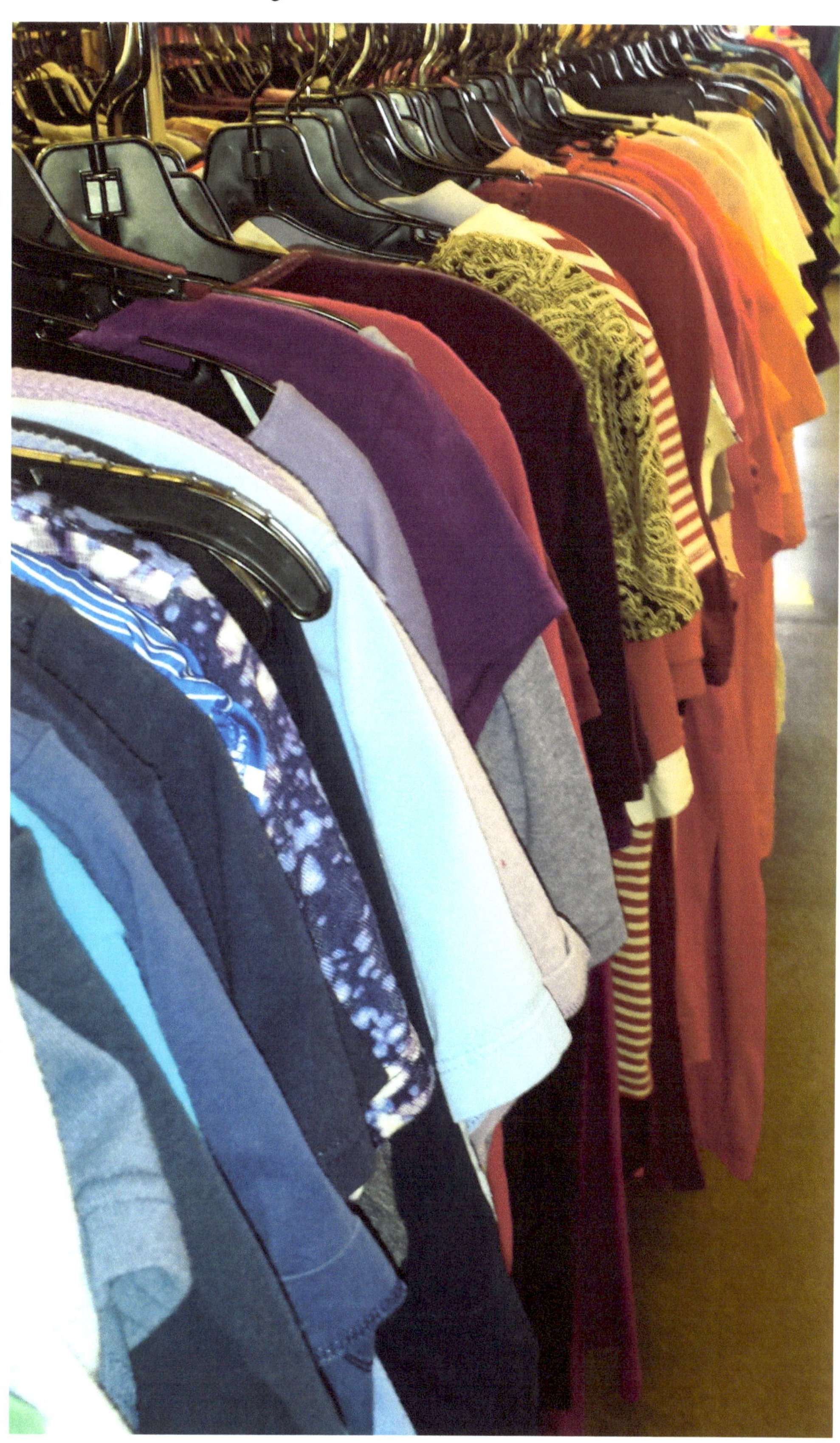

Makes you wonder what happens to all of those trendy togs? Admit it, there's a drawer in your very own bedroom, stuffed full of them. (And if there are other folks living in your house, a similar drawerful in each room!) Kids outgrow a mountain of them in their relentless march to adulthood. Pretty much every organization we associate with provides us with a T-shirt, from political campaigns to product promotion to sports teams to runs for breast cancer. Not to mention fashion garb, in every color of the rainbow and tie-dyed besides. Most of those perfectly good cotton tops end up in thrift stores or are exported to other countries.

When I look down at the aisles and aisles of T-shirts in my local thrift store, I don't see cast off fashions, I see COLOR. Like the world's biggest box of crayons, right in front of me. All I have to decide is which color to try first.

Remember when you were a kid, and you opened a brand-new box of crayons? There was just nothing like the thrill of creativity that you got from those waxy wands. There were no rules. No one to tell you how to color, *you just knew.* Like Harold and his wondrous purple crayon, you and your imagination were unstoppable.

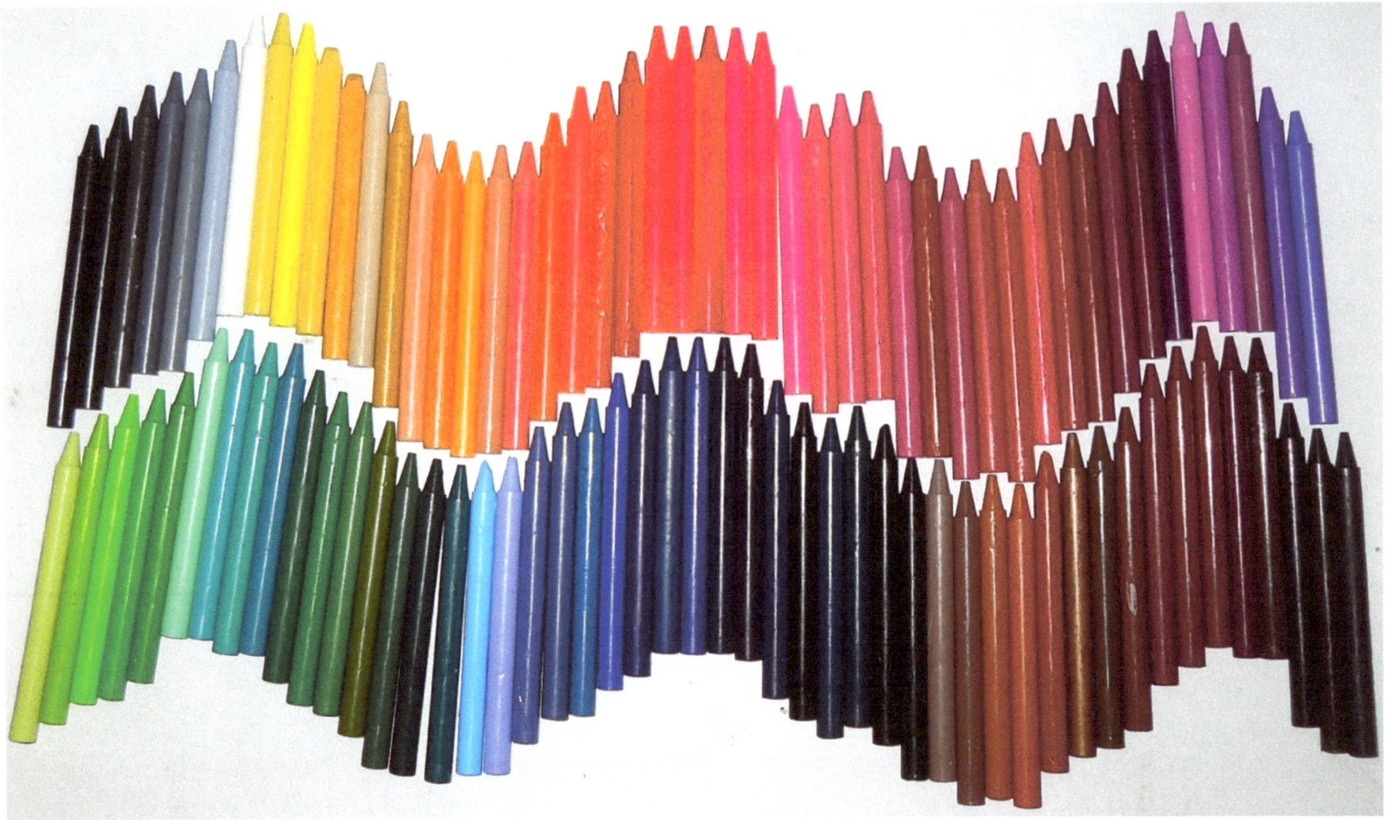

Now imagine I put in your hands a box of oil paints and a paintbrush. Would you dive in with abandon in quite the same way? Possibly not. When we grow up, we tend to fill our heads up with "no's." My goal with this book is to unlock your creativity, to get you to absolutely wallow in color, just like you did when you were a kid.

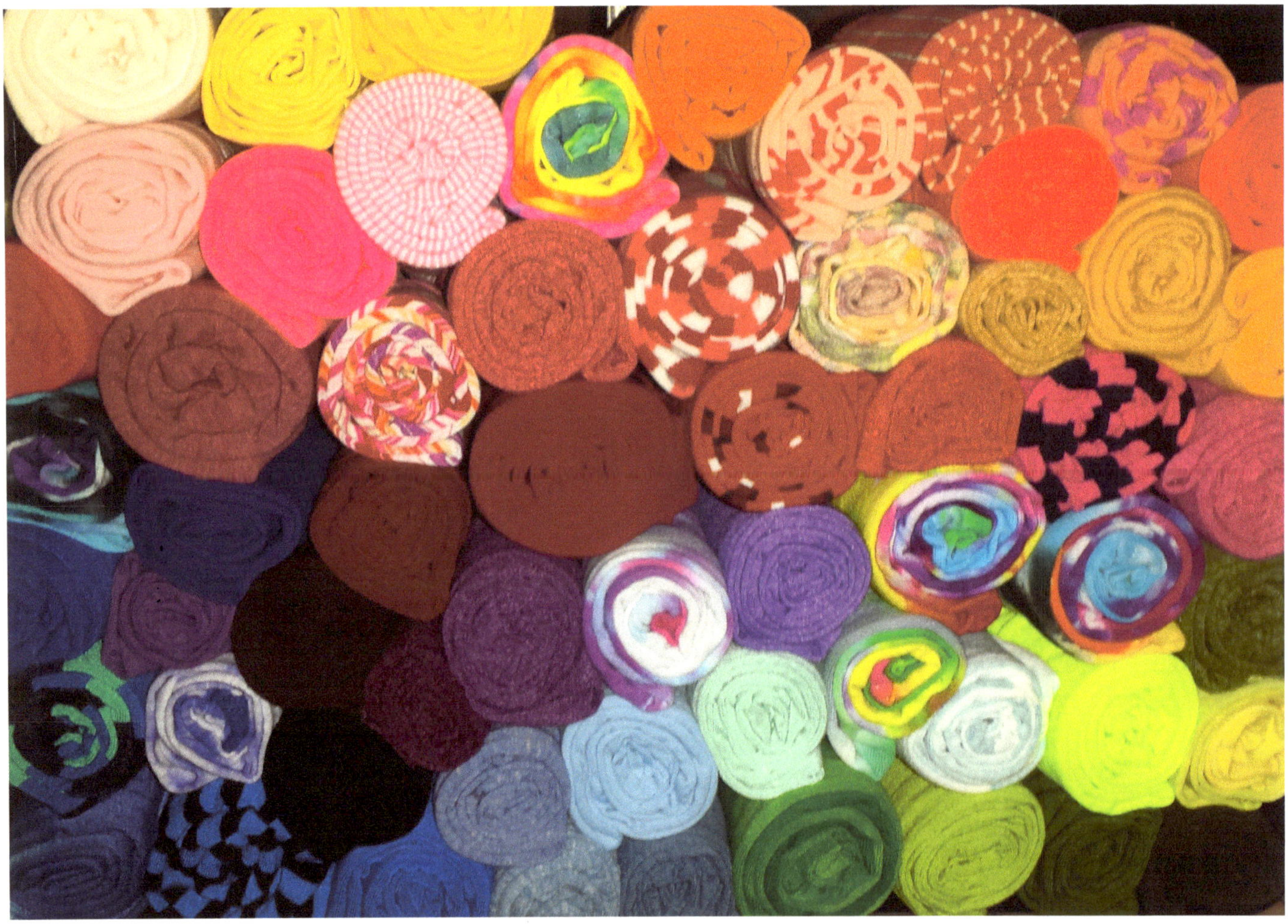

Why hook with T-shirts? Not only do T-shirts provide you with a nearly infinite color palette, that can trigger your imagination toward exciting adventures in new projects; they're also cheap, especially compared to yarn and wool fabric. And there's the fun of up-cycling, making something totally unique out of something totally ordinary. They already come in a kalidescope of gorgeous colors, so you don't even have to dye them.

T-shirt rugs are surprisingly tough and durable, and more importantly, they're machine washable (on gentle cycle with cold water, air dry). Rugs made with yarn or wool fabric have to be hand-washed, which can be a project, but the convenience of throwing a well-loved rug in the wash is hard to beat.

Hooking with T-shirts does present some challenges, though. If you think about it, a T-shirt is a relatively small amount of fabric. You'll need one extra-large T-shirt (5-6 oz) to hook a square foot of rug, so that takes some strategizing to work around the limited fabric available. In the Counting Sheep rug (right), I used different T-shirts to hook the background.

However, I got around that challenge when I realized that by hooking with slightly different shades of T-shirts, I could achieve a variegated effect. This made it possible for me to hook any size background, but also gave me that variegated, uneven effect I love when hooking with yarn. The "Demelza" rug on page 75 and *Ma Jolie Fleur* on page 1 show the effect of combining shades.

The easiest designs to start with are what I call "jar-of-jellybeans," or "hit-or-miss." These designs don't rely on one color, so you don't have to worry about running out, and if the rug ever has to be repaired, it's easy to substitute new colors.

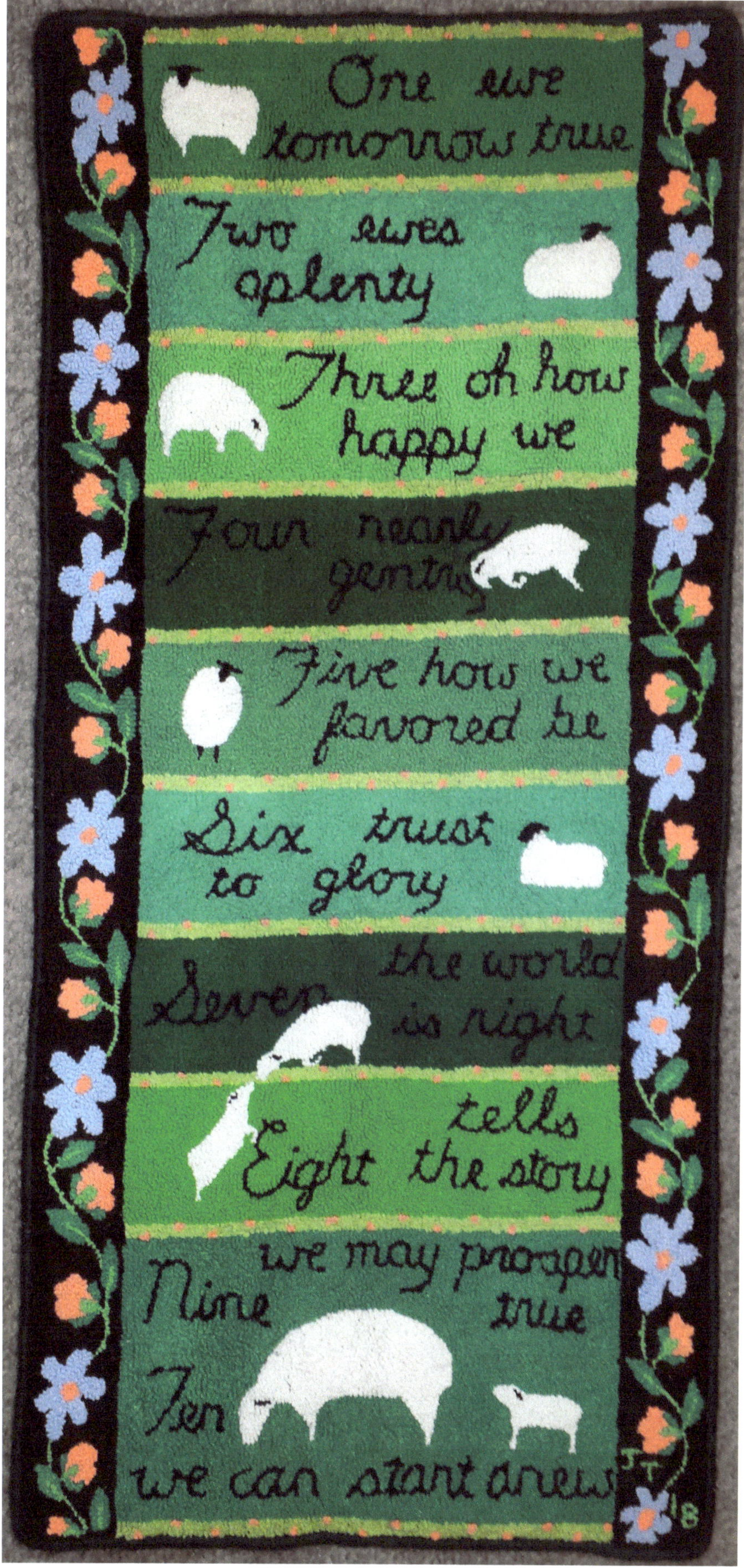

Counting Sheep, 17.5"x40"
Designed and hooked with T-shirts by Judy Taylor.

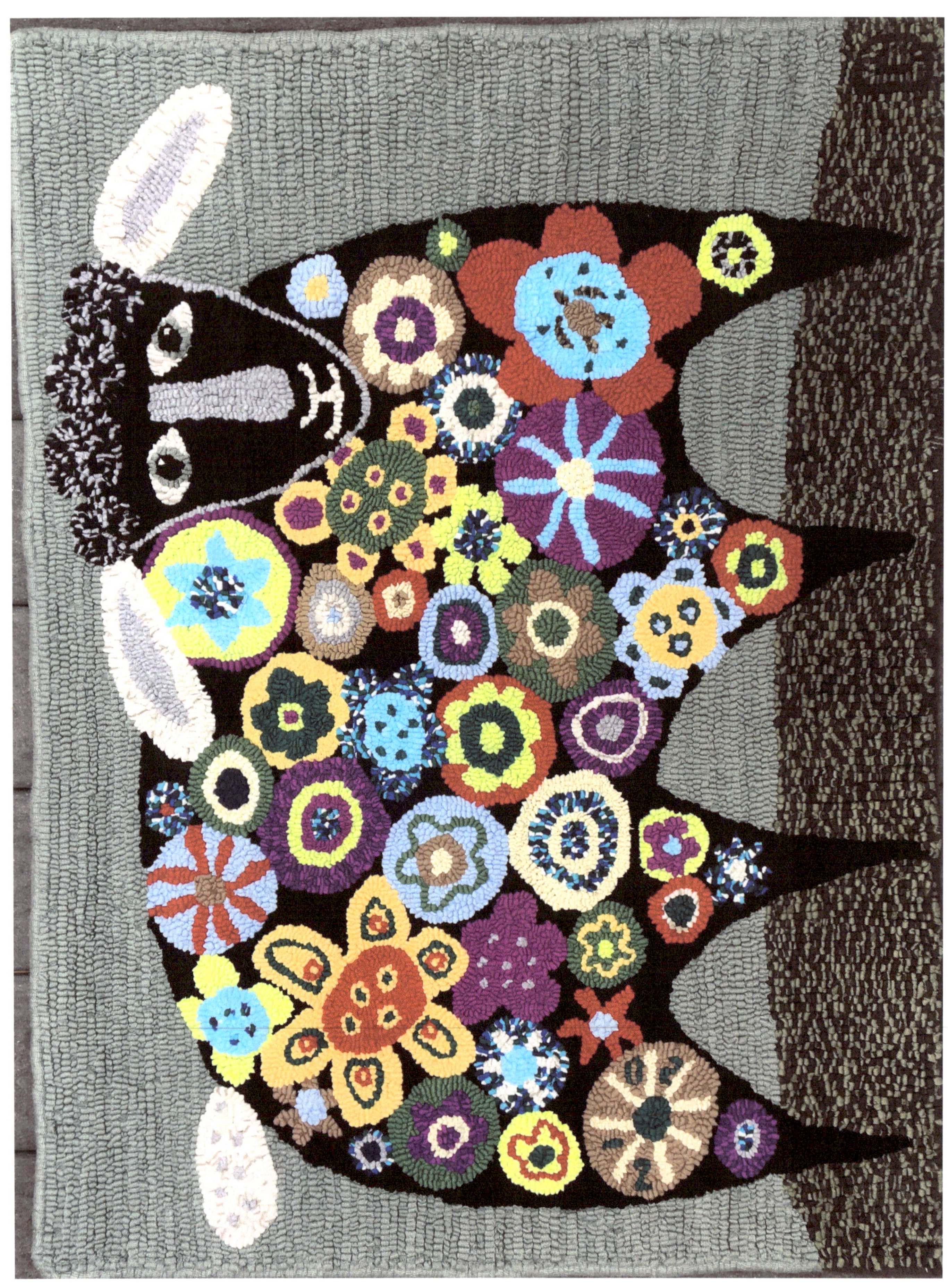

Psychedelic Sally, 37"x28" Design by Karla Gerard, hooked with T-shirts and cotton strips by Donna Culp. Photo by Donna Culp.

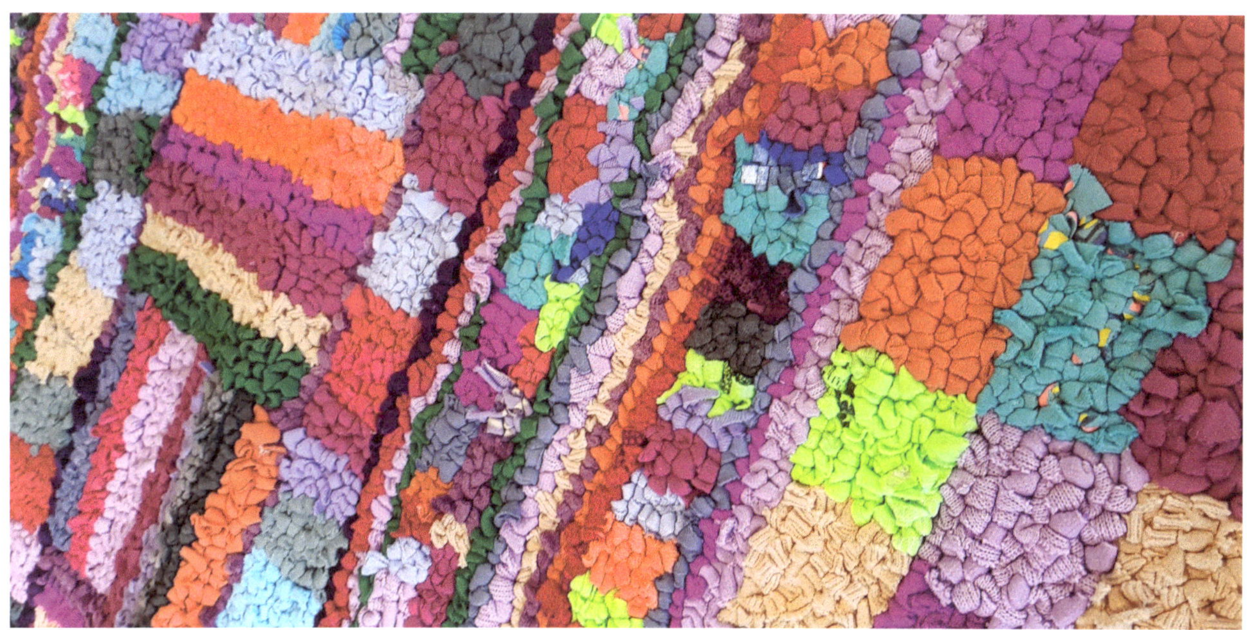

Close-up of a hit-or-miss rug hooked with T-shirts by Beth Cavendish. Photo by Beth Cavendish.

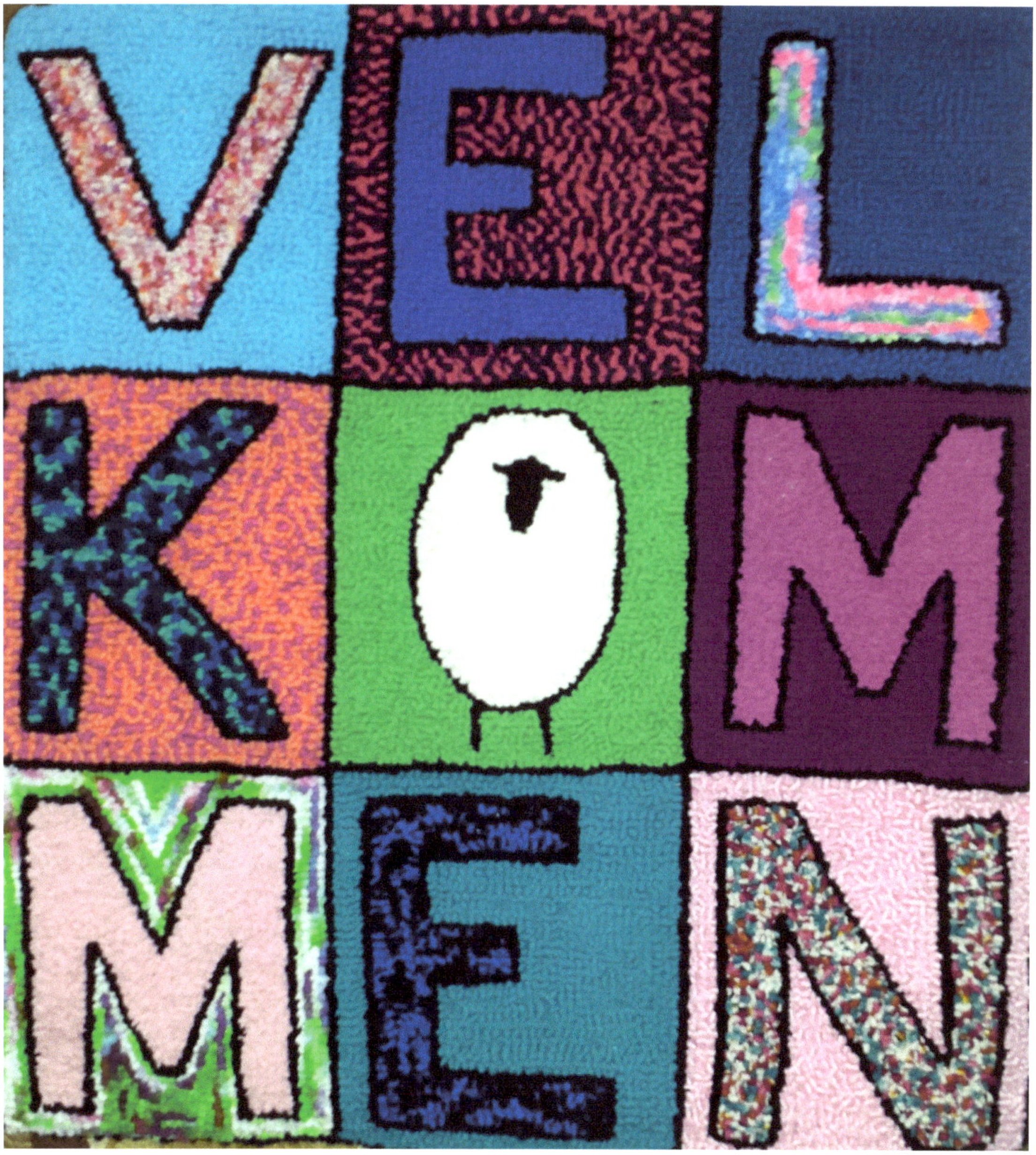

Velkommen, 16.5”x16.5”
Designed and hooked with T-shirts by Judy Taylor.

This is a great design that requires only a small amount of color for each square. You’ll find the template to make this mat, and many others, starting on page 25.

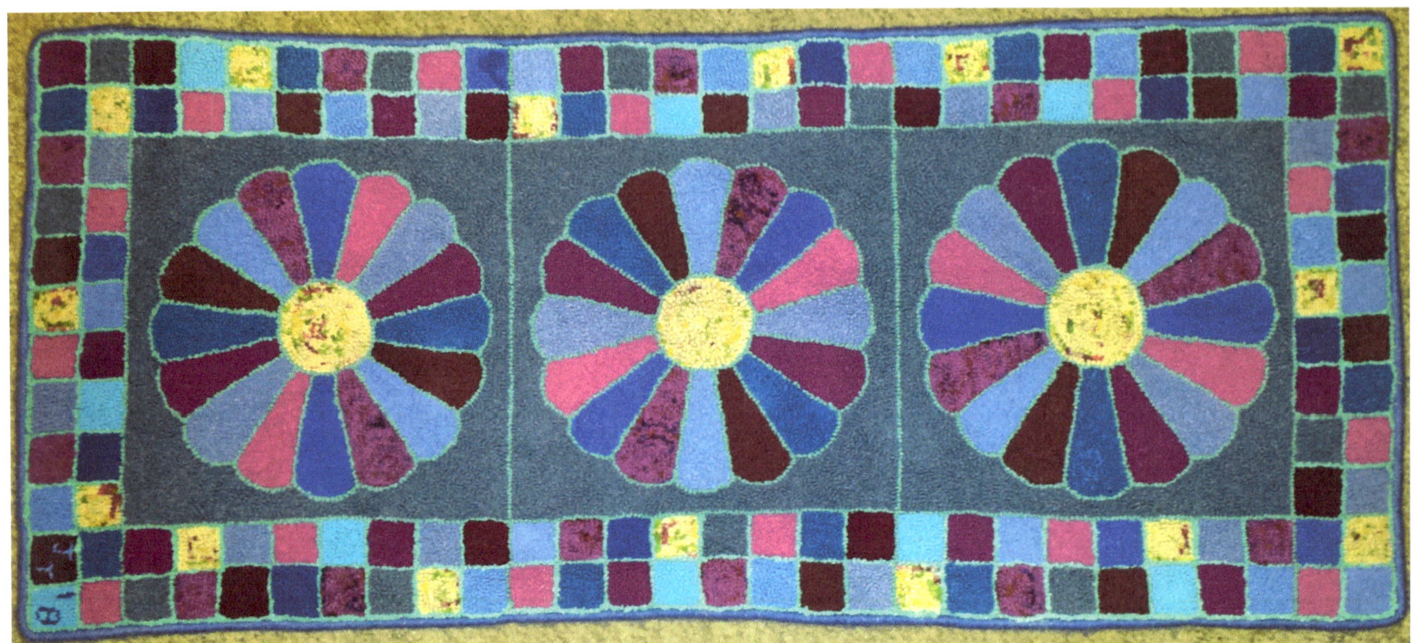

Dresden Plate, 19.5"x44"
Designed and hooked with T-shirts by Judy Taylor.
I call this the "Martha Stewart" approach; choose a pallete of colors that go together or to match your decor. Template on page 44.

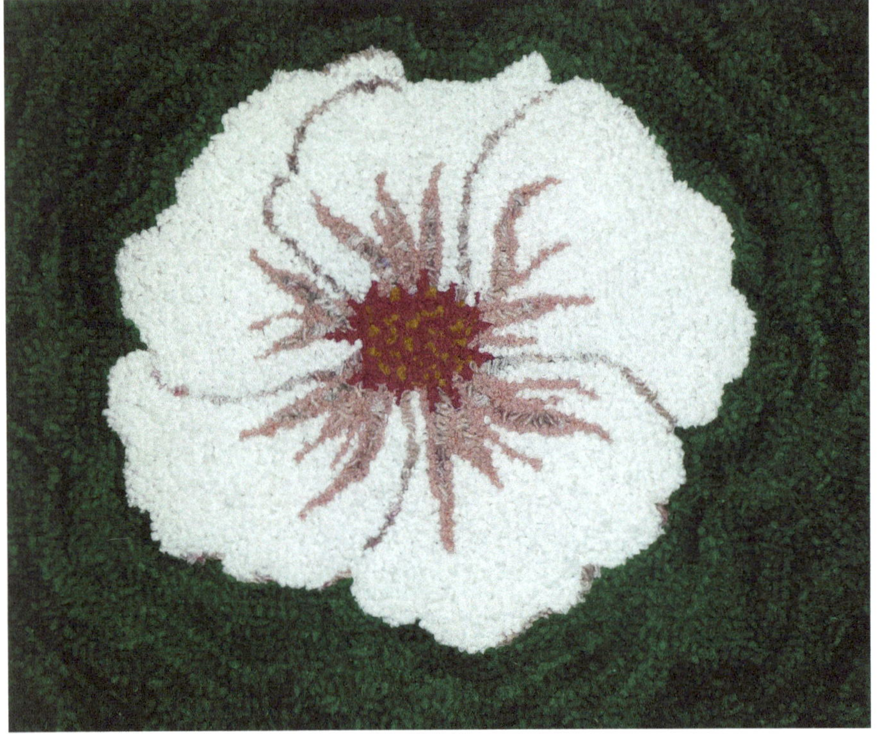

Peony, 9.5"x11.5" Designed and hooked with T-shirts by Judy Taylor.
Try adding shading to your T-shirt rugs. Template on page 47.

When you're shopping for T-shirts, don't forget to check out dresses and skirts that are made with T-shirt material. Sometimes you can even find sheets made with T-shirt material, so there you'll get yards of color to work with.

Okay, you could also just go to a fabric store and buy T-shirt fabric by the yard, but come on, isn't that cheating? Maybe, but if you want to have a one-color large background area, and you absolutely, definitely don't want to worry about running out, go ahead and buy your fabric by the yard, I'll never judge.

In this book, you'll learn everything you need to know to hook with T-shirts; how to prepare your strips, which backing to choose, how to hook with step-by-step instructions and how to hem your finished rugs. You'll find a whole bunch of templates you can use to create projects of any size. Then you can get insprired browsing the Gallery to see what other hookers are doing with T-shirts. You'll even find out how to make your own spiffy rug hooking frame. All you have to do is collect the T-shirts in the colors you prefer.

Remember, you can always change your mind on color. Unlike with crayons, you can "erase" and rehook if the colors aren't working for you. Sometimes you just don't know how the colors will work together until you try.

So without further ado, let's start coloring!

Choose Your Backing

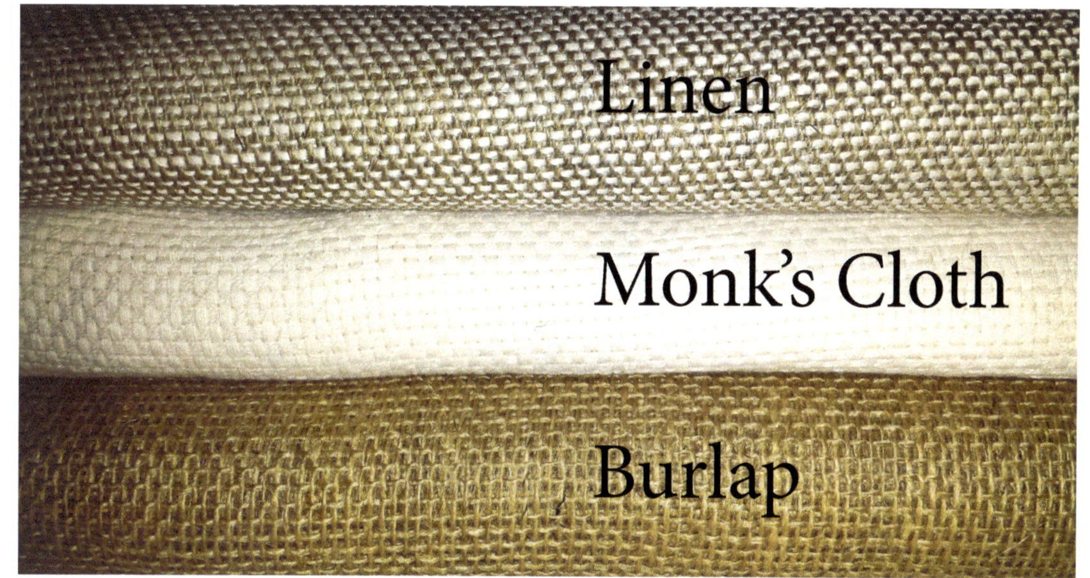

These are the three main types of fabric that we use in rug hooking. Which backing you choose depends on the type of project.

Burlap is good for small projects that won't need to be washed, like wall-hangings or other decorations. It is made from the jute plant, which is wonderfully biodegradable (if you've ever bought a large shrub, you might have noticed the root ball was wrapped in burlap, which goes right into the ground, to disintigrate into the soil). It is not suitable for floor rugs for this reason. However, at around $4.00/yd, burlap is great for practice. When you're ready to design a rug for the floor, you'll want linen or monk's cloth.

Monk's cloth is pretty easy to find in most fabric stores, so that's handy, but if you're willling to search online, you can find "rug warp" which is tougher than monk's cloth. Monk's cloth and rug warp are made from cotton, which is a brittle fiber when exposed to wear and tear. I'm sure you've noticed how you wear holes in your jeans after a certain point (even without climbing trees!). That's the nature of cotton. The fibers tend to break over time. I repair old rugs, and I often come across rug damage when the cotton backing has deteriorated, unravelling the hooked part, so that can be a concern if the rug is intended for a high traffic area. Monk's cloth will cost you about $15.00/yd, while rug warp will run around $27.00/yd.

I prefer linen for floor rugs, because it's not only washable, it's practically indestructible! When the flax plant is prepared for spinning, it is soaked in water, and everything that doesn't rot is what is spun into linen. It costs $36.00/yd. Before you balk at the price, remember that by far, the greatest value that goes into a hooked rug (much more than the backing material plus the T-shirts, yarn or fabric strips) is your *time*. You will spend exactly the same amount of time hooking the rug, whichever backing you choose, but linen gives you far more lasting value.

How long do you want that rug to last? The backing material is what holds the rug together. It has to withstand wear and tear. There's a big difference in durability between burlap, cotton or linen. Burlap rugs might survive ten years on the floor, cotton 25-50 years, but a rug made with linen will last 100 years or more!

Breaking it down by price per square foot is perhaps a better way to compare the types of backing fabric. Burlap costs about 33 cents per square foot, monk's cloth goes for a little more than $1.00/sq. ft., rug warp around $2.00/sq. ft., and linen will run you $2.75/sq. ft. My rugs sell for $100.00 per square foot, so you can see that my labor is by far the greatest investment I put in the rug. If someone buys a rug from me that is hooked on linen, it's the very best guarantee I can give them that the rug will last many generations. That's worth an extra 75 cents in my book.

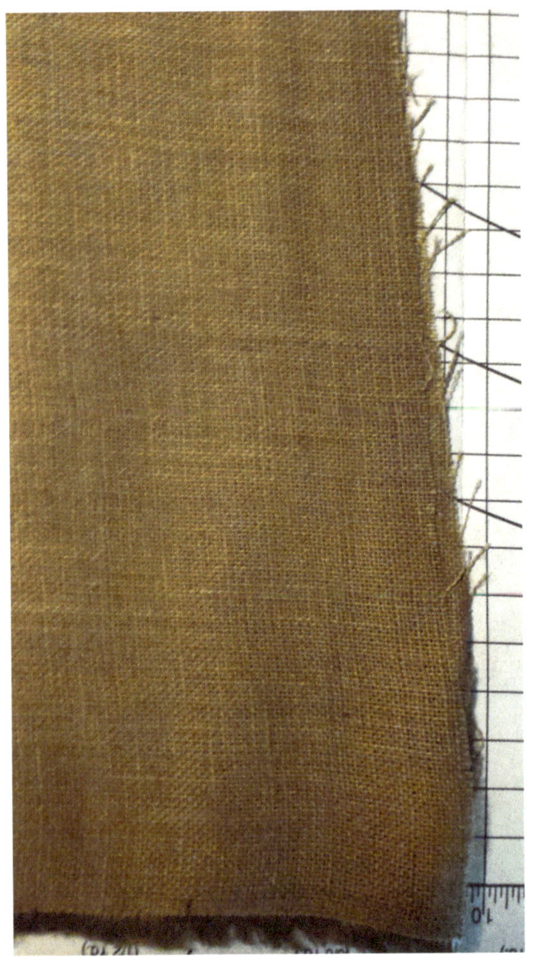
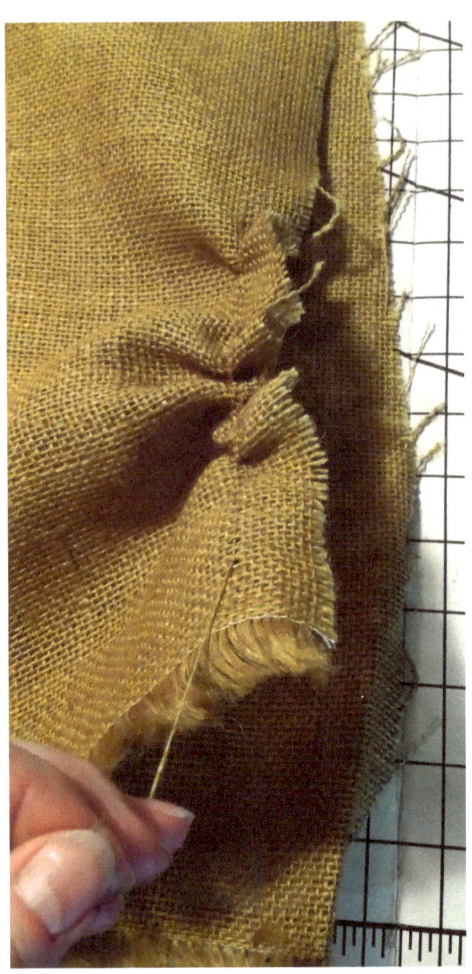

It is important to identify the grain on your backing fabric. Here you see how uneven the burlap is, because of the way it is wrapped on the bolt (above left). If you cut your backing fabric based on the cut edge, you might find your design is significantly off the grain. This is true of all types of backing fabric, but is easily remedied. Tug on a weft strand (along the cut edge) and pull it out (above right). Then just cut along the gap that gets left behind (below). Press the backing with a steam iron to correct any stretch in the fabric before you draw your design.

If you want your finished rug to be machine washable, it's best to prewash your linen or monk's cloth before drawing your design (don't put burlap in the washing machine). In that case, you should hem or zig-zag all the rough edges before washing.

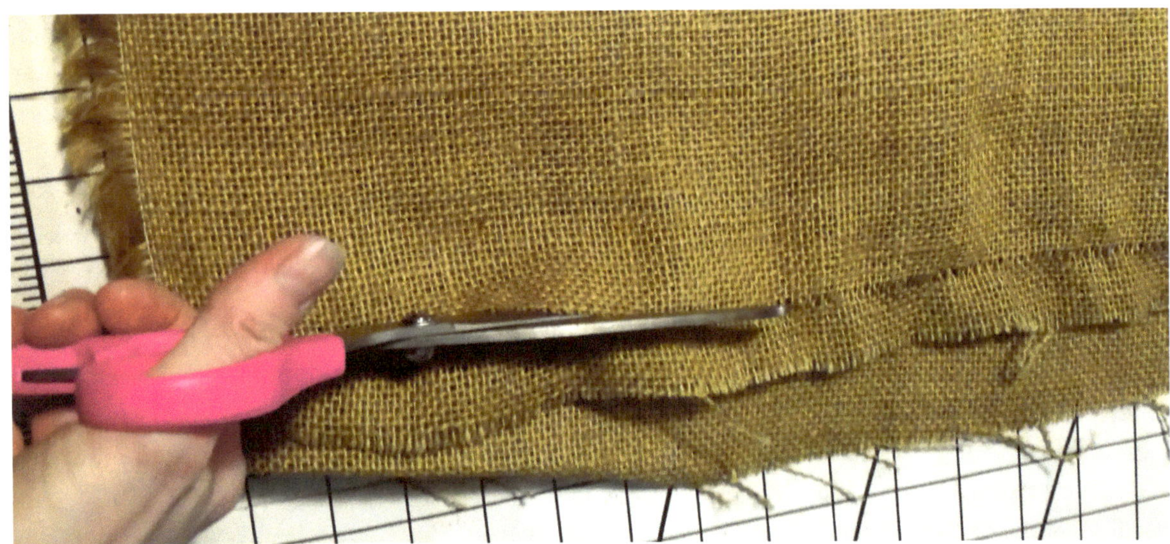

Cutting Your T-Shirts

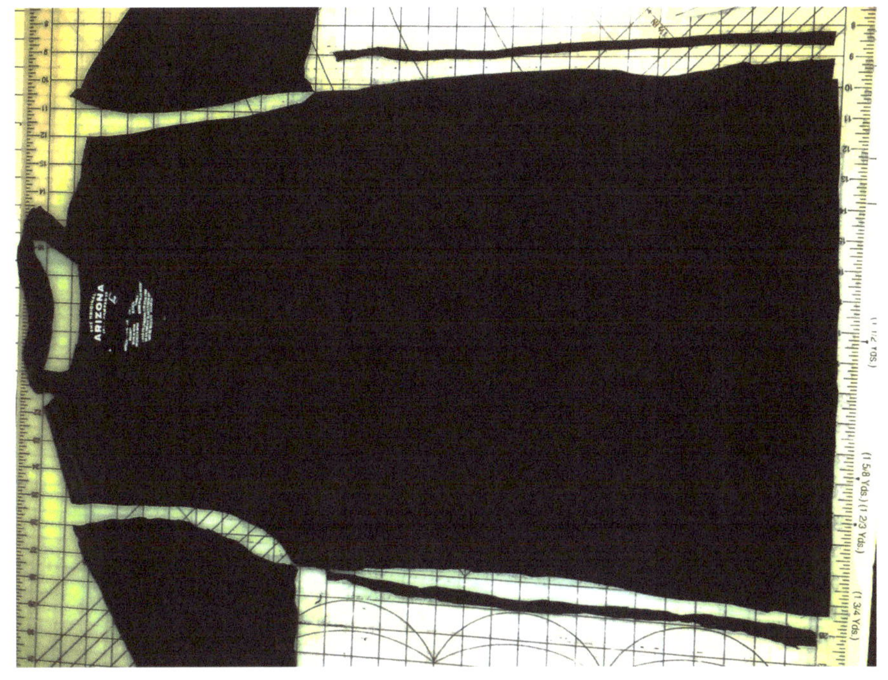

To prepare your T-shirts for cutting, first remove the side seams, sleeves and collar. If there isn't a side seam, you'll still want to open up one side. If a T-shirt has an iron-on decal, you'll want to remove that before you cut it into strips.

Be sure you smooth out the T-shirt before you cut (if there are creases in the fabric, you'll get a jagged edge). I start at the bottom edge of the T-shirt and cut horizontally. I cut the hem off first, and use that to bundle up my strips when I get done cutting.

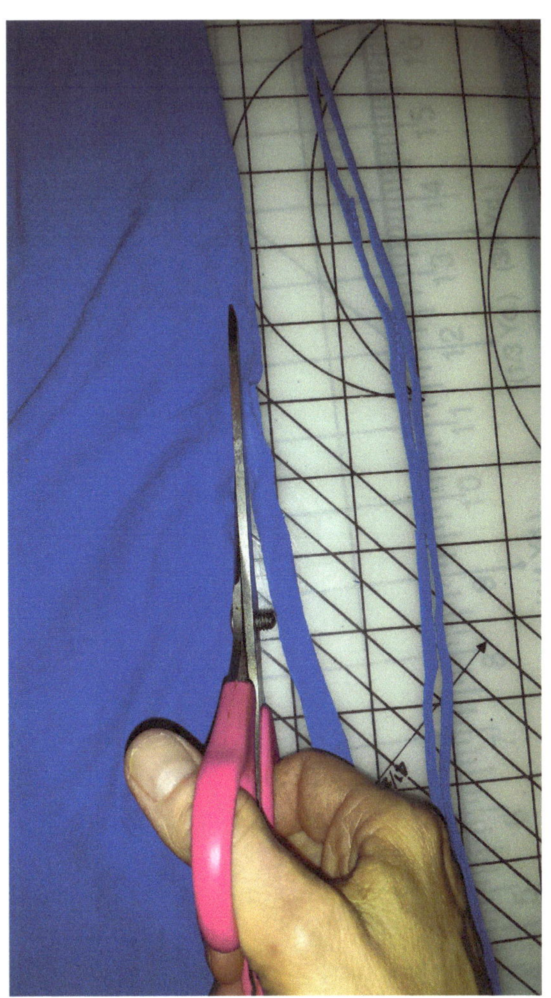

You can cut your T-shirts with scissors (left), but I find that a rotary cutter (like they use for quilting) and a cutting mat is much faster and more accurate (right). I usually work with strips that are 3/8" wide, although when I want finer detail, I will go as thin as 1/4." Using a yardstick to line up your strip is a great way to guide your cutter so the strips are even and just the right width for your project.

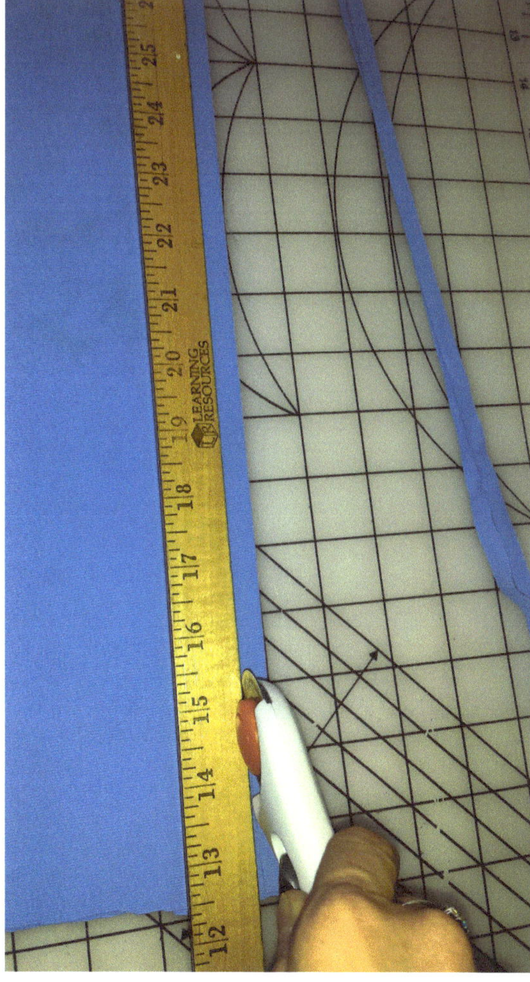

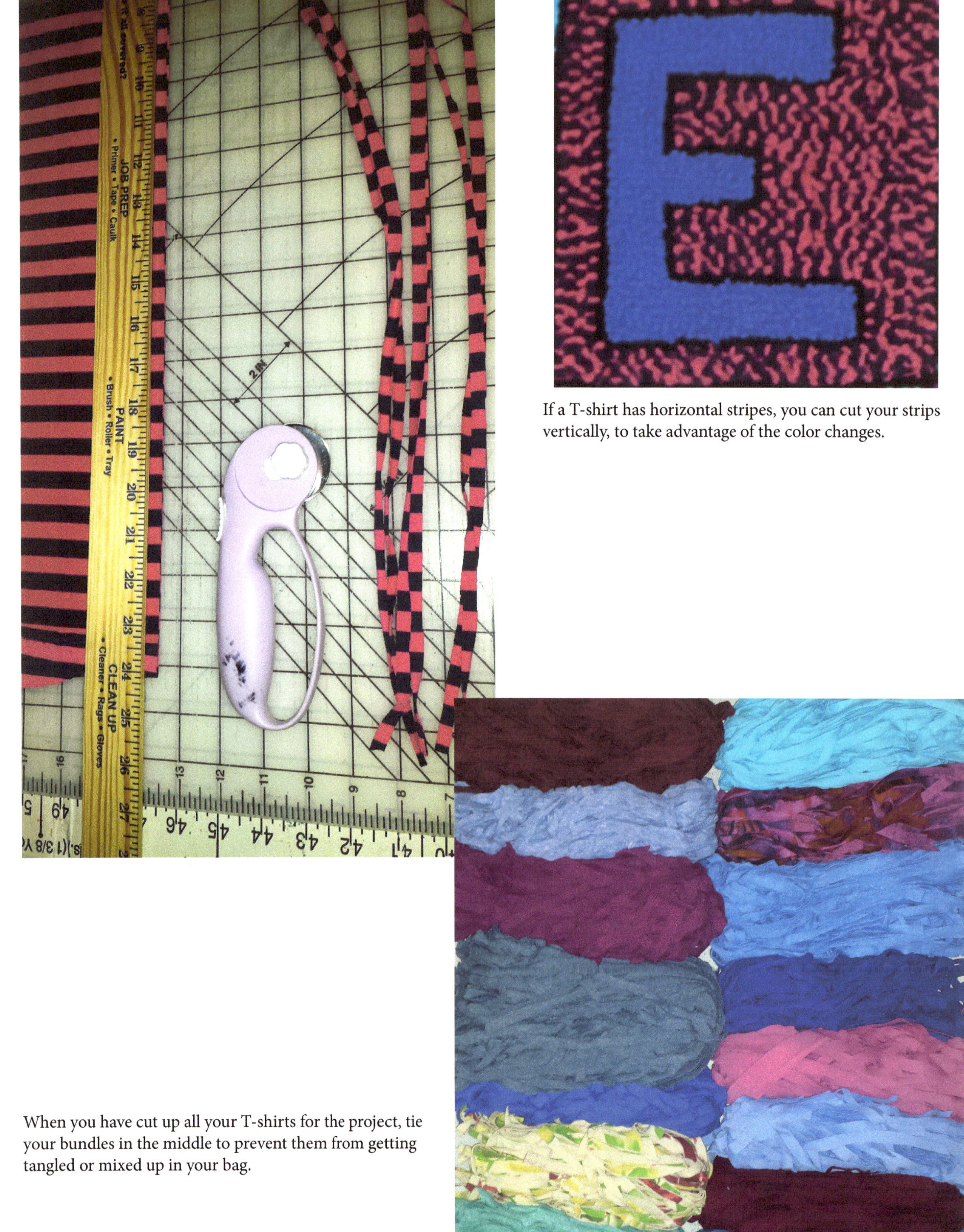

If a T-shirt has horizontal stripes, you can cut your strips vertically, to take advantage of the color changes.

When you have cut up all your T-shirts for the project, tie your bundles in the middle to prevent them from getting tangled or mixed up in your bag.

When you cut your T-shirts, you might notice that some strips curl up when you tug on them, and others don't. I assume this has something to do with the knitting process (is that what they call "double knit?"). T-shirts that curl when you cut them into strips will look like round dots when hooked into the rug, while the other kind looks more textured when hooked.

You can tell if a T-shirt will curl or not when cut into strips if you check for the stretch; if the T-shirt stretches from side to side as well as from top to bottom, the strips will curl. I have found if it only stretches from side to side, not top to bottom, it won't curl. Personally, I like both, so as long as the T-shirt is the color I'm looking for, I'll use it.

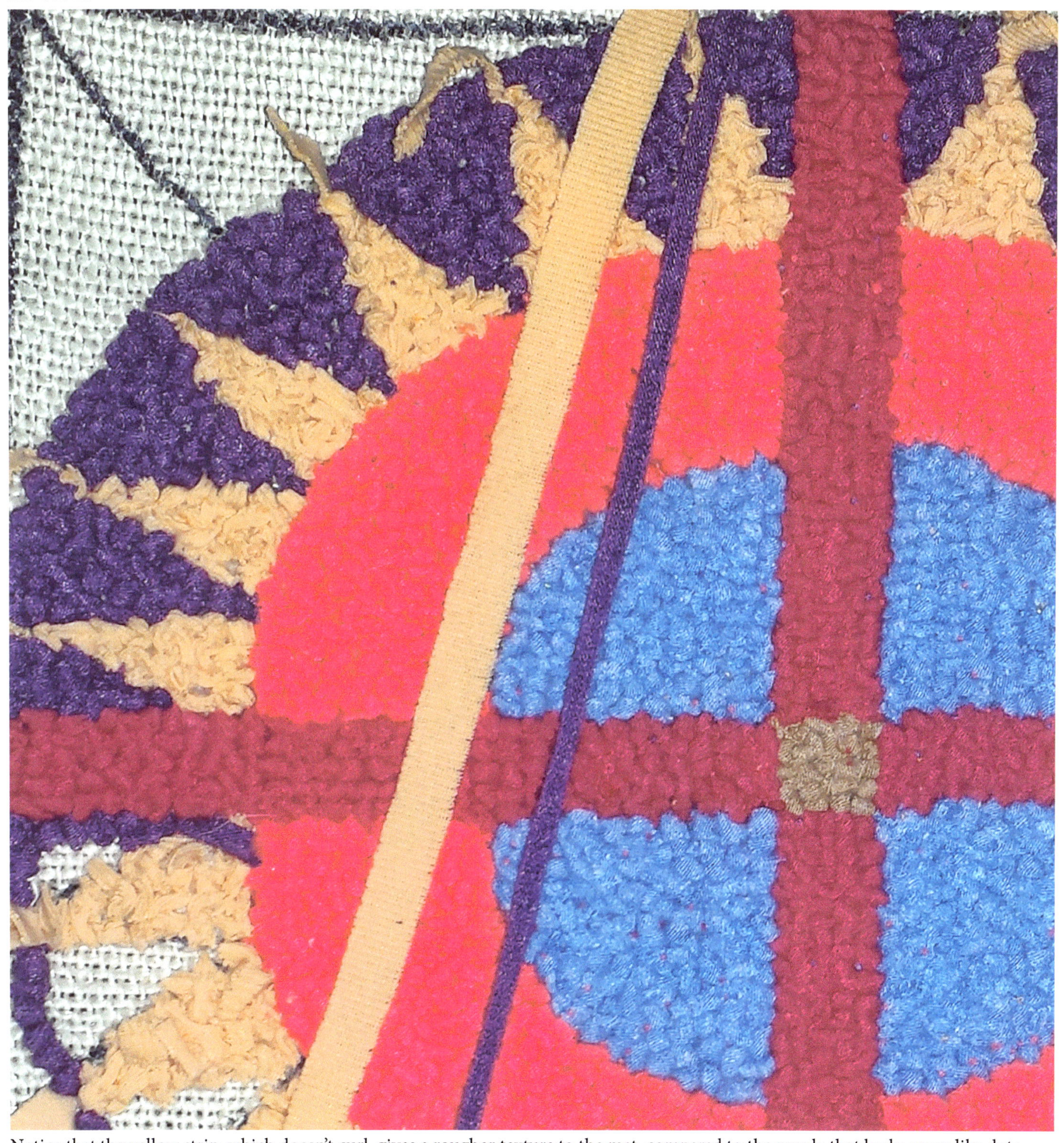

Notice that the yellow strip, which doesn't curl, gives a rougher texture to the mat, compared to the purple that looks more like dots. To me, it's like the difference between handspun yarn and commercially spun in my rugs, I like them both.

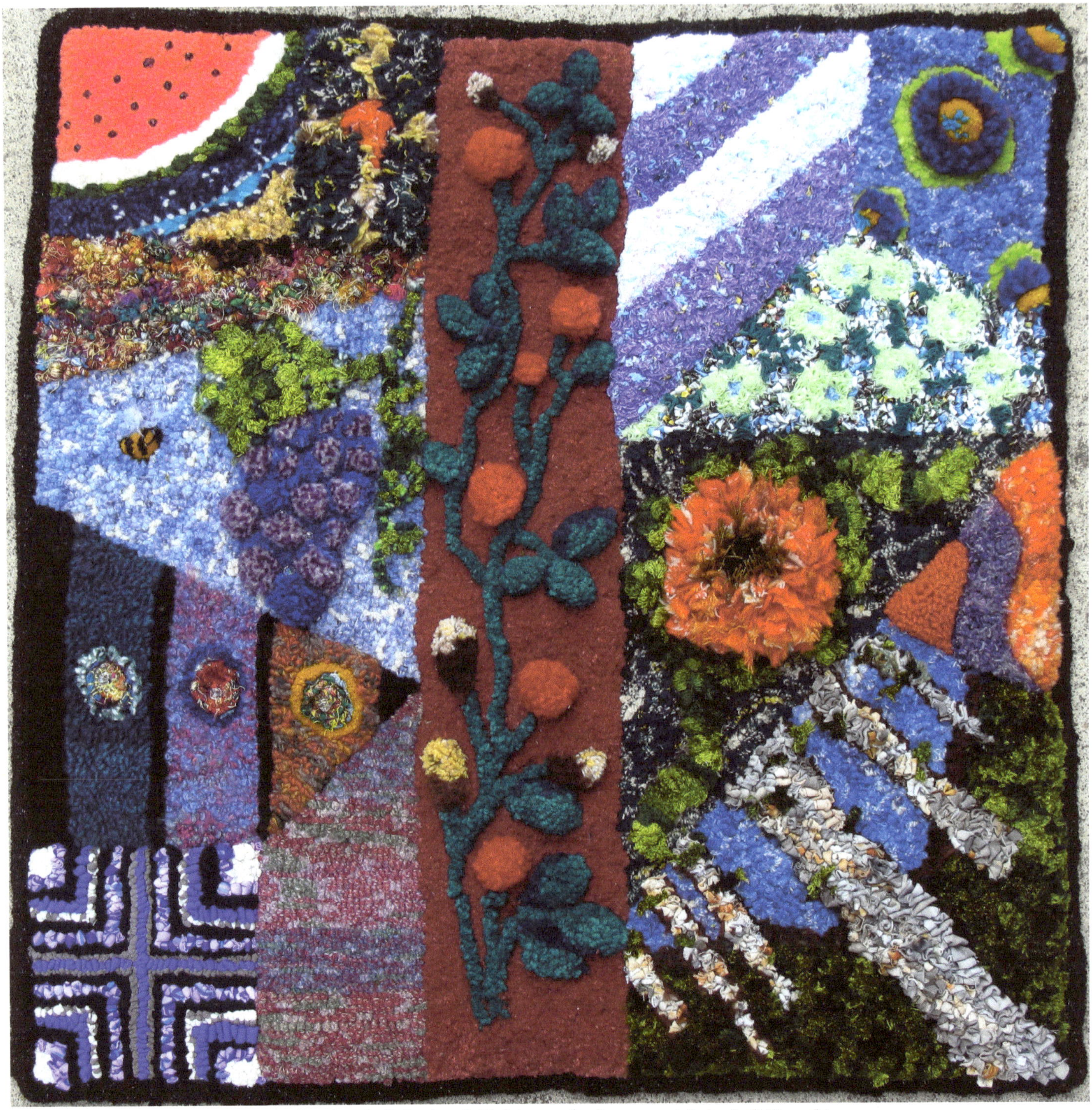

Bitzer, 35"x35" Designed, hooked and embellished with T-shirts and other materials by Judi Tompkins.
Photo by Judi Tompkins.

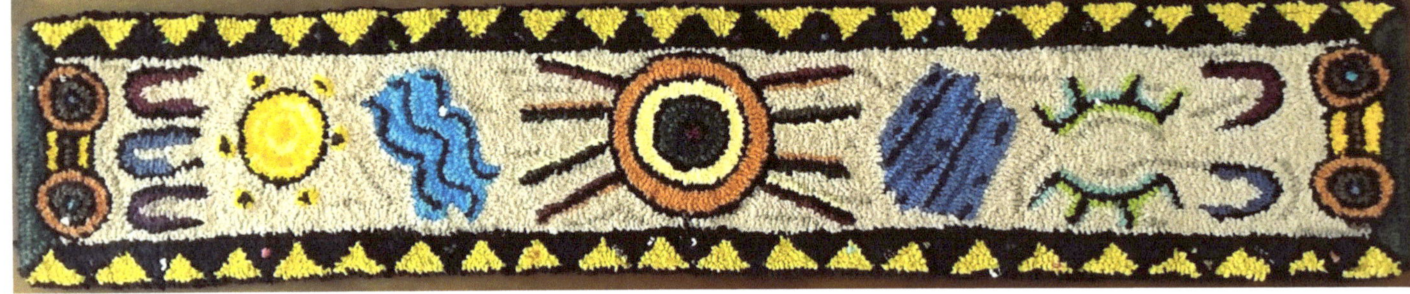

Old Aussie Welcome, 40.25"x8" Designed and hooked with T-shirts by Laura Salamy.
Photo by Laura Salamy.

Hooking With T-Shirts

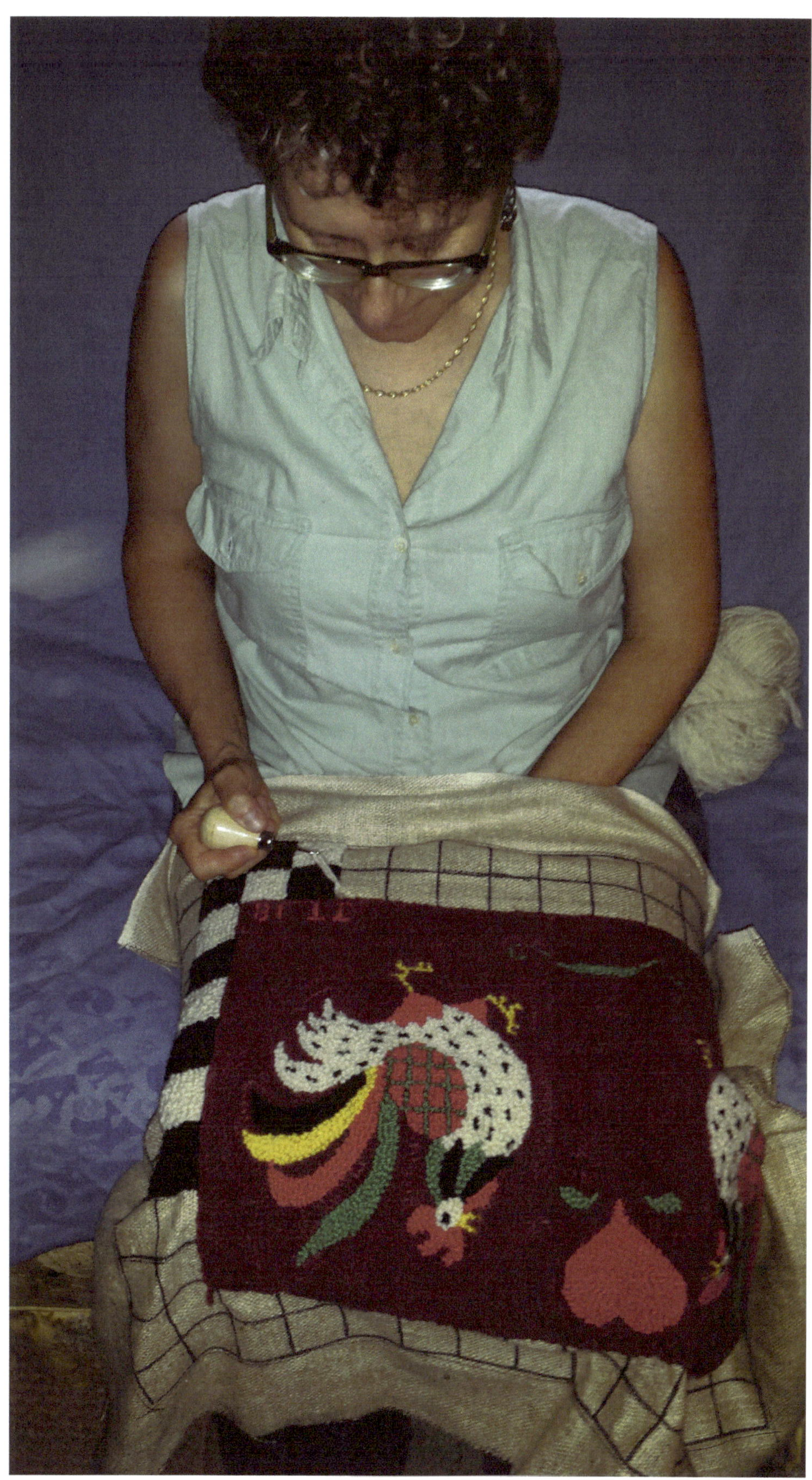

To begin, wrap the backing around your legs, design side up. You can also hook with a frame (see page 89), but for starters, all you need to do is tuck the backing around the outside of your legs, knees slightly apart. When I teach rug hooking, this is how my students do it. It's handy to find out if you like rug hooking before you have to invest in a frame.

In the picture (left) you can see I'm hooking a rug with yarn. Hooking with T-shirts is almost exactly the same technique. In the pages that follow, you'll find step-by-step instructions. Take your time at first. There's a rhythm to it. You'll speed up gradually. Before you know it, you'll be hooking without even thinking about it anymore.

I'm right-handed, so I hold my hook in my right hand above the rug. You can see my left hand is under the backing, where the white yarn is coming up from underneath (the ball of white yarn is right next to my left hip, but you can also just let it drop to the floor underneath). My left hand does most of the work, feeding the yarn or strip onto the hook, making sure it gets pulled snug up to the back.

My favorite hook is 2 mm wide (the metal part), and I rather like the one pictured here, with the bulbous handle. It keeps my hand very relaxed.

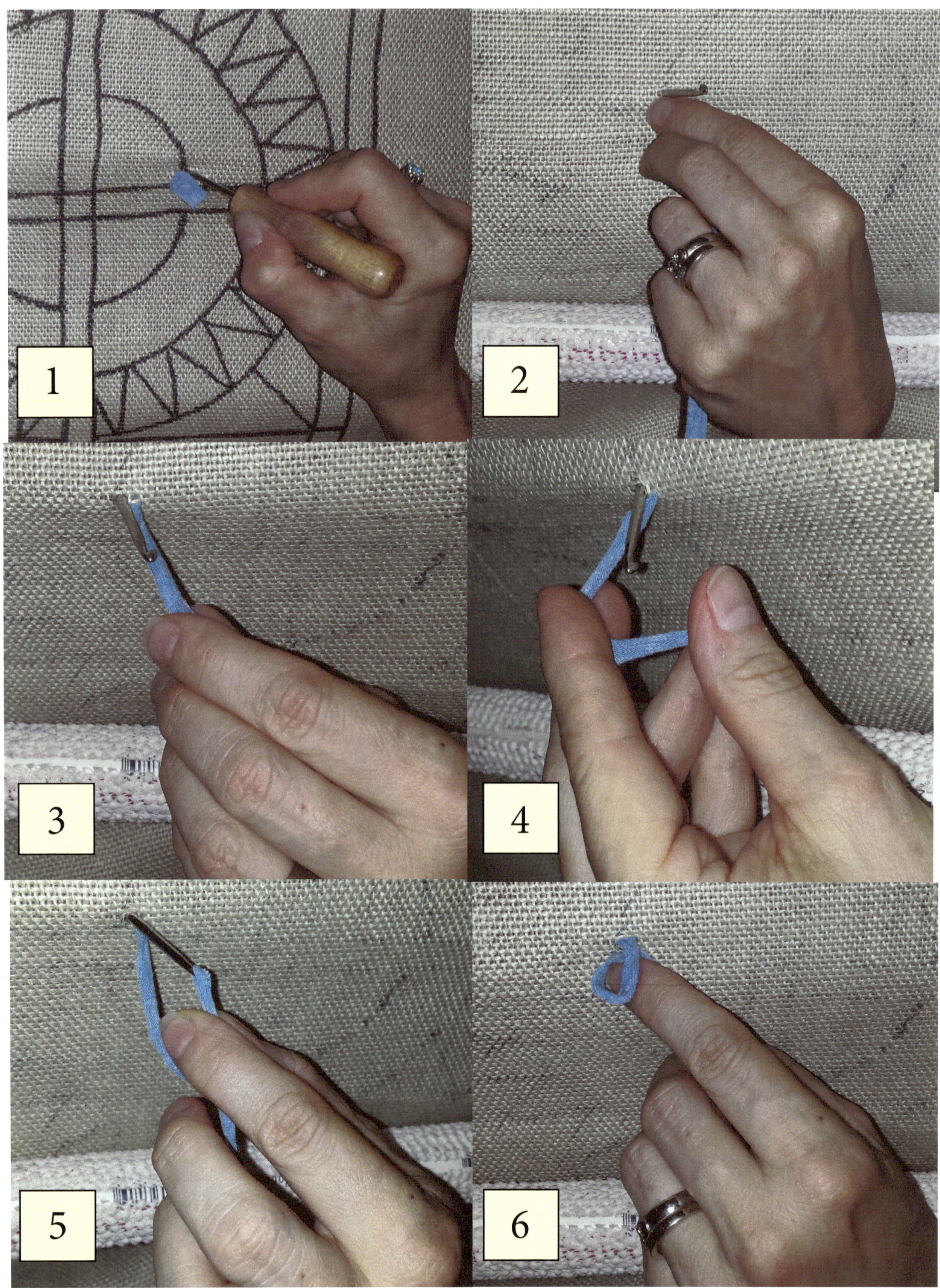
1
2
3
4
5
6

Step 1: Push in your hook where you would like to begin. Grab onto a strip from below with your hook and pull it up to the surface. With your left hand, pull the strip down from below until you have a 1" tail sticking up. The picture shows the hook next to the tail, ready to push in for the first loop.

Step 2: This shot is from below. It shows how my left hand pushes up against the backing while I'm poking the hook in. It gives me something to push against.

Step 3: (view from below) Here you see my left hand sliding down the strip. I'm not *pulling down* on the strip, I'm just letting my fingers guide me down at bit. This is to give myself some slack, so I don't pull out the previous loop or tail when I'm pulling the strip up with my hook.

Step 4: (view from below) Spreading the strip out with my fingers, I am raising a section of the strip up to meet the hook. If while you are hooking, you find you're pulling out the previous loop or tail, give yourself more slack.

Step 5: (view from below) Here you see I have folded the strip over the hook. I pinch it with my left hand and give gentle downward pressure to keep it on the hook, until I have pulled the hook up to the top.

Step 6: (view from below) As I pull up on the strip with the hook, my left hand is feeling with my index finger for the loop that is being pulled up. I'm *feeling* it disappear (underneath), so the strip gets pulled tight against the back.

A picture may be worth a thousand words, but there's no substitute for seeing the process in real time. If you can't make it to a class, check out my YouTube video. Search for "Rug Hooking With T-shirts" to see the process in motion.

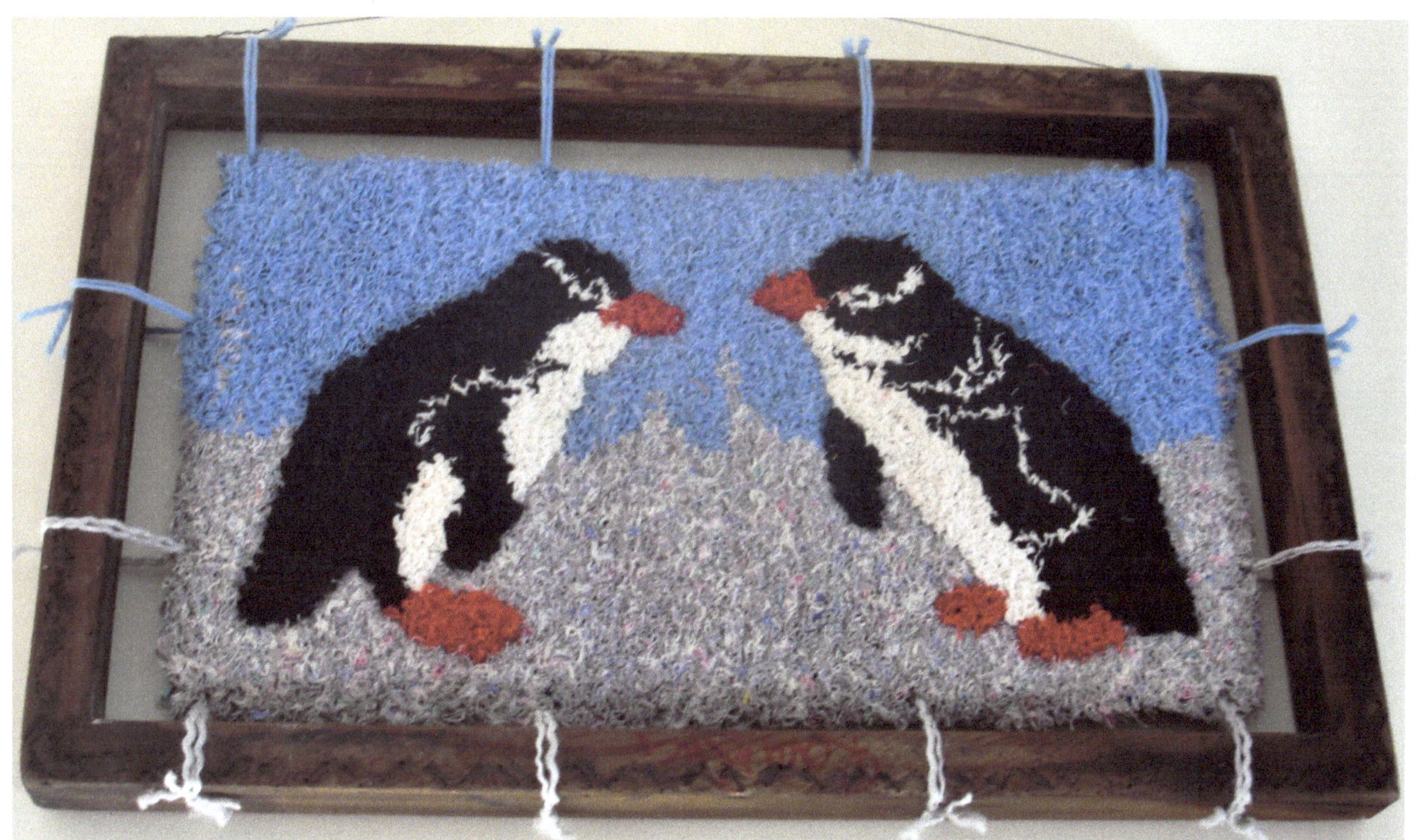

Penguins, 9"x16" Designed and hooked with T-shirts by Renate Kirkpatrick.
Photo by Judi Tompkins.

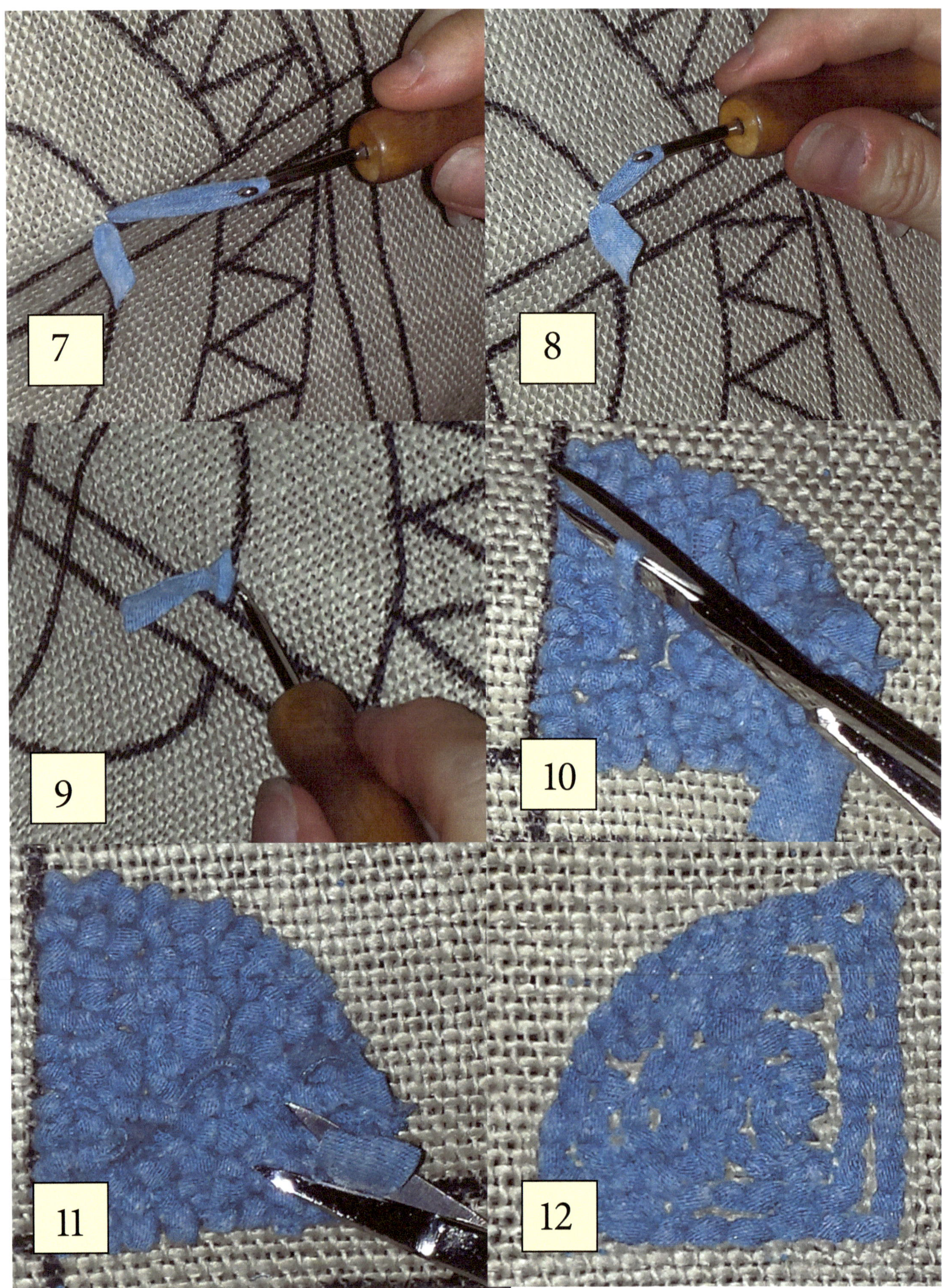
7
8
9
10
11
12

Step 7: Here is the view of Step 6 from above, as I pull up on the strip with my hook. My left hand (underneath) is feeling the strip pull tight against the back. While I'm feeling the slack pull tight in back, I'm also noticing the tail or the previous loop shift just a bit. Then I know to stop pulling up with the hook.

Step 8: With some T-shirt strips, it is necessary to leave the hook in the loop while you pull down from below with your left hand. Otherwise, you may find the strip drags itself down, leaving a loop in the back. When you leave the hook in the loop, don't pull up from above, a little resistance is all it takes. Only pull down with your left hand, and let the strip glide down over your hook.

Step 9: Here you can see the loop has been pulled down to the desired height (about 1/8"). You see how it spreads out, that's important. As it takes up space, it is anchoring itself (if your loops aren't spreading out on top, they're not high enough). Once that loop is surrounded by other loops, they hold themselves in place.

Step 10: When you have filled in the area you want to hook, bring up one last loop, but before you pull it down, cut it from above with scissors, leaving a 1" tail, just like when you began. Then pull the rest of the strip out.

Step 11: As soon as all the tails are surrounded by loops, they can be cut off, even with the surrounding loops.

Step 12: Take a look at the back. You should be able to see some gaps where the backing shows through (but it doesn't show through from the front). It's important that the loops have room to spread out on top, that's what keeps them in place. If you don't find some gaps in the back, you're probably overpacking your loops, which might prevent the rug from lying flat. You have to hook for a little while to get the hang of how far apart to go.

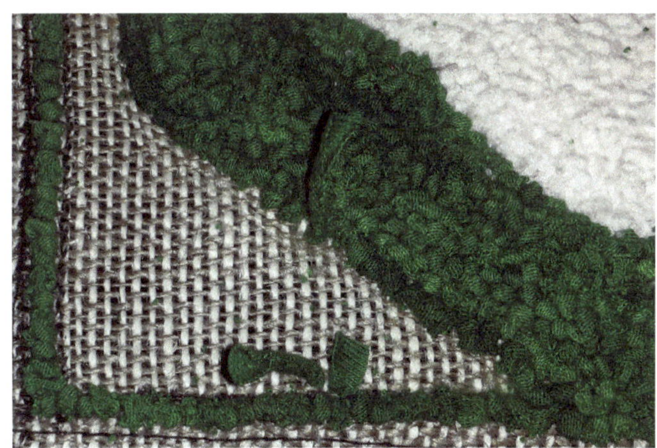

While it may seem as if there are many steps, in fact, the whole thing becomes fluid with practice. Anytime you find you're having a problem, just slow down and do one step at time, and don't go on to the next step until you're satisfied. It's like learning to knit; you feel all thumbs at first, then when you get the hang of it, it becomes automatic, rather meditative.

(top left) It's a good idea to start your outside row just inside the line. That way, all of your tails will be surrounded and secured.
(bottom left) Check the back periodically for any loop that got dragged to the back.
(bottom right) Just gently pull the extra up to the top, then trim the loop.

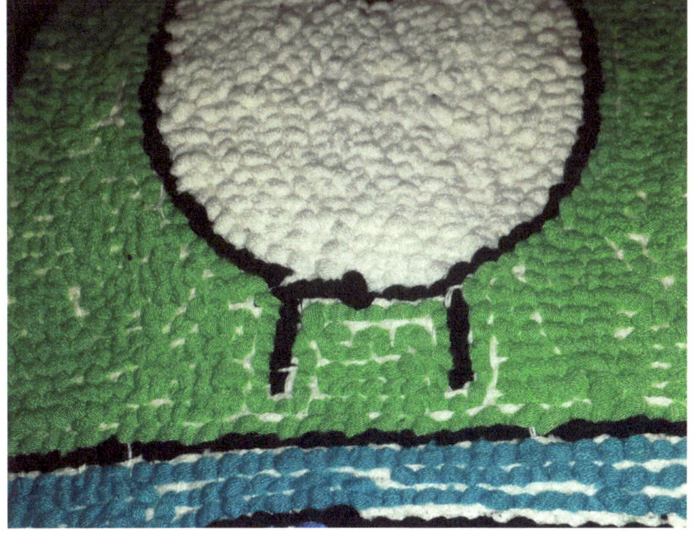

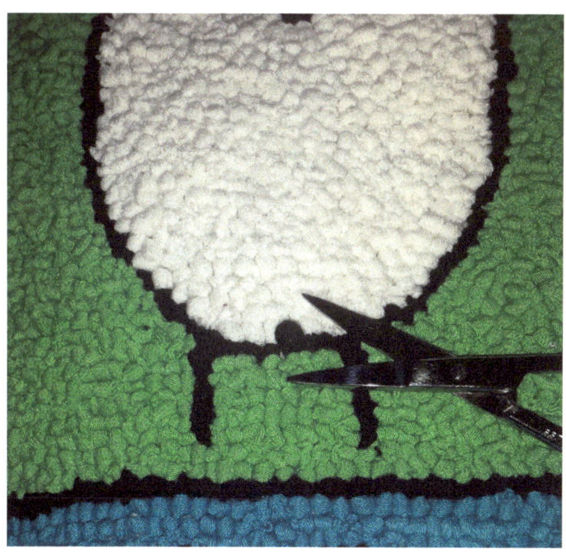

Whats Old Is New, 26"x45" Designer unknown. Hooked with T-shirts by Laura Salamy. Photo by Laura Salamy.

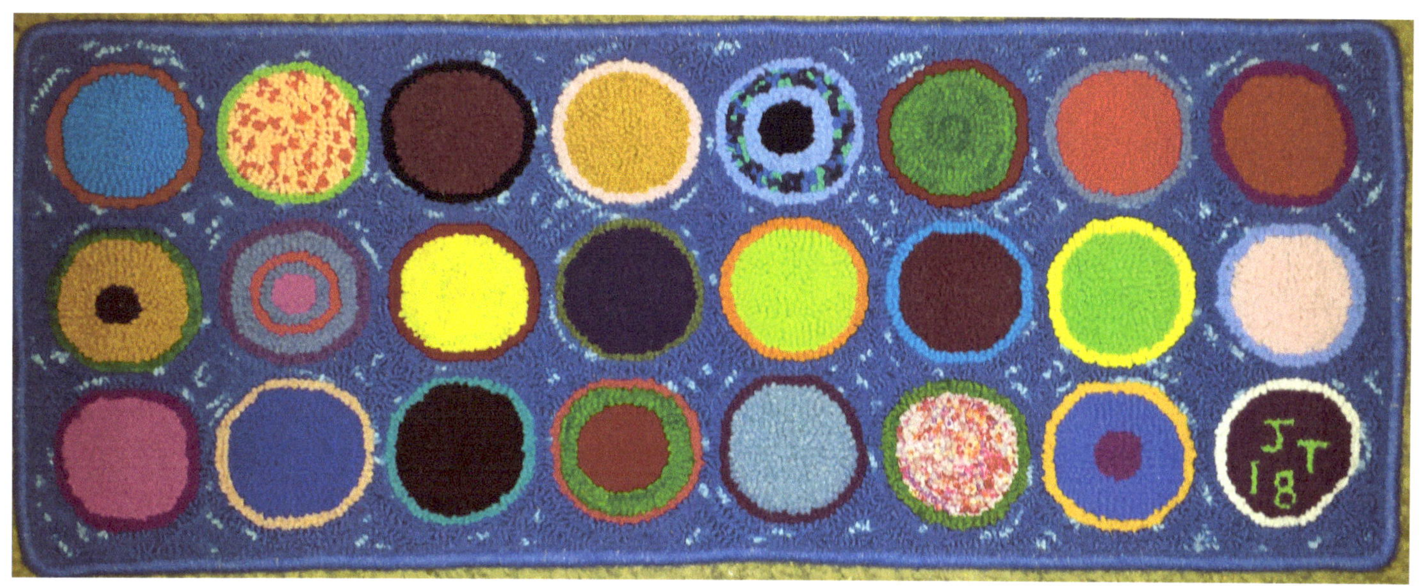

Projects

Now you're ready to dive in. These seven easy projects will let you try your hand at hooking with T-shirts. You can use the templates to create rugs small or large. Go wild with color! Experiment! Have fun!

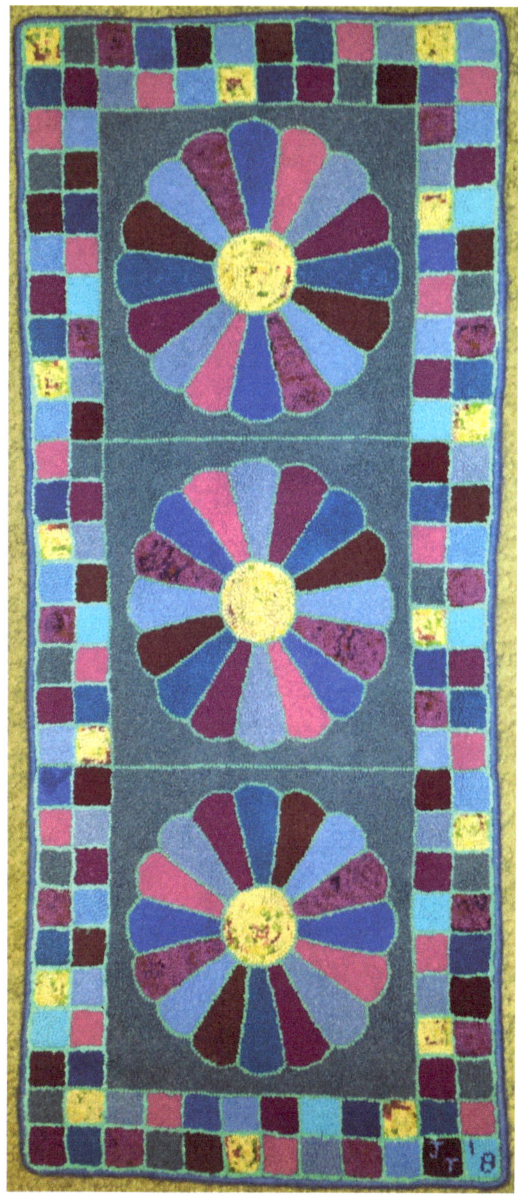

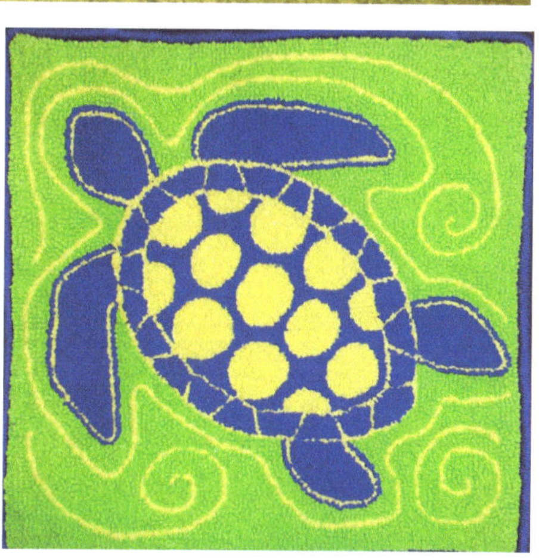

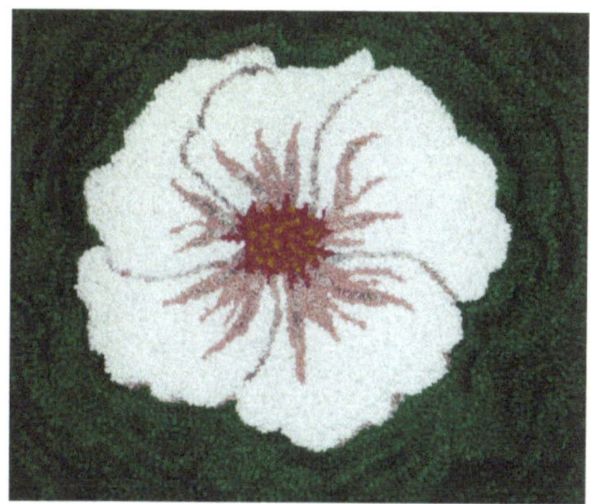

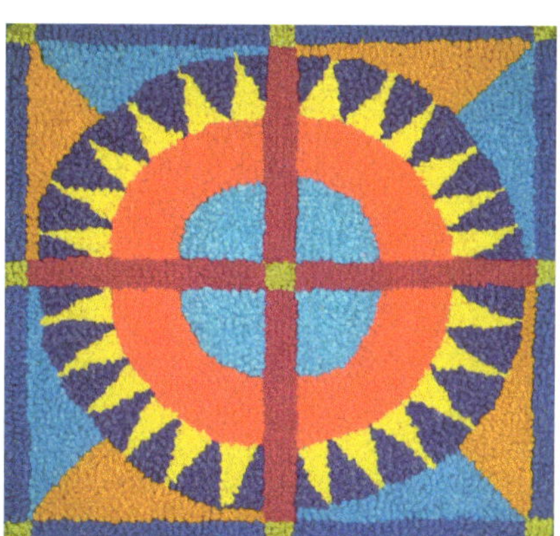

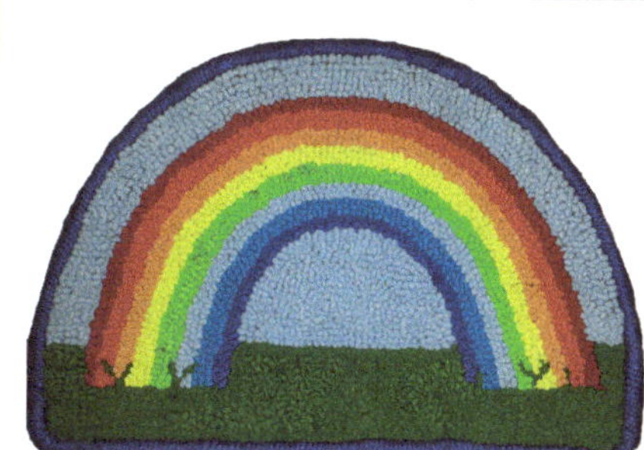

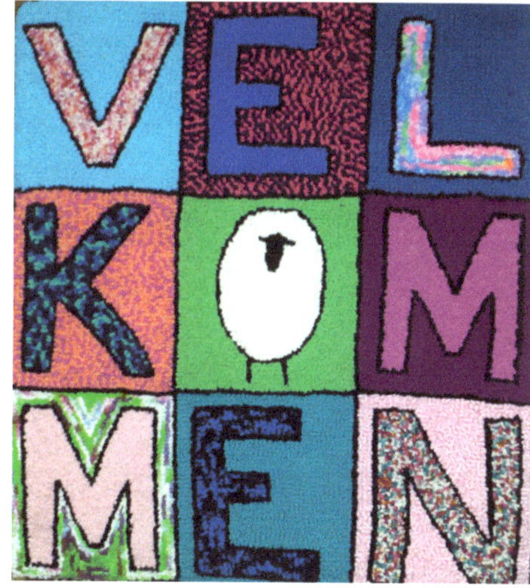

Transferring Your Designs

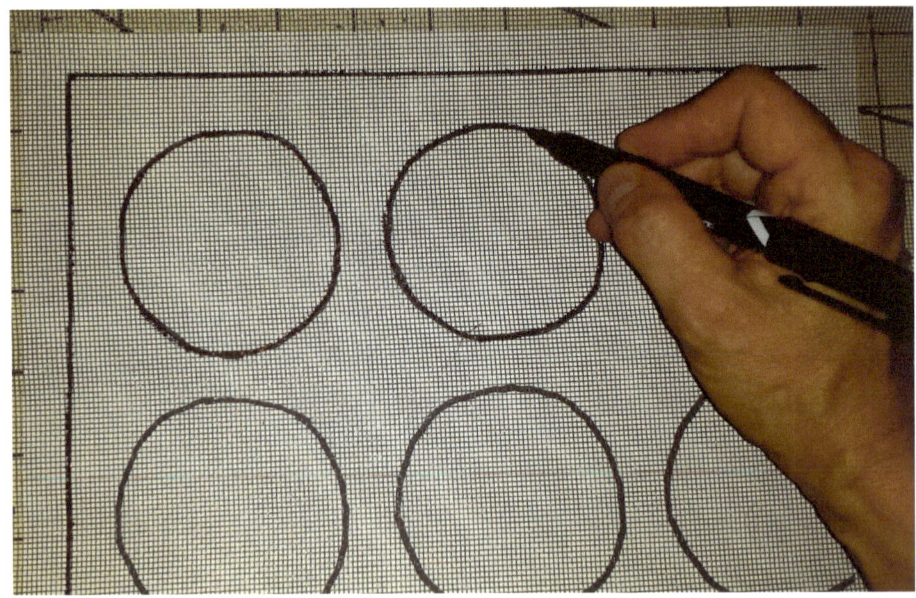

Lay a small piece of windowscreen over your copied template and trace over all the lines with a Sharpie pen.

Before you draw your pattern, pre-wash your backing material (if it's going to be machine washed in the future). All of the projects in this book start with a template.

The easiest way to use the template is to make a copy of the page, then lay a piece of fiberglass windowscreen over the paper. (You can buy this by the roll at a hardware store.) With a Sharpie pen, draw over all the lines, transferring the drawing to the windowscreen.

All the projects in this book are perfect for practicing your skills. They are intended for personal use only. Depending on the project, you can use the template to make a small pillow or a larger rug. In that case, you will want larger paper on hand, as big as the final project.

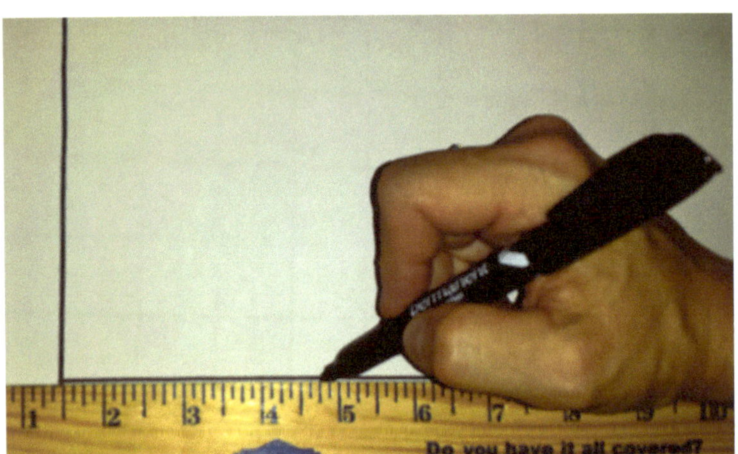

To extend your template to create a larger project, on paper big enouth to accommodate your ultimate design, mark out a square edge with your yardstick (above).

Next take your windowscreen template and line up the corner, then start drawing in all the lines (right).

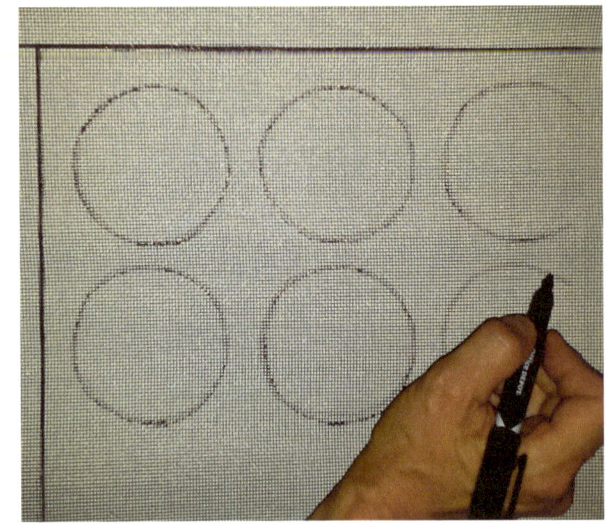

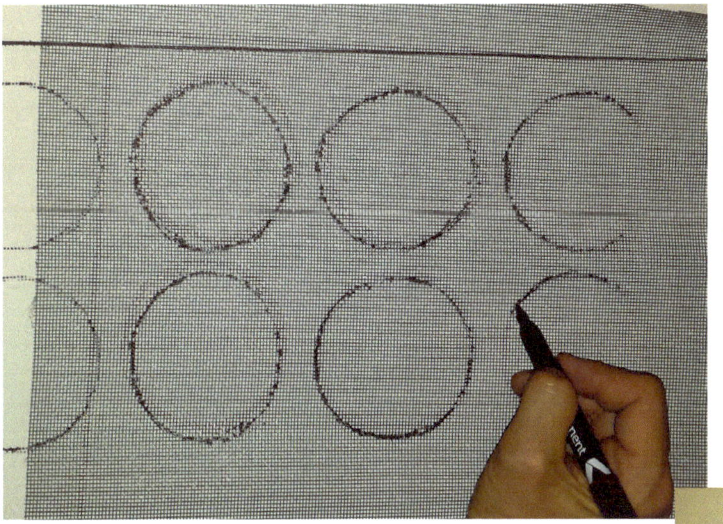

(left) Here you can see I have moved the windowscreen down along the edge, lining up with the pennies I already transferred to the paper below. You can continue to extend the pattern in this way until you have the length you want.

I decided I wanted to make a table runner, with eight pennies along the length and three on the width. When I got to the last row, I flipped my windowscreen template over (you can still see the lines on the other side), and used it to draw my ending borderline (right).

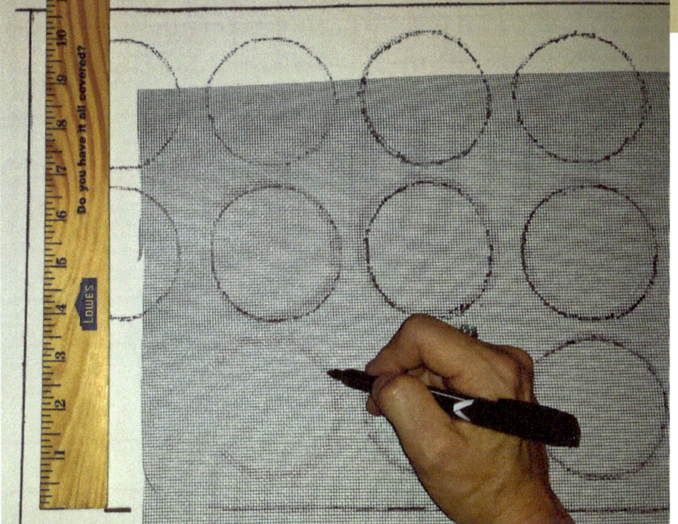

Lining the template up with the pennies I'd already transferred to the paper, I drew my third (final) row. With my yardstick, I measured out my lower borderline, and used that as my guide to draw that last row (left).

Below you see I have cut a new piece of windowscreen to lay over the pattern I drew on paper. I trace over all the lines again with the permanent marker, transferring the paper design to the new windowscreen template (below).

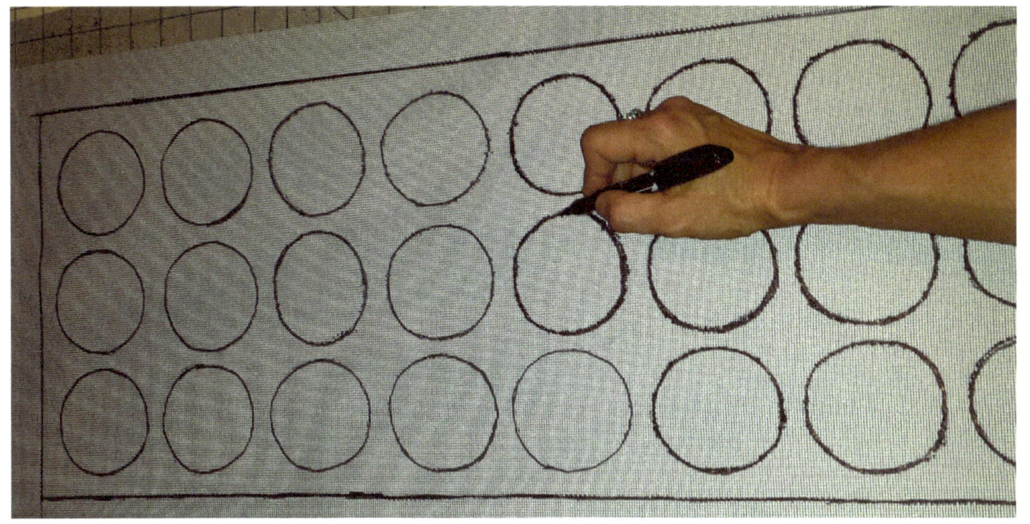

Don't be afraid of making mistakes with the Sharpie. You get to change your mind. The design you draw is not going to show on the finished rug, but you need a permanent marker so it doesn't rub off during hooking, or doesn't bleed through when washed.

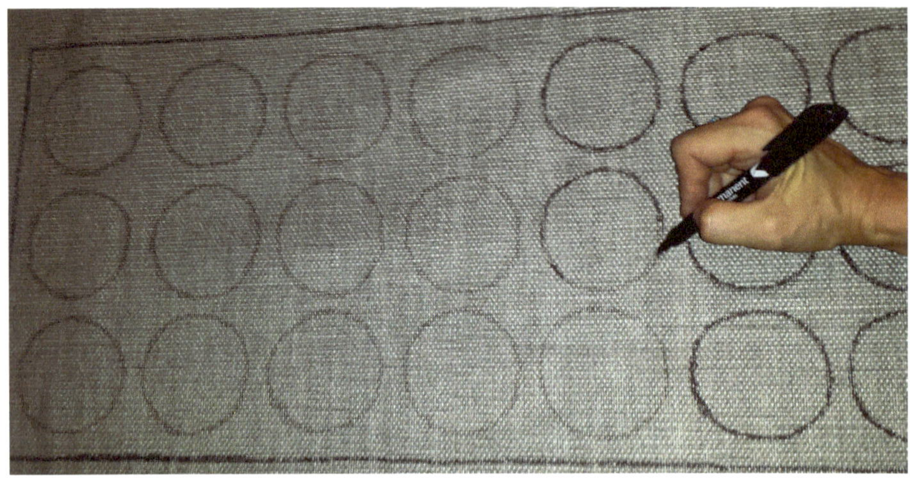

Lay the new windowscreen template over your pre-washed backing, and trace over all the lines, transferring the design onto the backing (left).

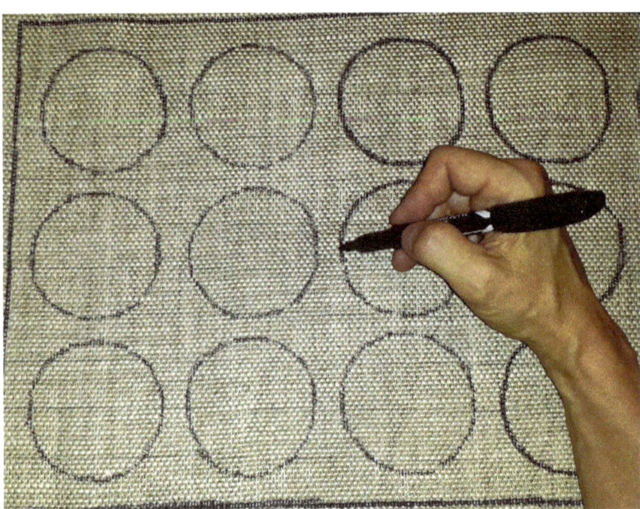

When you have removed the windowscreen template, you will want to go over all the lines one more time on your backing with the permanent marker, so they are clearer (left).

I have actually washed a linen pattern that was already drawn out, and the pattern was fine, I just needed to go over the lines again with the pemanent marker. So even if you buy a pattern on linen or monk's cloth, you may still pre-wash it for hooking with T-shirts (you might ask if they use permanent ink first!).

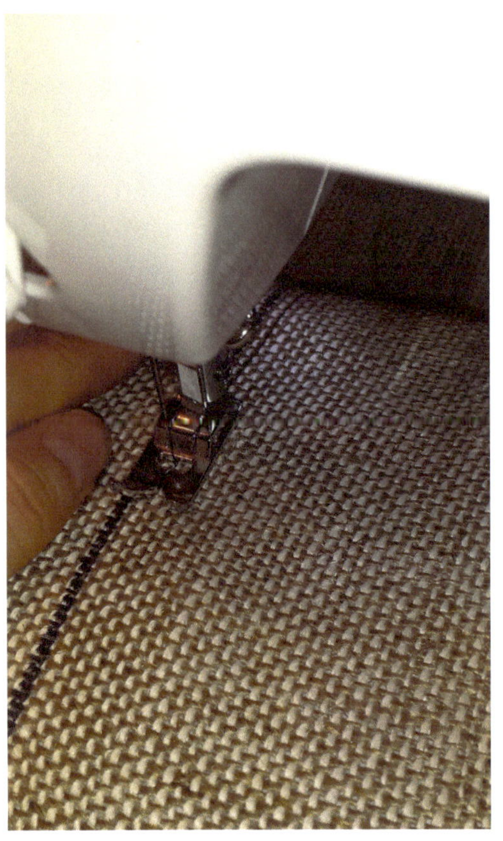

After I have drawn my pattern on the backing, I like to do a running stitch all around my borderline. This supports the linen so it doesn't lose it's shape on the hooked edge (left).

And if I haven't already, I do a zig-zag stitch along the cut edges of the fabric, so they don't fray while I'm hooking (right).

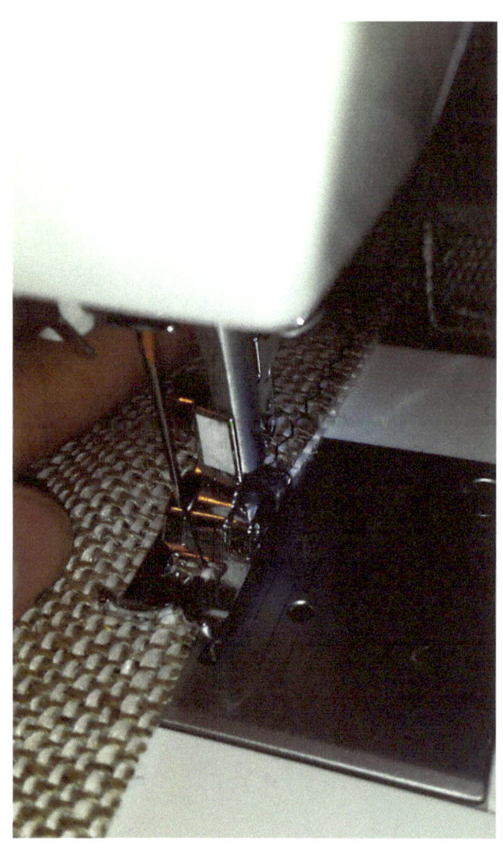

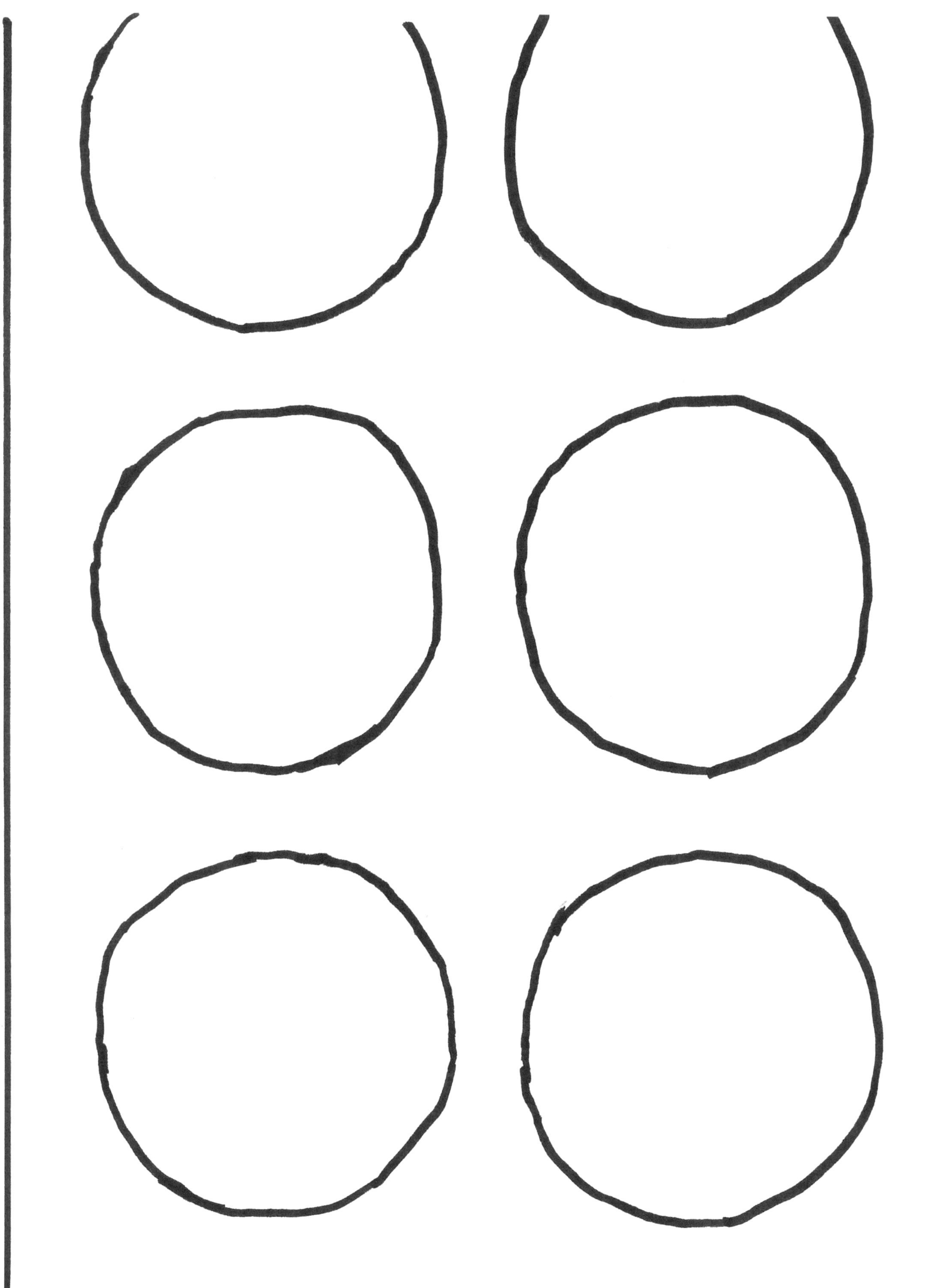

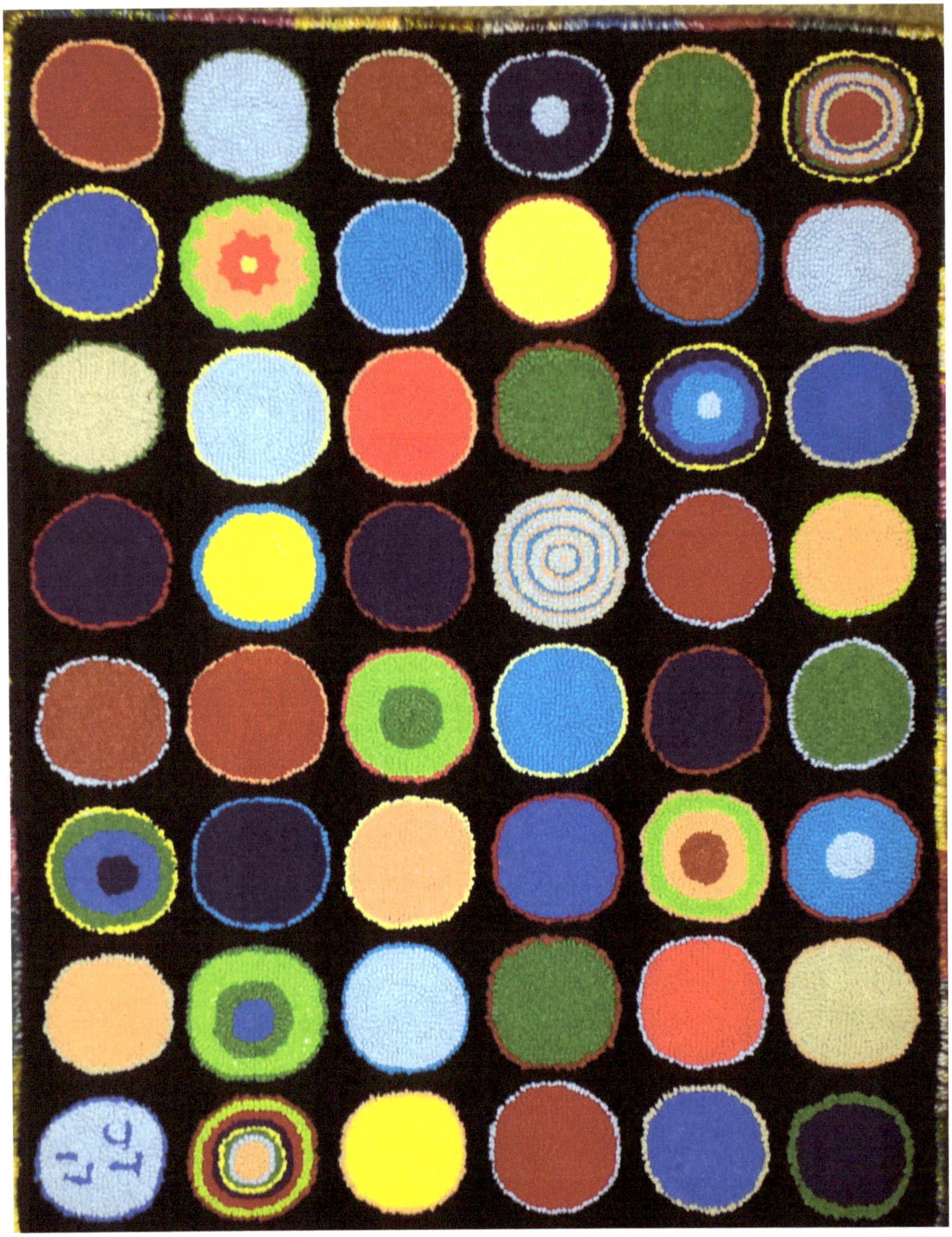

Use the template to make a penny pillow, runner, or rug of any size.

You will need .3 oz for each penny, and for the background, figure 10-12 oz of T-shirt strips for the rug to the left, and around 6 oz for the background on the runner below.

(left) Penny Rug 21"x28.5"

(below) Penny Table Runner, 29.75"x11.25"

Both designed and hooked with T-shirts by Judy Taylor.

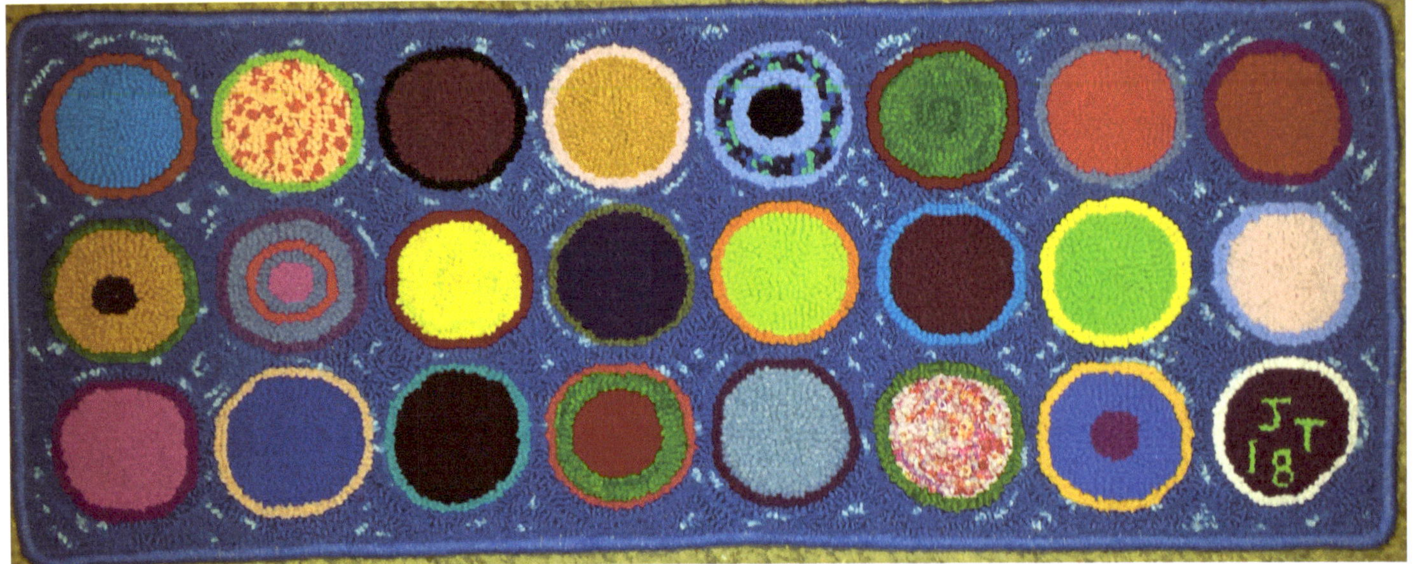

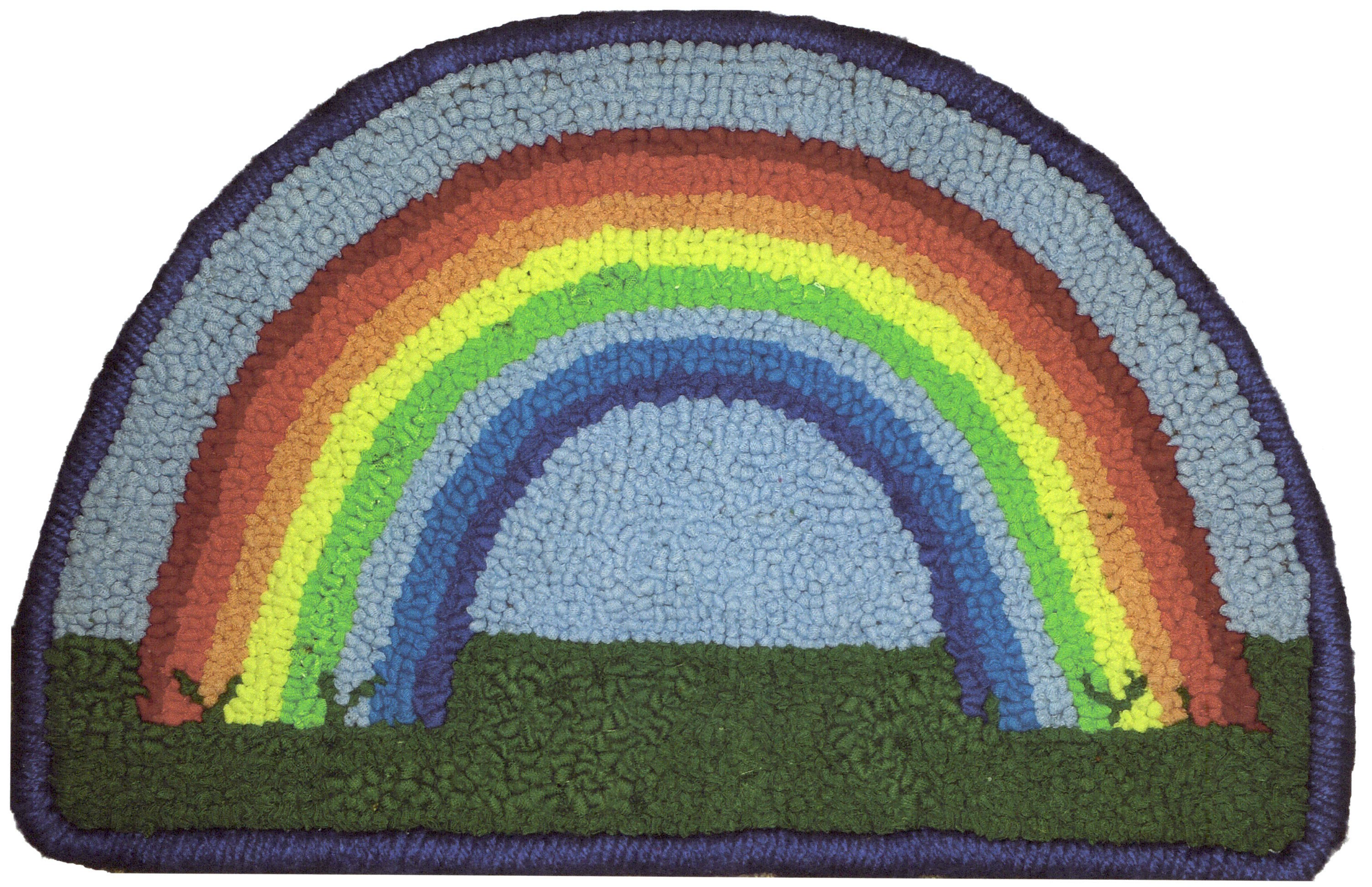

Rainbow Mat, 7”x10.5” Designed and hooked with T-shirts by Judy Taylor.
You will need 3 oz for the sky, 2 oz for the grass and .2 oz each for the colors of the rainbow.

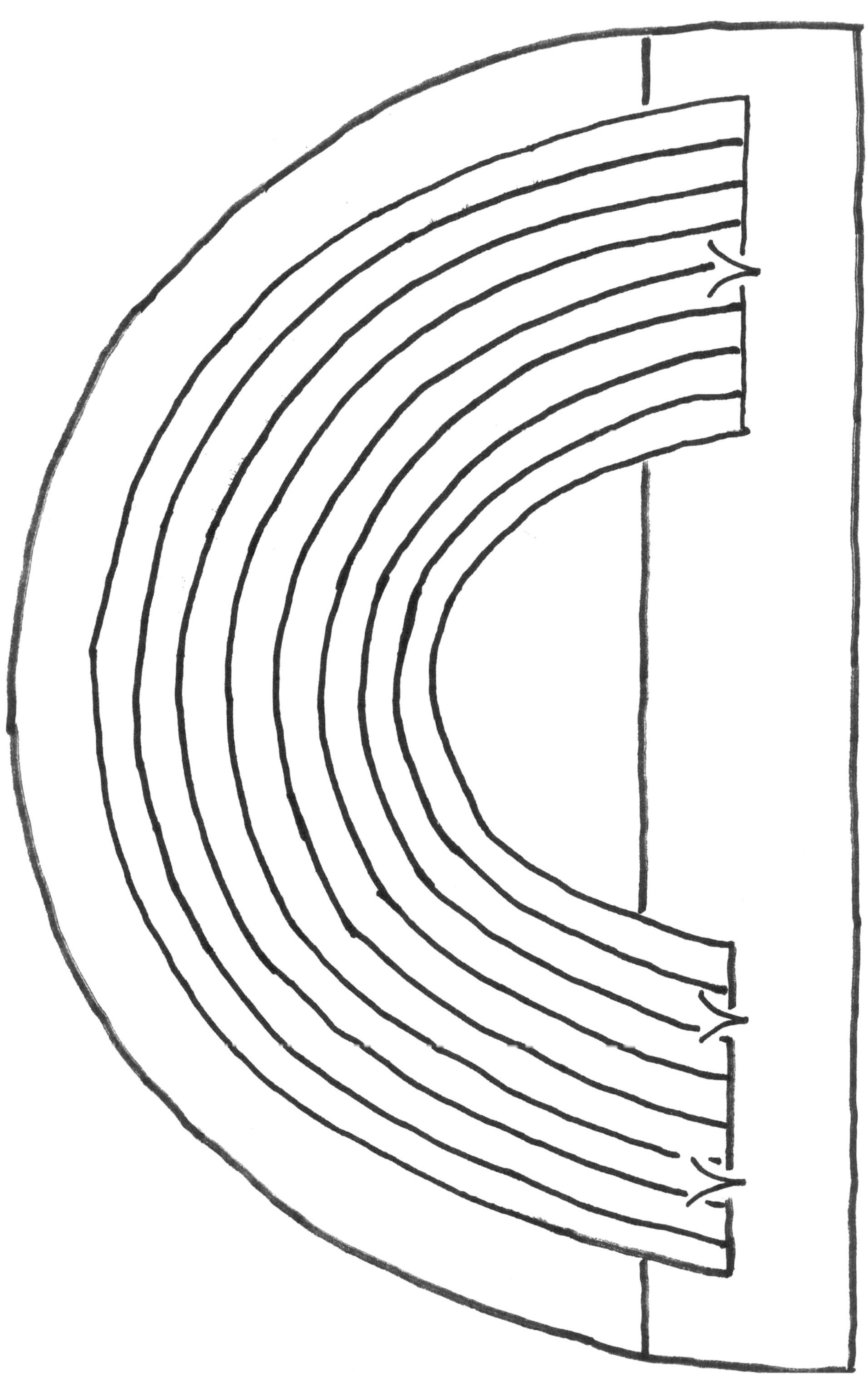

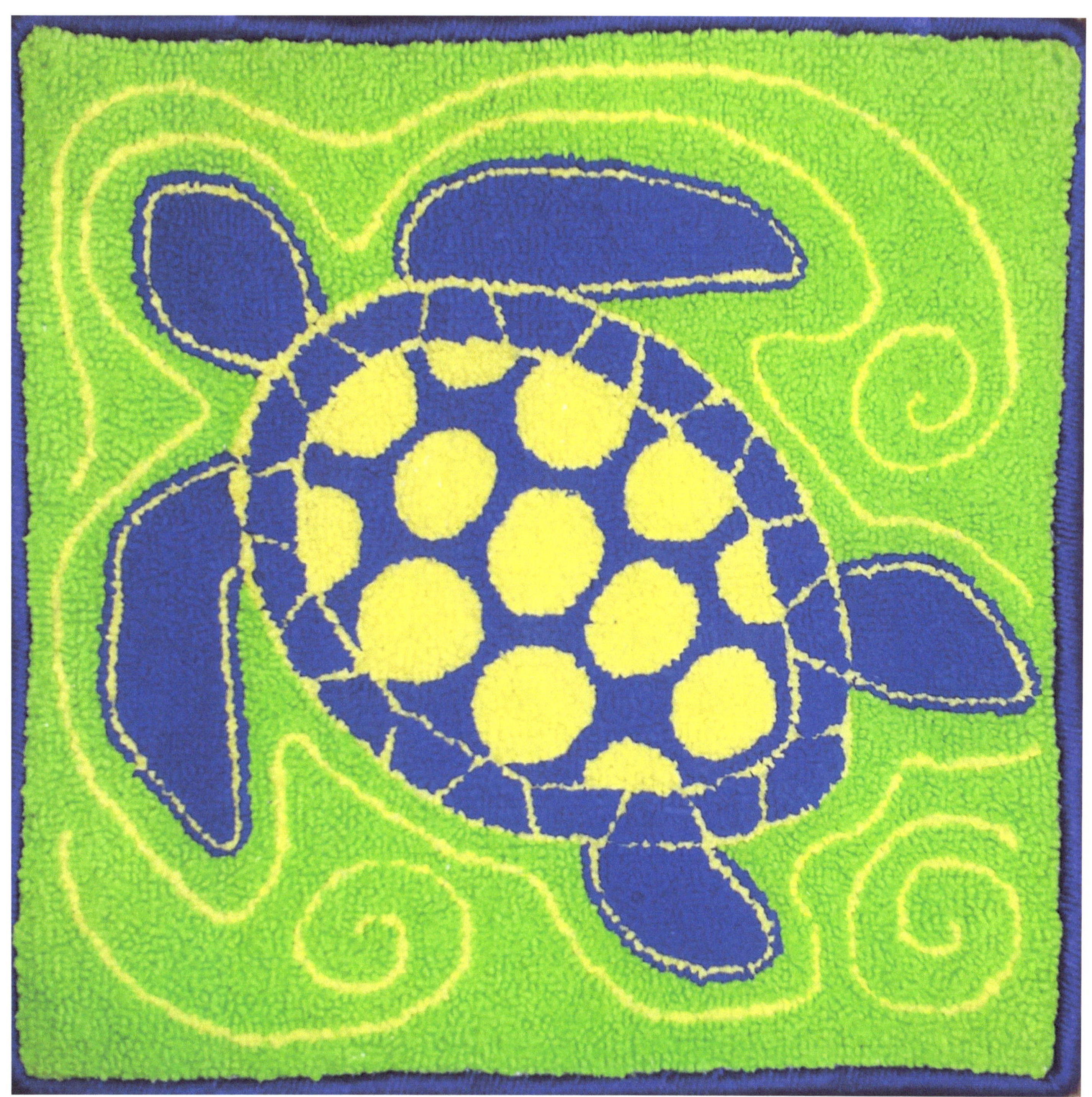

T-shirt Turtle, 12"x12" Designed and hooked with T-shirts by Judy Taylor.
You will need 6 oz for the background, 4 oz for the turtle, and 3 oz for the detail (yellow).
Copy all three design pages and tape them together to create the whole template.

With all of these designs, use my drawing as a guide. I'm not a machine, and I'm not overly concerned about getting things exact. Even if I draw something perfectly on paper, I'm always tracing it by hand, so there's bound to be imperfections. Use my somewhat wonky designs as suggestions for the lovely projects you will make!

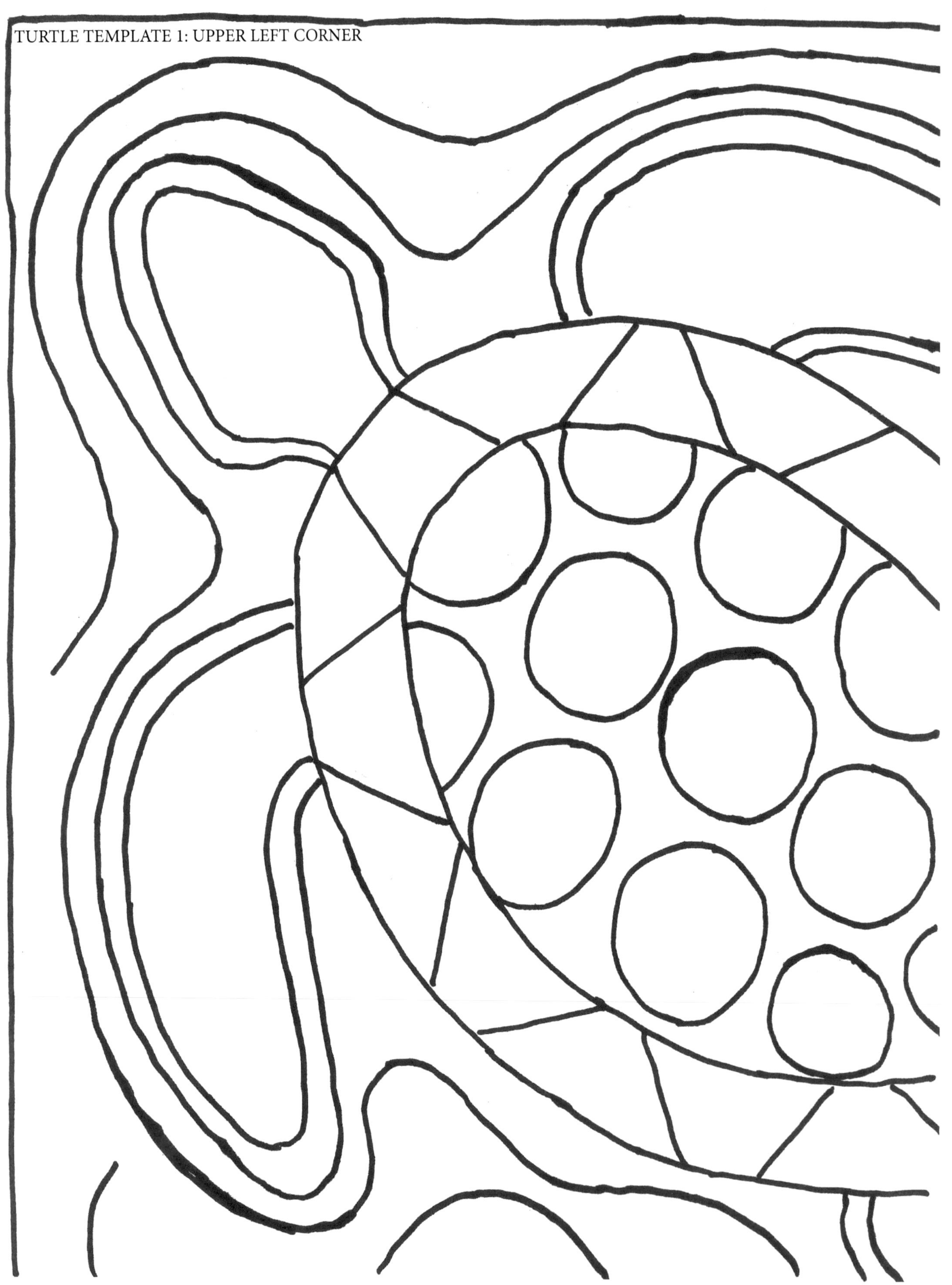
TURTLE TEMPLATE 1: UPPER LEFT CORNER

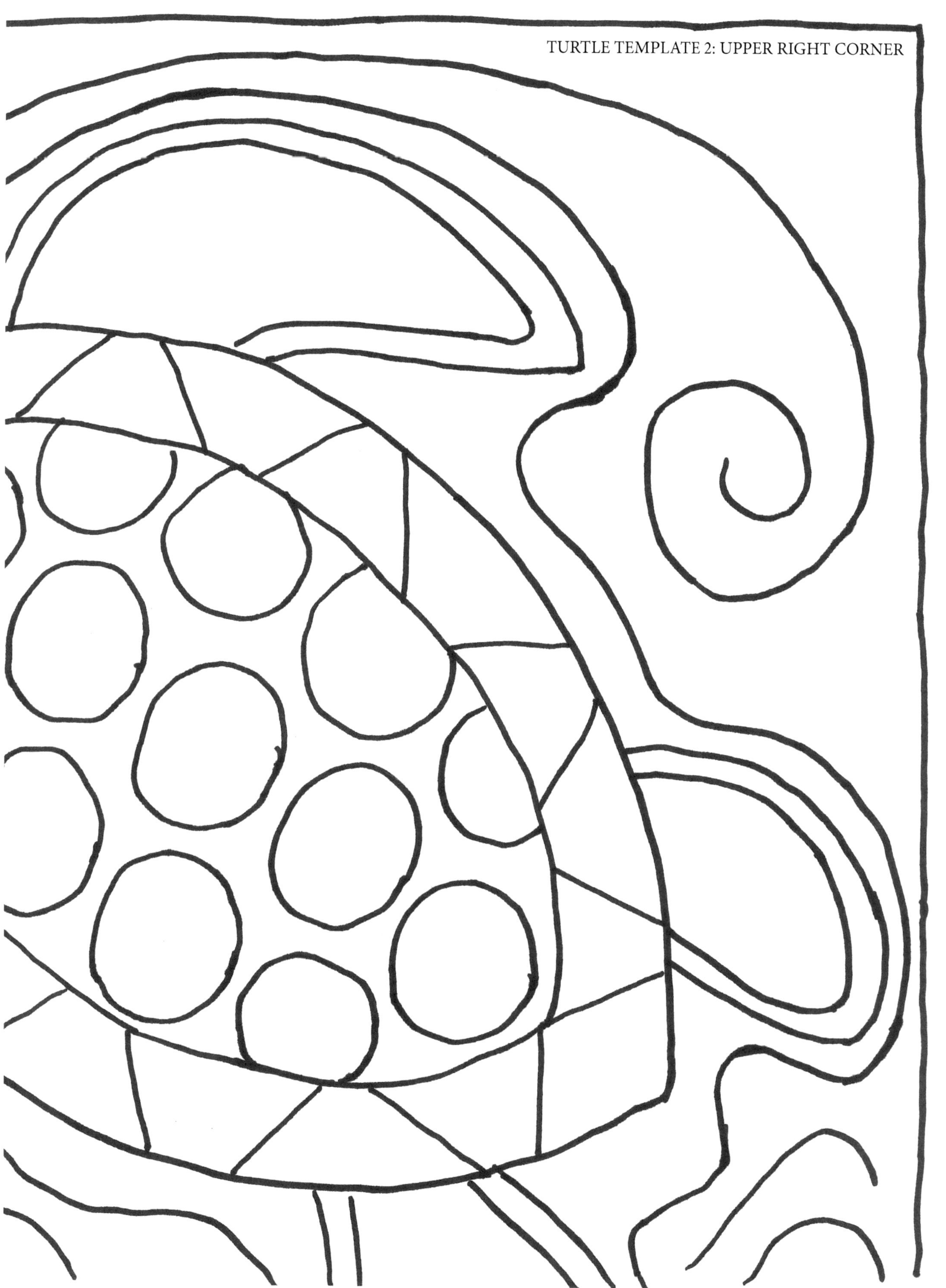
TURTLE TEMPLATE 2: UPPER RIGHT CORNER

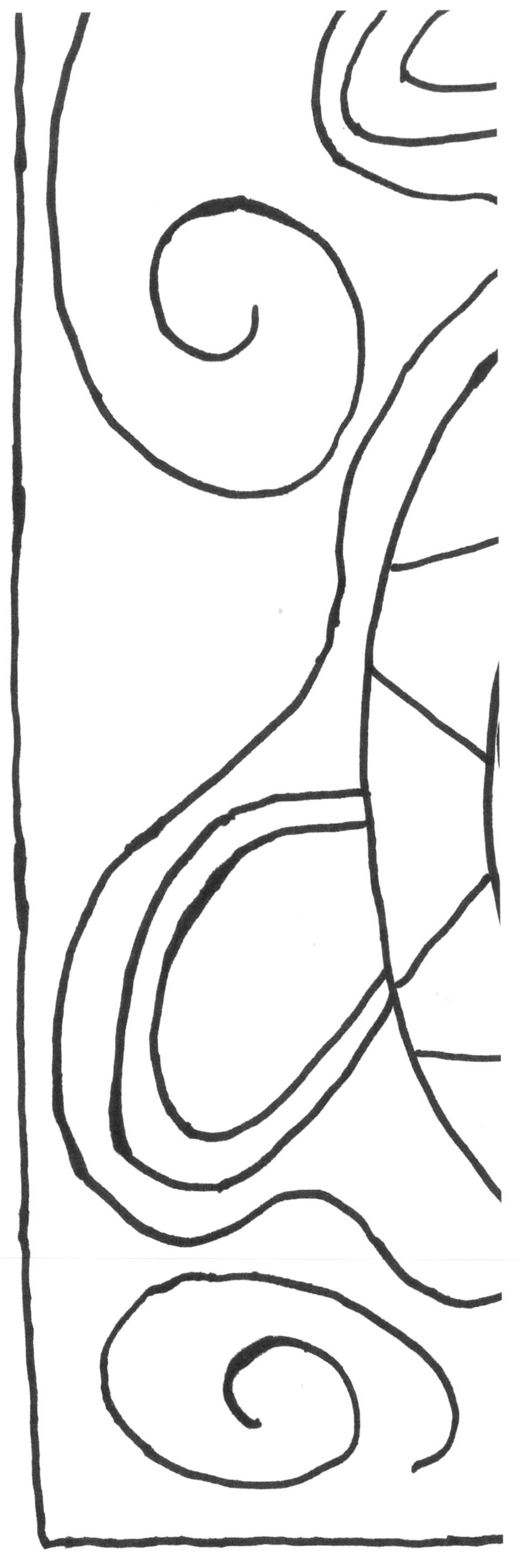

TURTLE TEMPLATE 3: LOWER RIGHT CORNER
(The lower left corner will be obvious when you tape them together.)

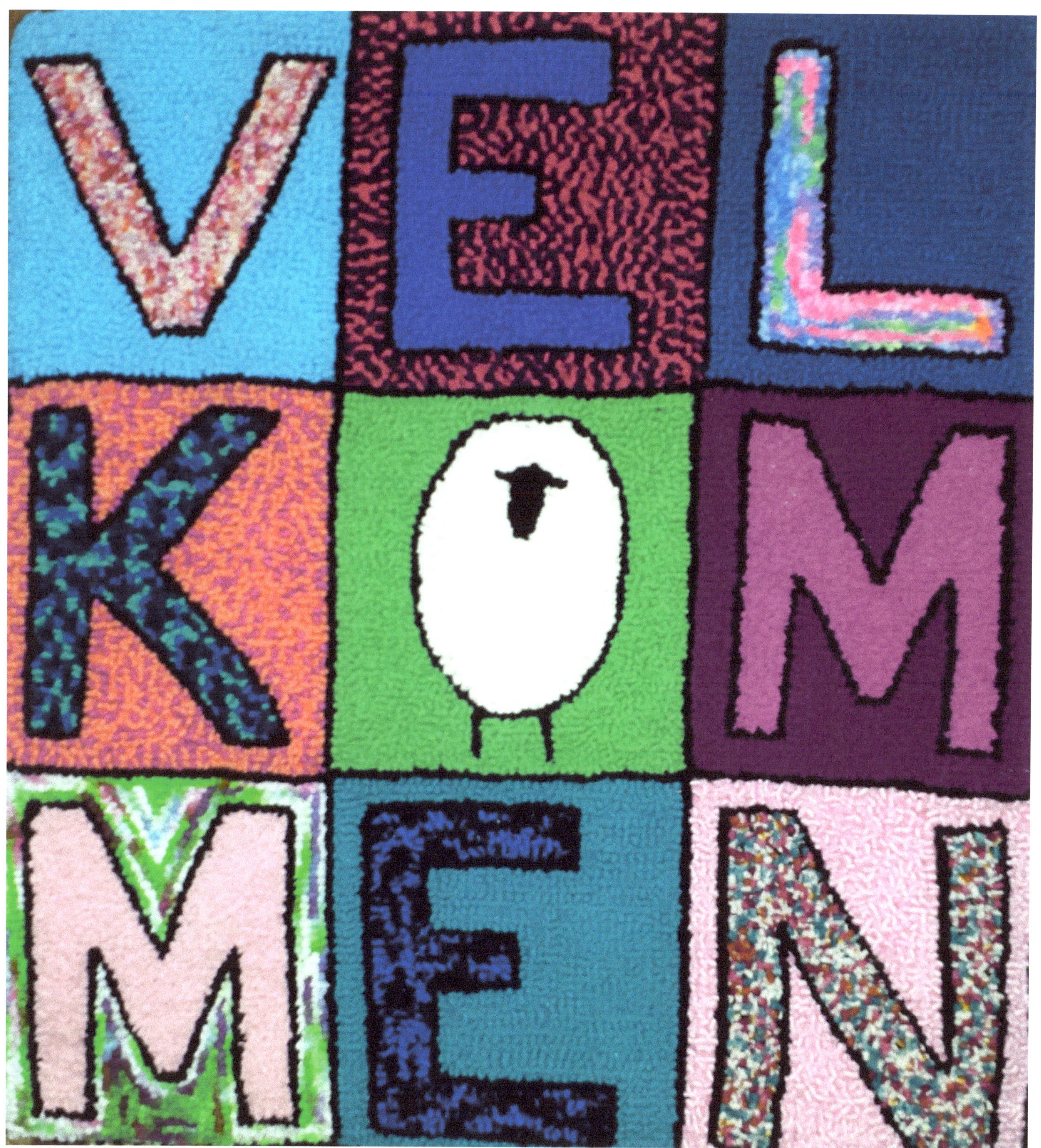

Velkommen, 17"x18" Designed and hooked with T-shirts by Judy Taylor.
For the backgrounds, you will need 1.5 oz each, letters .7 oz each and 1.8 oz for the outline.
Copy all four design pages to create the template.

VELKOMMEN TEMPLATE 1: UPPER LEFT CORNER

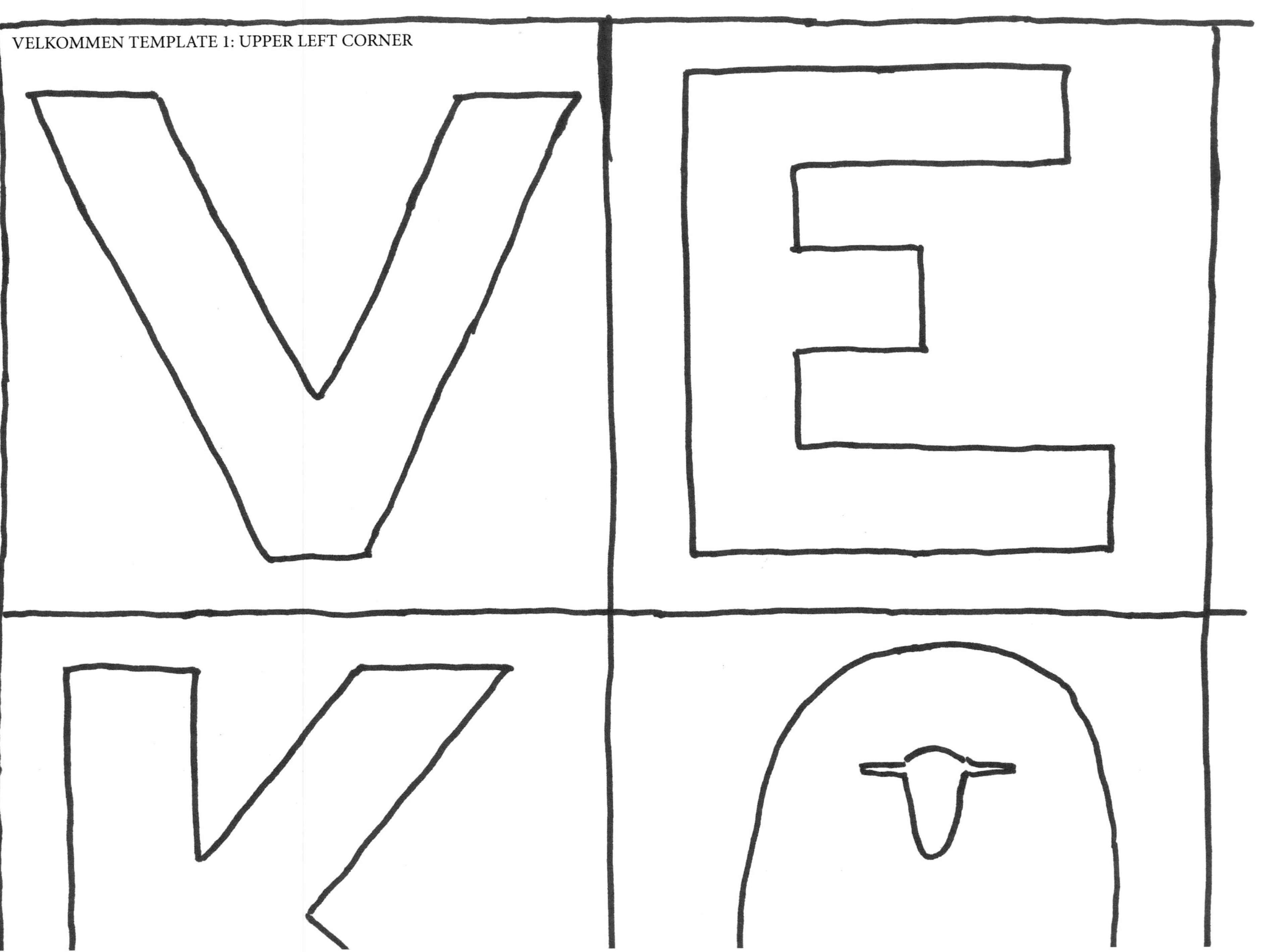

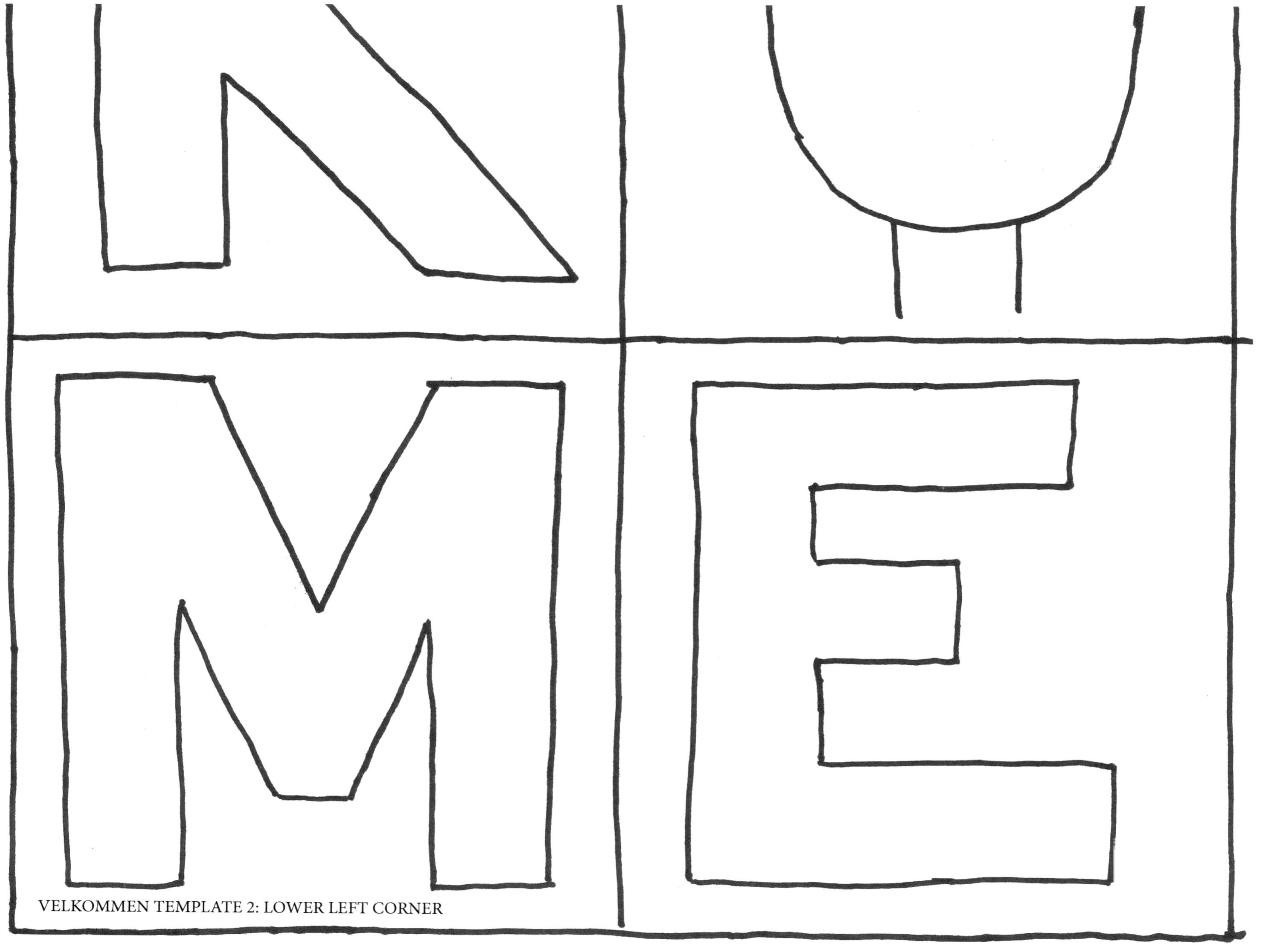

VELKOMMEN TEMPLATE 2: LOWER LEFT CORNER

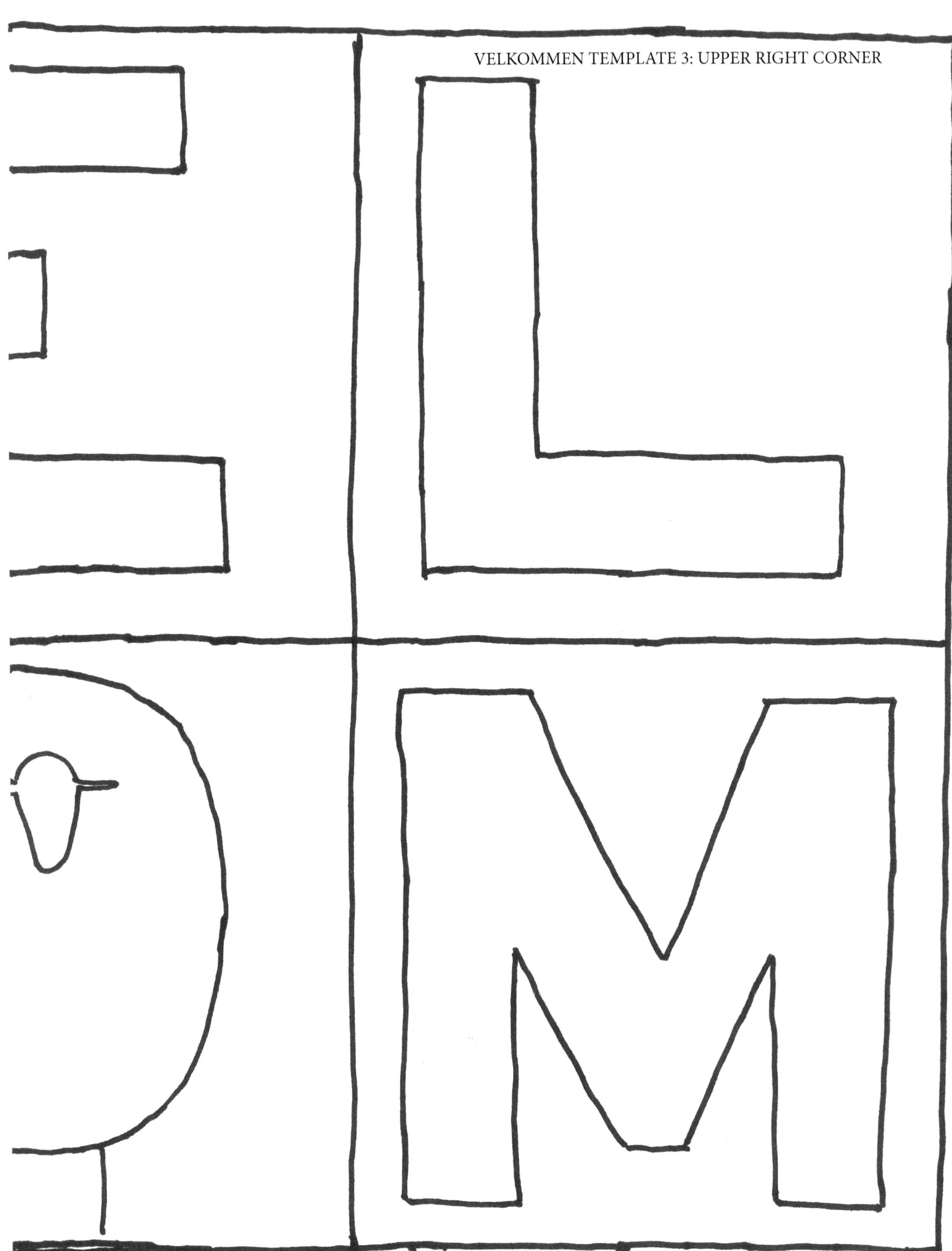
VELKOMMEN TEMPLATE 3: UPPER RIGHT CORNER

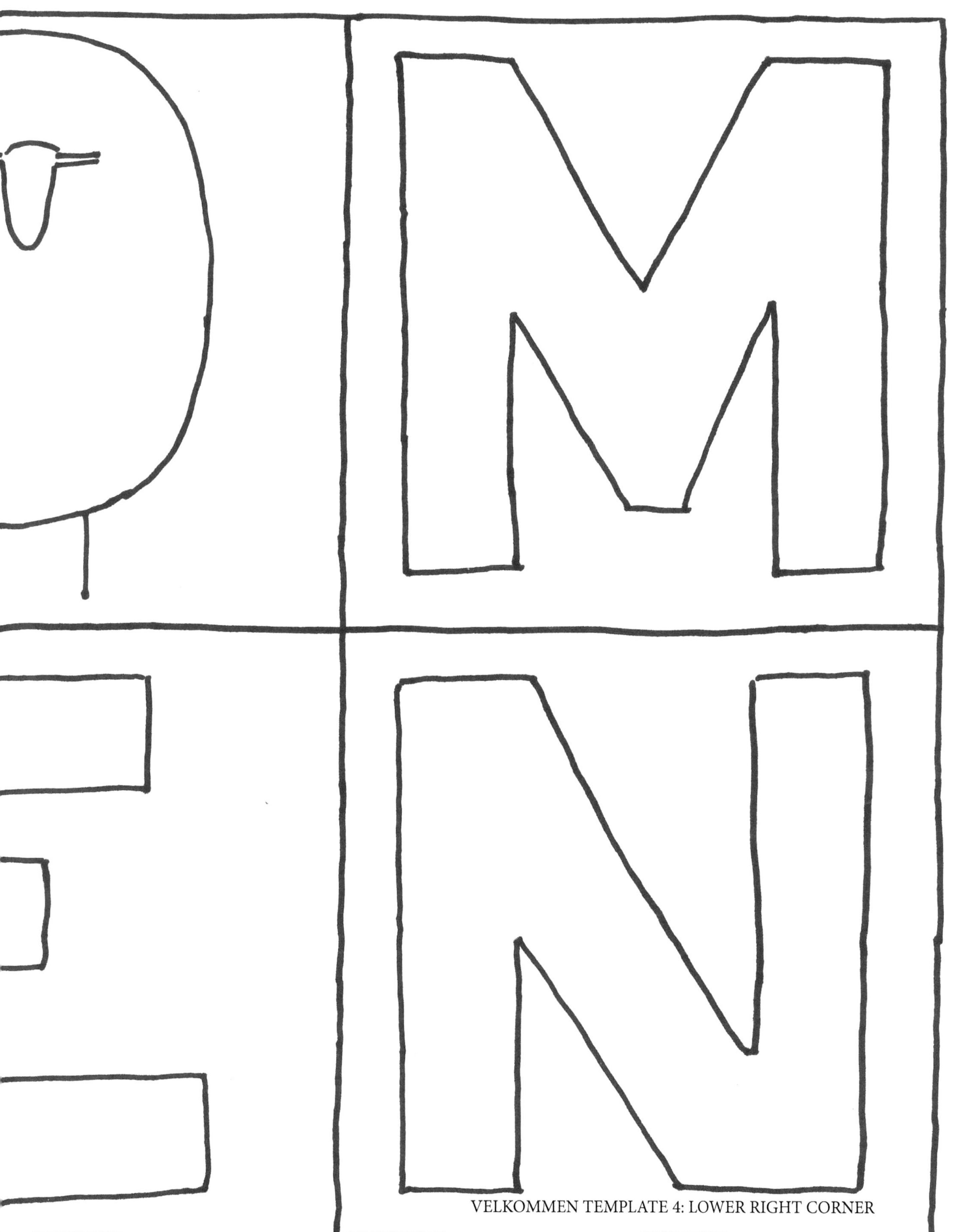

VELKOMMEN TEMPLATE 4: LOWER RIGHT CORNER

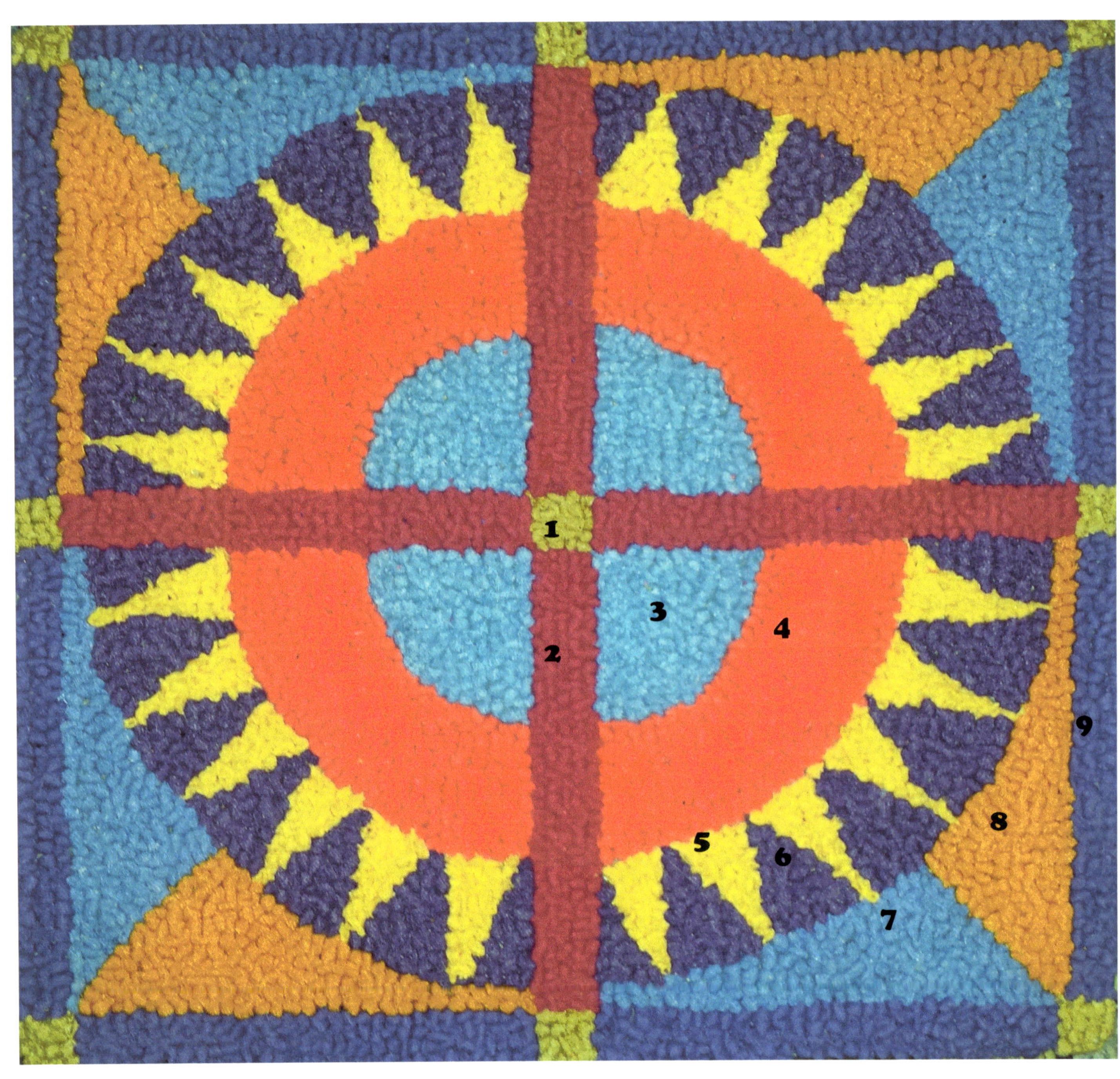

Crown Mat, 9.5"x9.5" Designed and hooked with T-shirts by Judy Taylor.
To make the Crown Mat in this size, using the above numbers as a guide, you will need:
1: .1 oz 2: .4 oz 3: .4 oz 4: .5 oz 5: .7 oz 6: .8 oz 7: .4 oz 8: .4 oz 9: .5 oz.

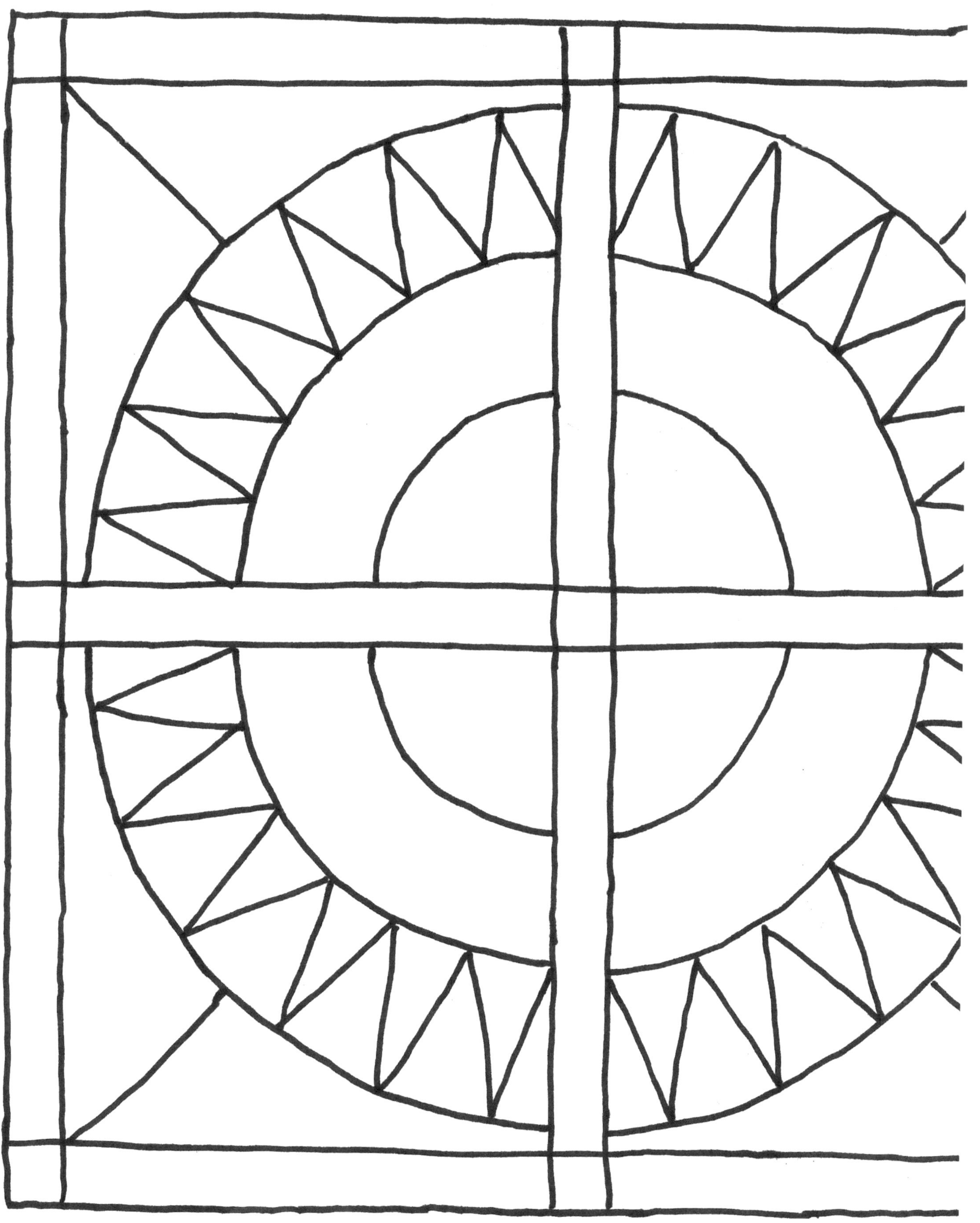

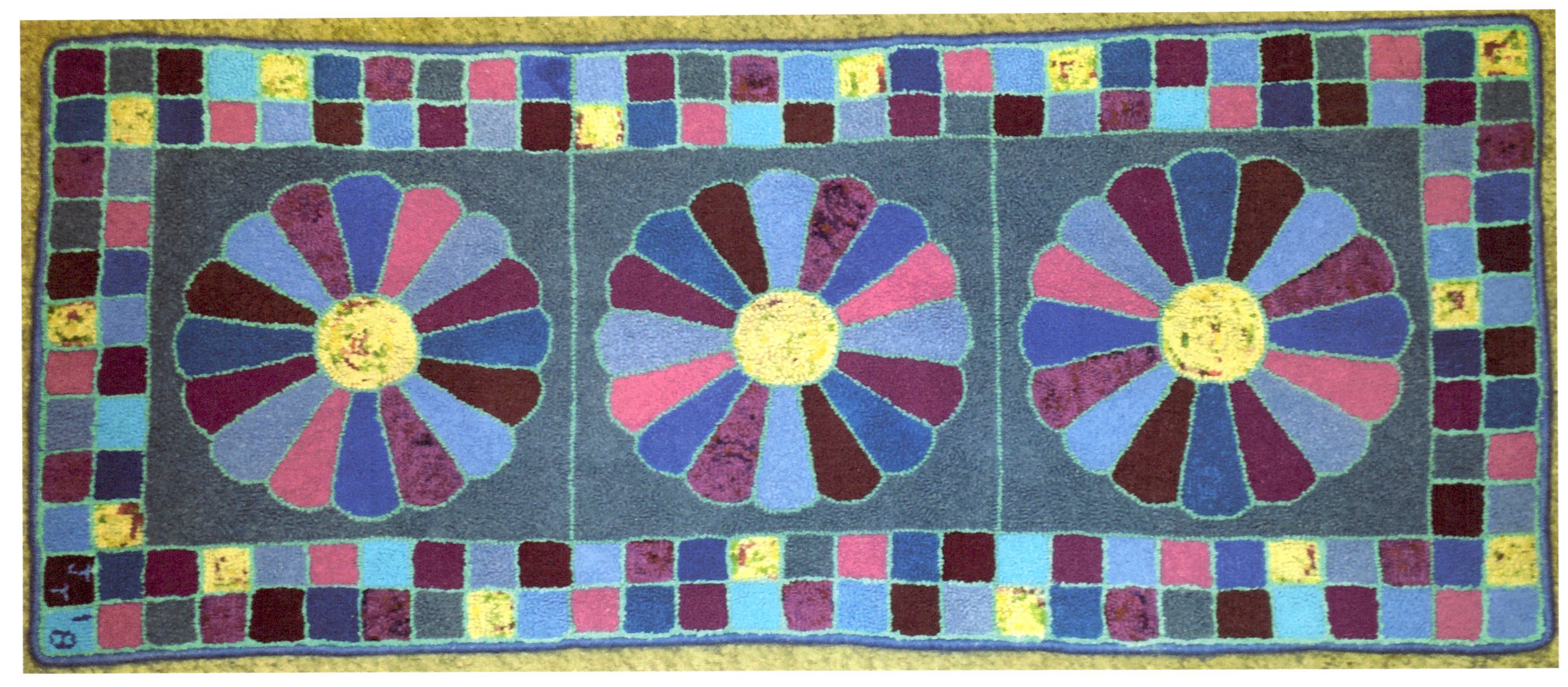

Dresden Plate Rug, 19.5”x44” Designed and hooked with T-shirts by Judy Taylor.
For the background of each panel you will need 2.4 oz (for a total of 7.2 oz), and for the remaining 14 colors, plan to have 2.6 oz of each color.

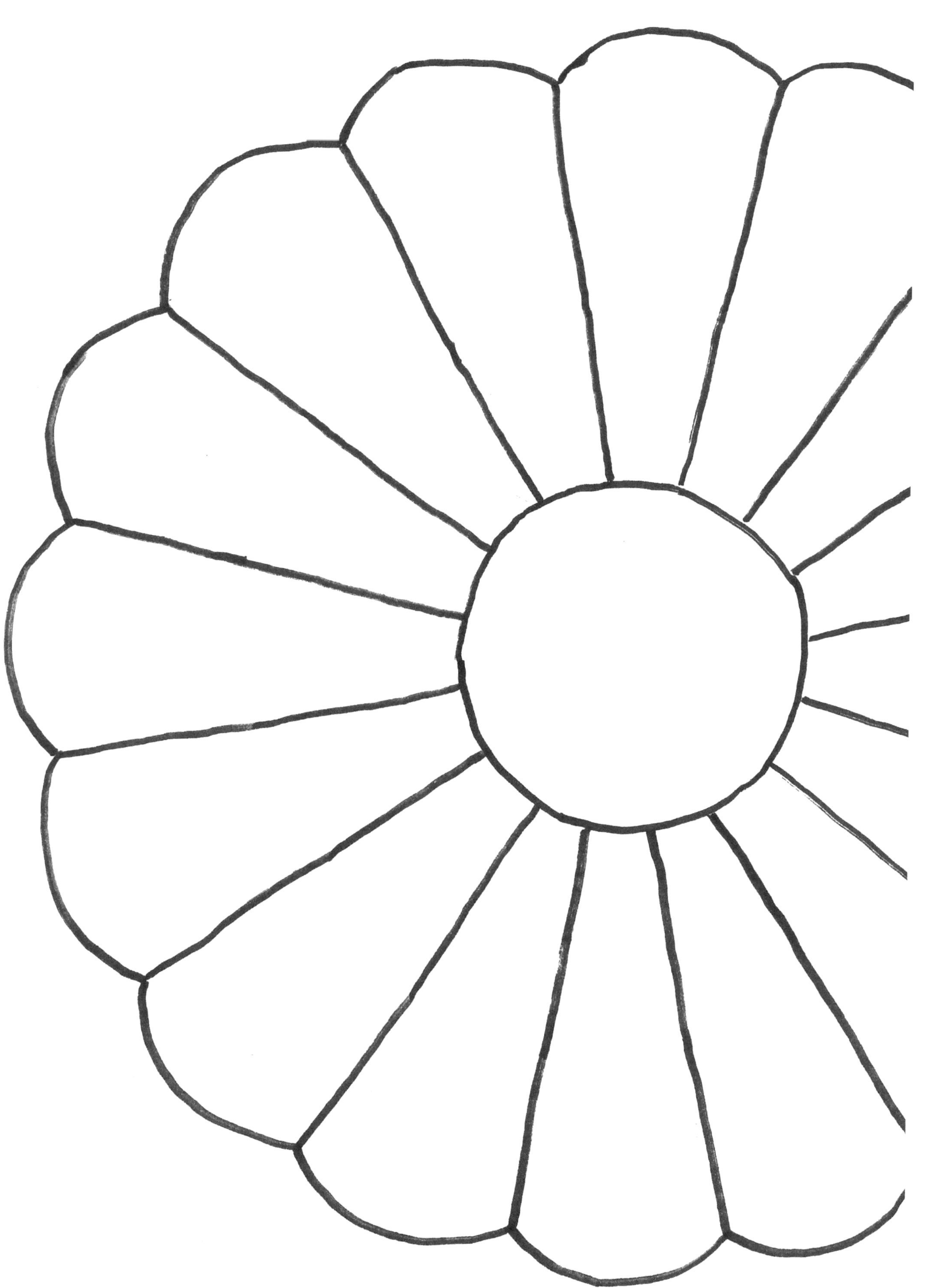

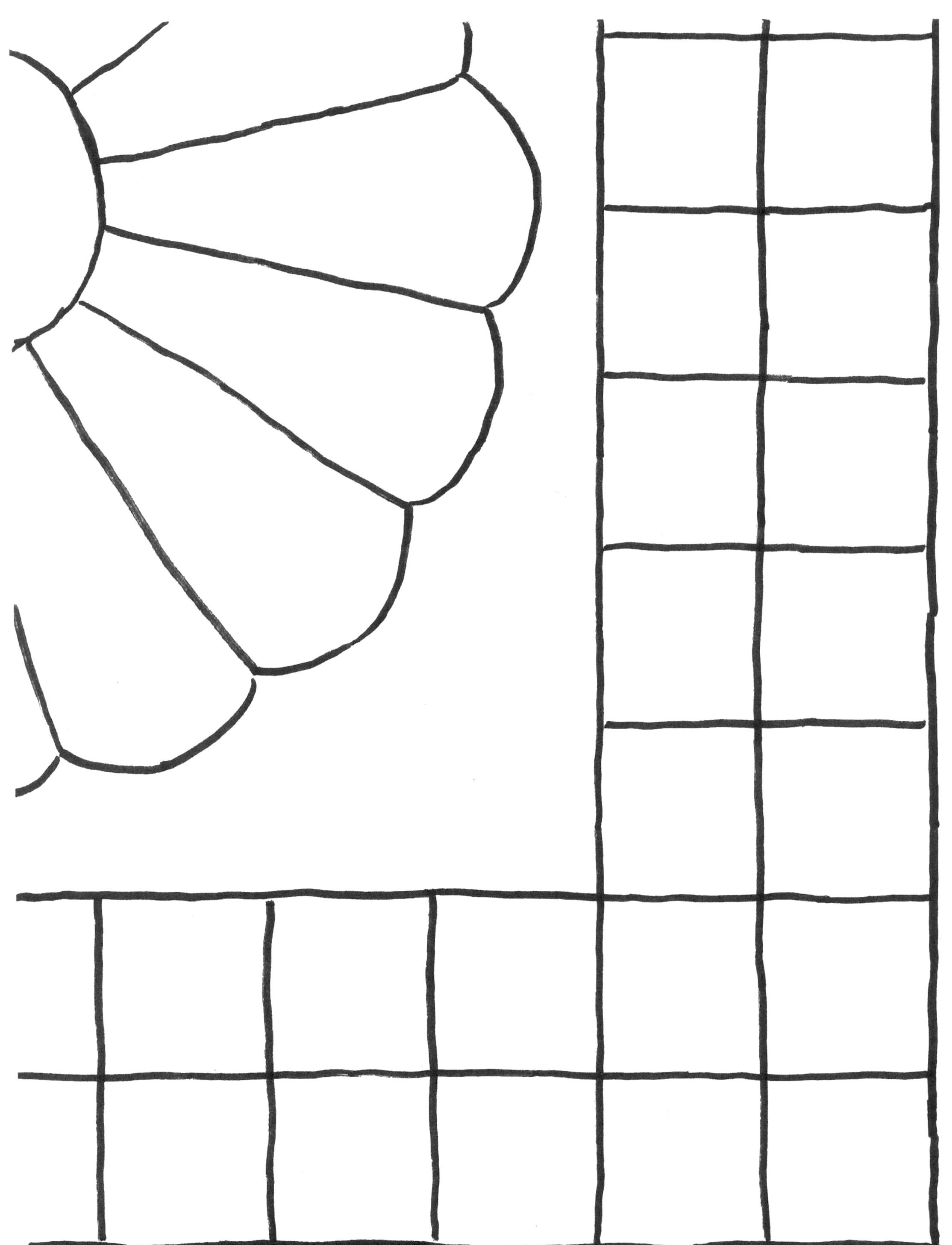

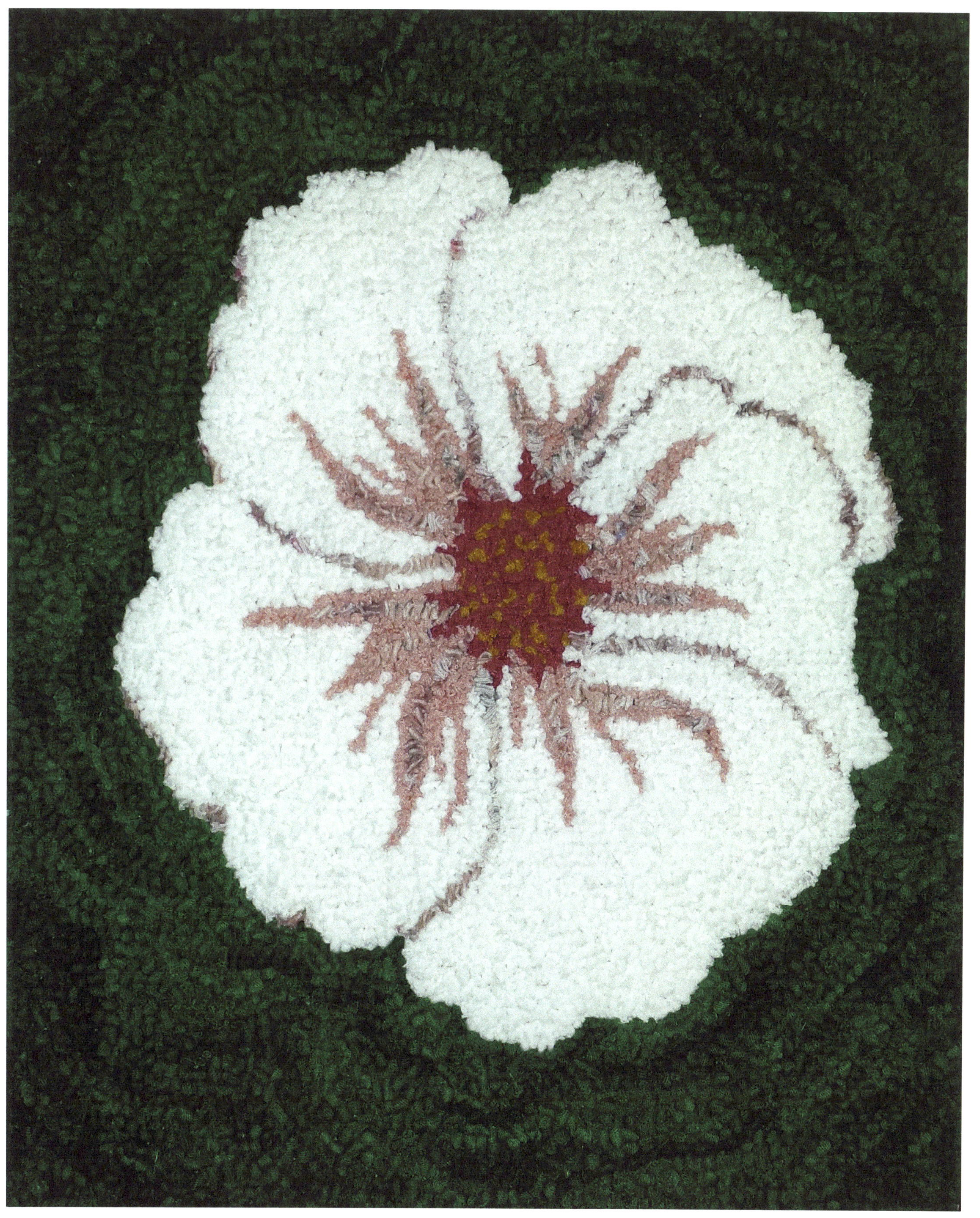

Peony, 9.5"x11.5" Designed and hooked with T-shirts by Judy Taylor.
For this piece, you could start out with a 9.5"x11.5" rectangle, or an oval or circle.
You will need 2.2 oz for the background, 1.35 oz white, .2 oz red, 1.5 oz pink, .45 oz pink/gray, .1 oz gold.

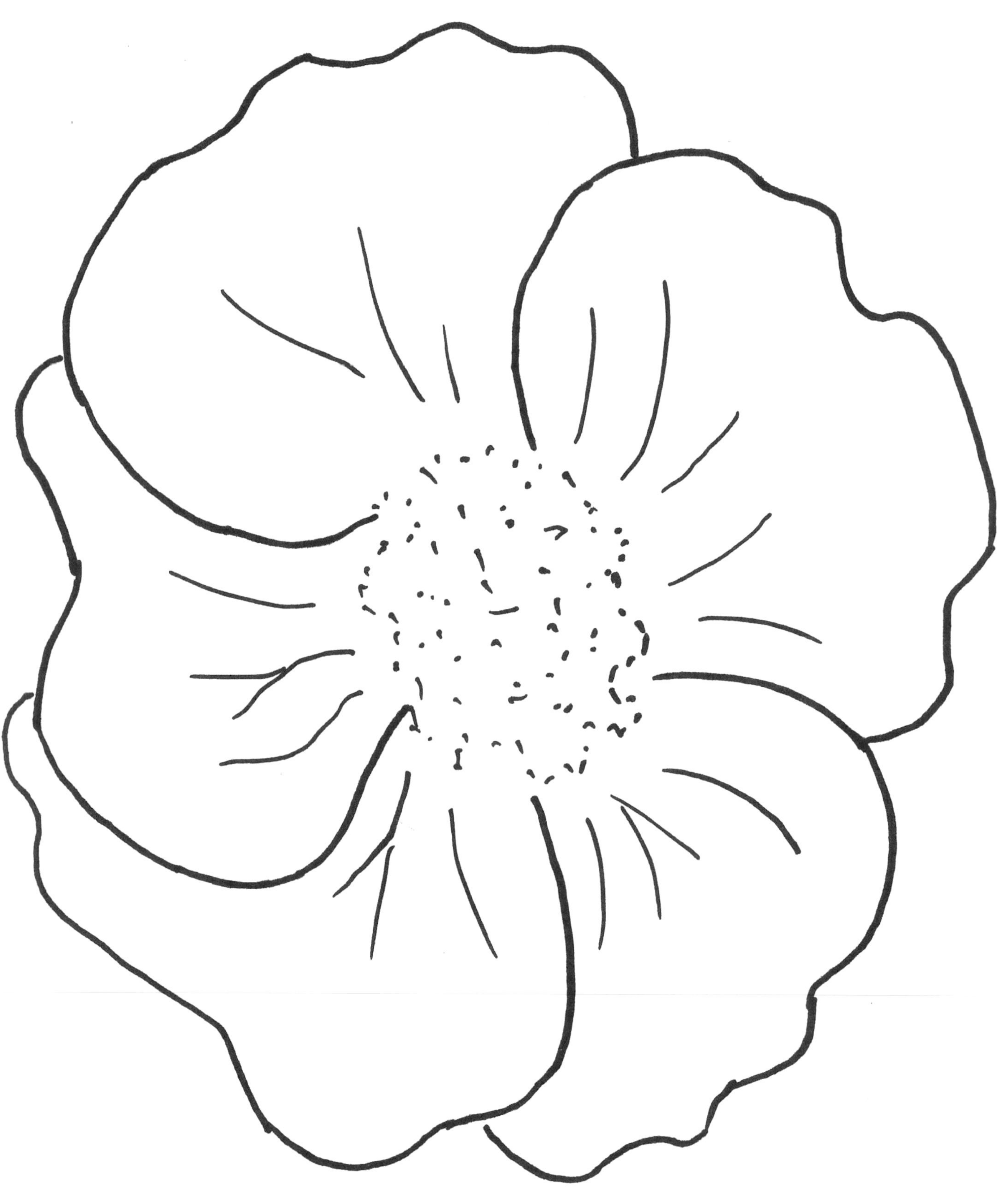

Hemming Your Projects

How you hem your project depends on what it's going to be used for. If it's going to be a wall hanging or table decoration (so not exposed to wear and tear or frequent washing) then you can just turn the selvedges over and do a simple hem. You'll want to cut off the excess, about 1" from the hooked corner (right), and about 3" from the hooked edge all around. It's a good idea to do a running or zig-zag stitch along the cut edge to reinforce it.

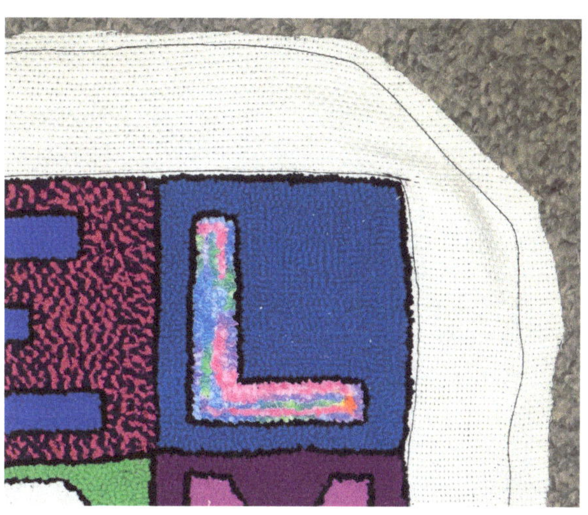

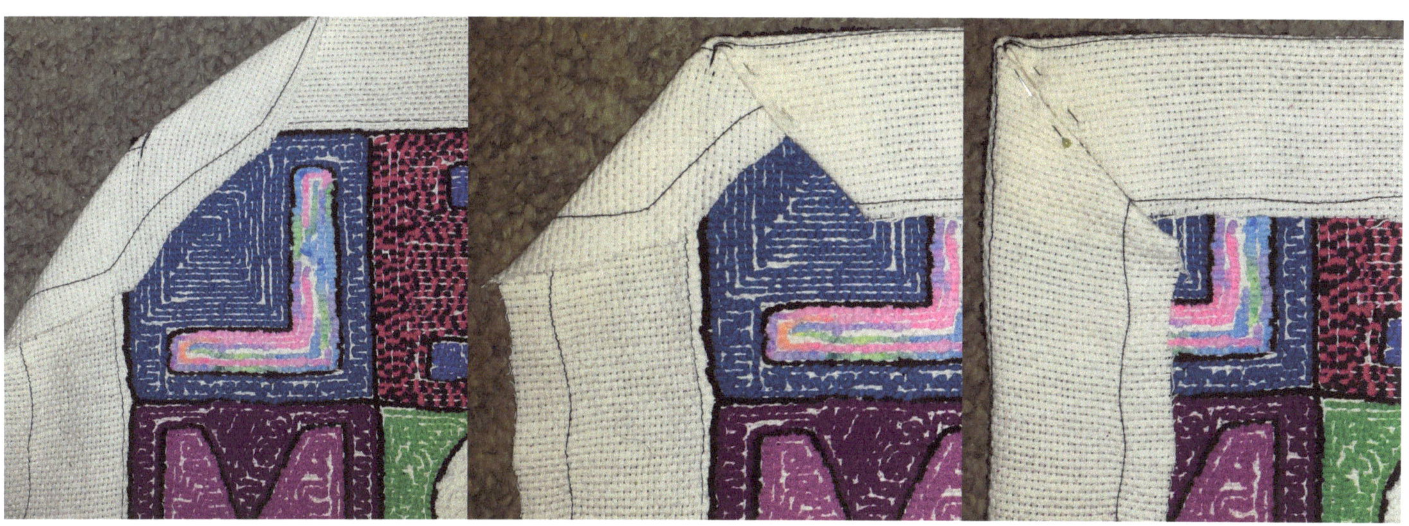

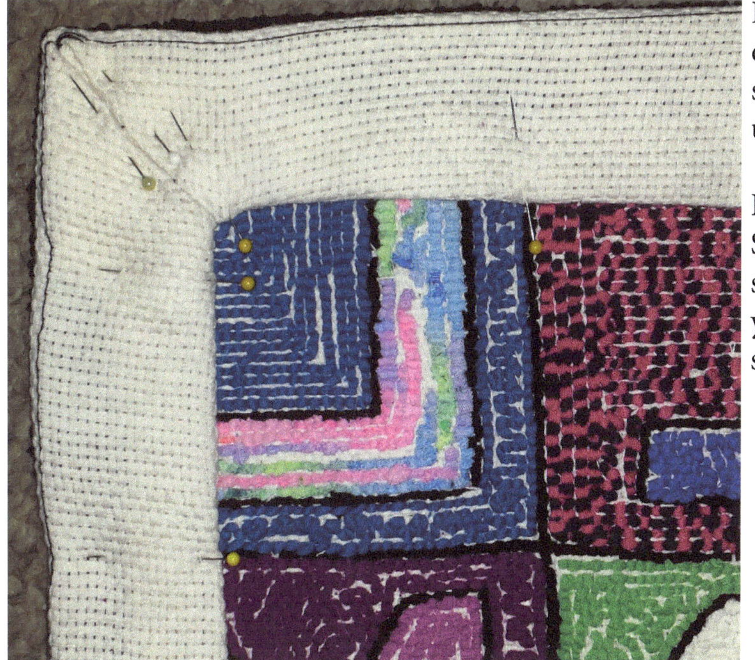

Fold down the corner diagonally (above left), fold down one side and pin it (above center) and do the same for the other side so the mitered corners meet up nicely and lie flat (above right).

Fold under the selvedges and pin them down (left). Sew the mitered corners together, and when you sew the hem, be sure you are digging deep with your needle, so you're grabbing the backing, not the strips.

If you're making a rug for the floor, you will want to bind the edge. This make such a big difference to the life of the rug, because on an old floor rug, the first place to wear out is the edge. And if you do a simple turned-under hem on a rug that has to withstand wear and tear (like with the Velkommen project on the previous page), the edges will become brittle over time and when they fall apart, the hooking along the edge will unravel. We prevent that damage by simply binding the edge to protect it.

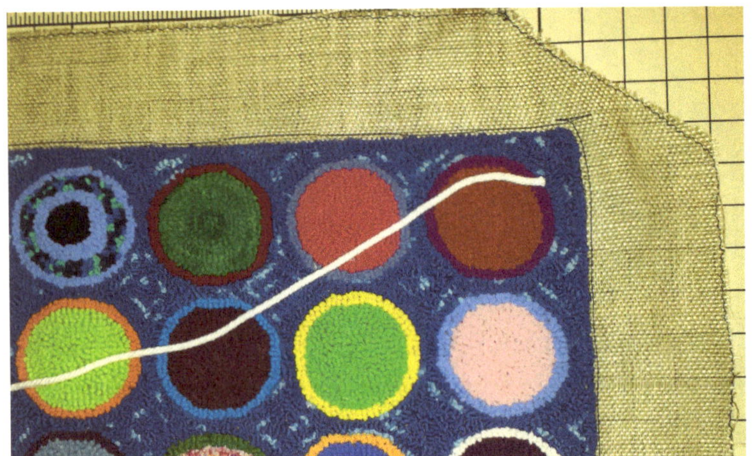

Just like we did with the Velkommen mat, trim off the excess backing and do a running or zig-zag stitch on your sewing machine to protect the raw edge from unraveling in the wash. But this time, you will wrap the selvedge around a cotton cord which you can find in the upholstery section of the fabric store (5/16") (you will need to pre-wash the cording at the same time you wash the backing material).

Do a basting stitch with a needle and thread to hold the cording in place, close to the hooked edge of the rug.

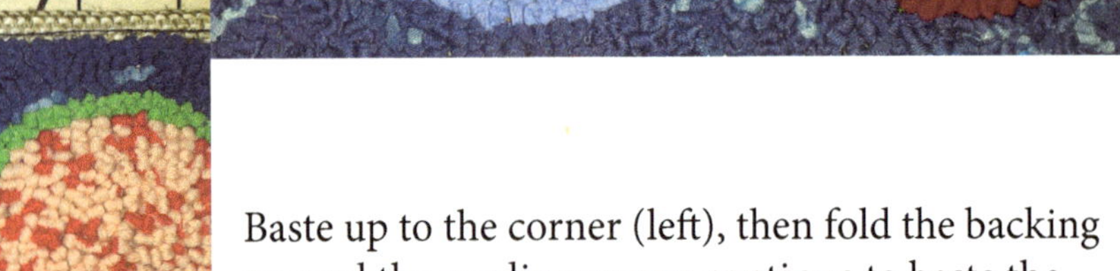

Baste up to the corner (left), then fold the backing around the cording as you continue to baste the cording in place (below).

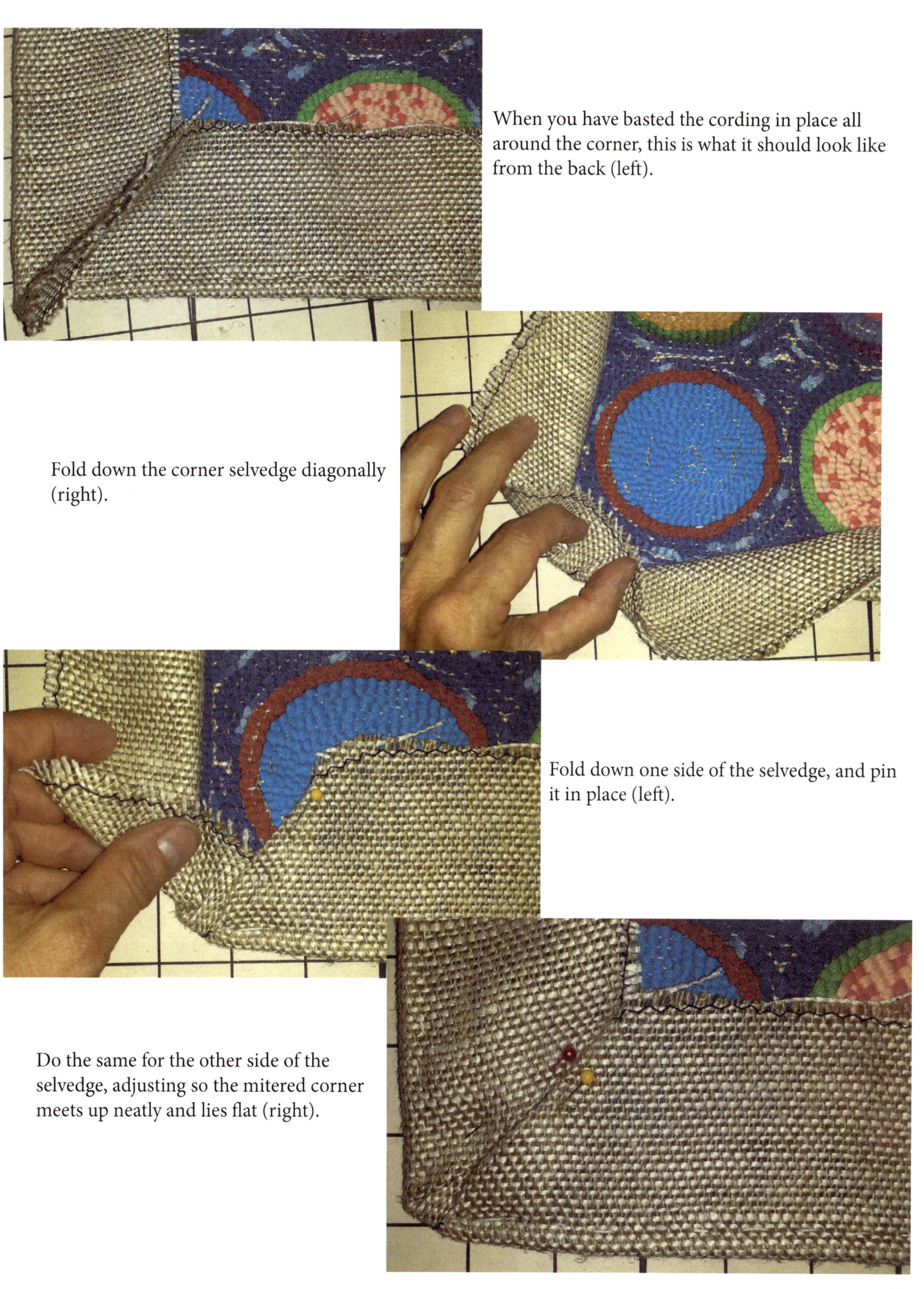

When you have basted the cording in place all around the corner, this is what it should look like from the back (left).

Fold down the corner selvedge diagonally (right).

Fold down one side of the selvedge, and pin it in place (left).

Do the same for the other side of the selvedge, adjusting so the mitered corner meets up neatly and lies flat (right).

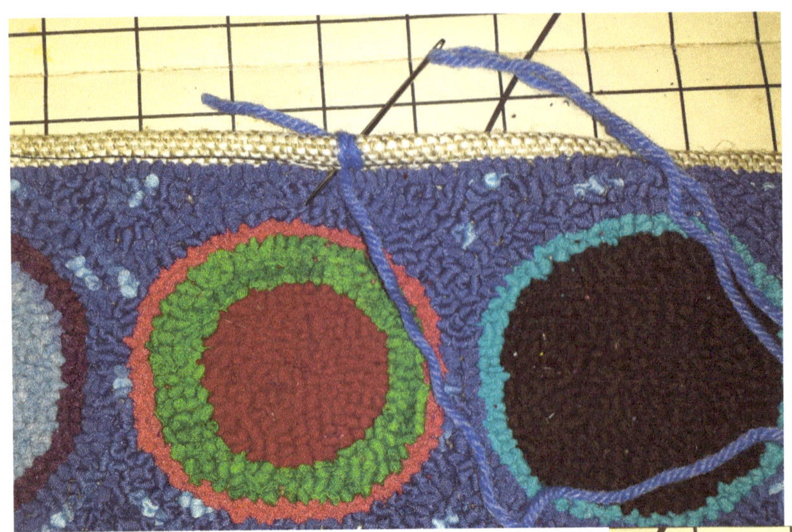

Using acrylic yarn (so it will be machine-washable) and an upholstery needle, come in from behind and whip stitch a few times over the end of the yarn. You won't need to tie knots with the whip stitching, you will sew over all the ends (left).

Once you've established the stitching, you will want to turn your needle around, so the final end of the yarn will also be in the back. Instead of whipping around with your needle, this one time you will come in from the front to the back with your needle (right).

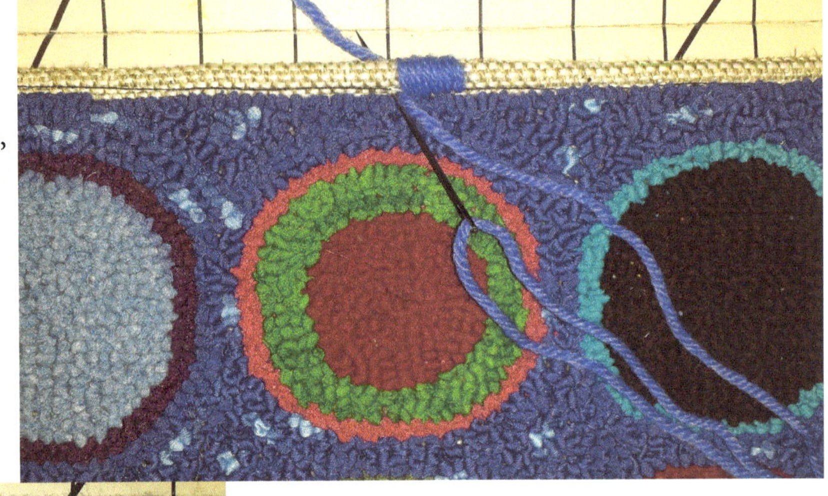

When the yarn runs out, start a new strand coming in from the back, as you did above, but this time you'll be sewing over two ends. Then turn the needle around so the next end comes out in the back.

When you have whip-stitched all around and you've come to the first stitches, run your needle under the stitching in the back for about one inch (left). When you pull it through, you can cut off the extra yarn, so all the tails will be secured without knots.

Fold under the excess selvedge and pin down (right). Sew the mitered corner together, and when you sew the folded hem down, be sure you are digging deep, grabbing the backing, not the strips.

By the way, if you have any old rugs around the house, and if the edges weren't bound before, you can extend the life of that old rug by protecting the edge in this way!

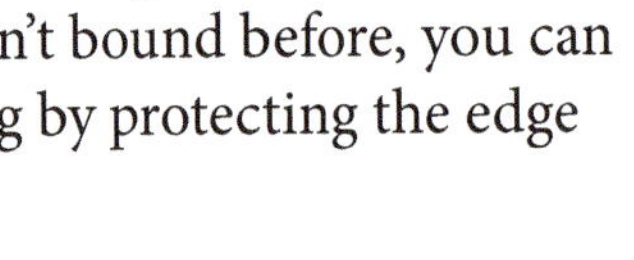

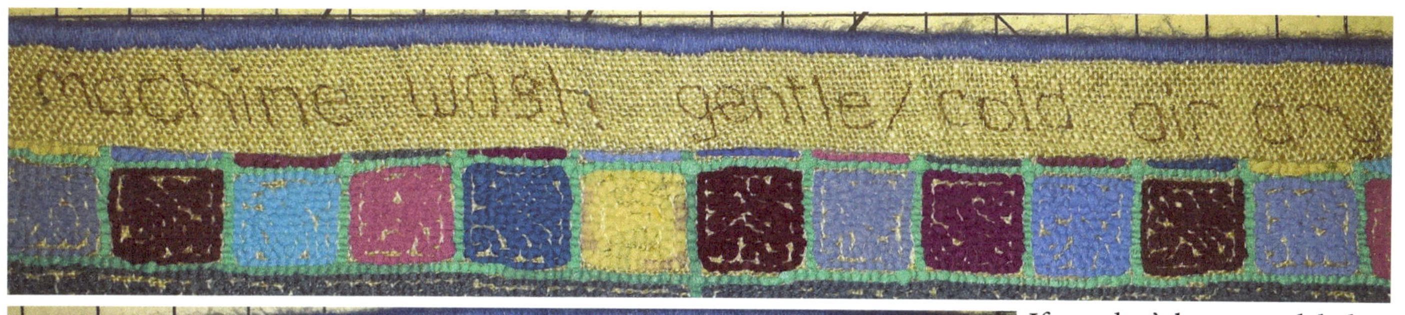

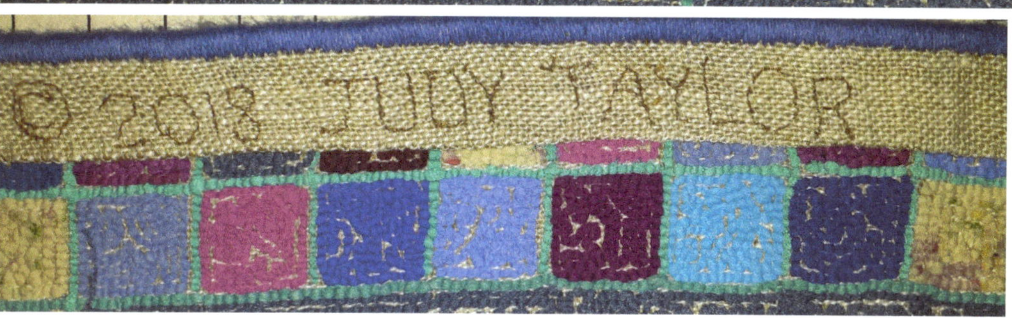

If you don't have care labels for your rugs, it's a good idea to sew the care instructions in the hem. You could write them with a Sharpie pen, but that could fade with repeated washing. Remember, this rug will be in use for a long time!

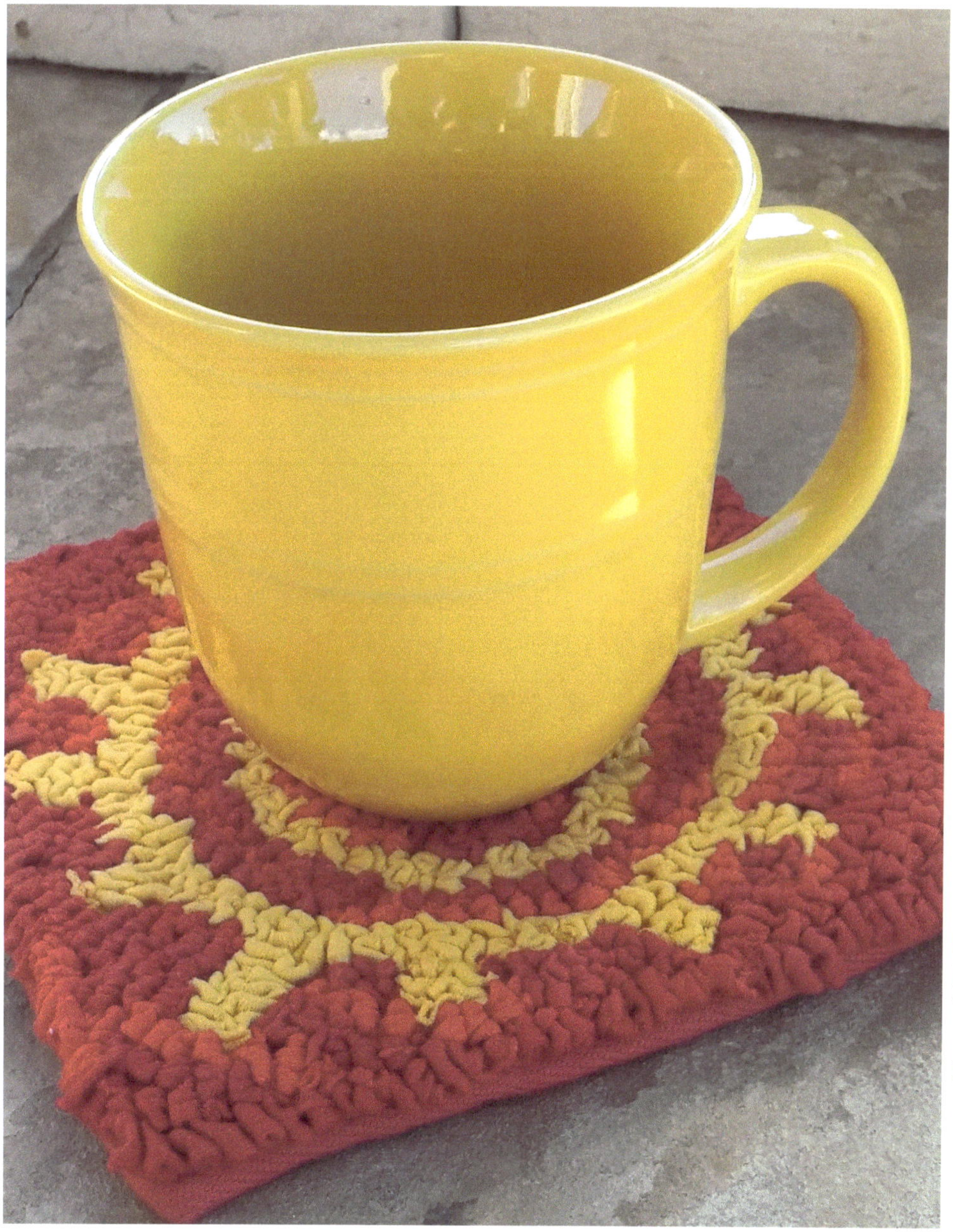

Petro Mug Rug, 6"x6"
Designed and hooked with T-shirts by Laura Salamy.

Photos by Laura Salamy.

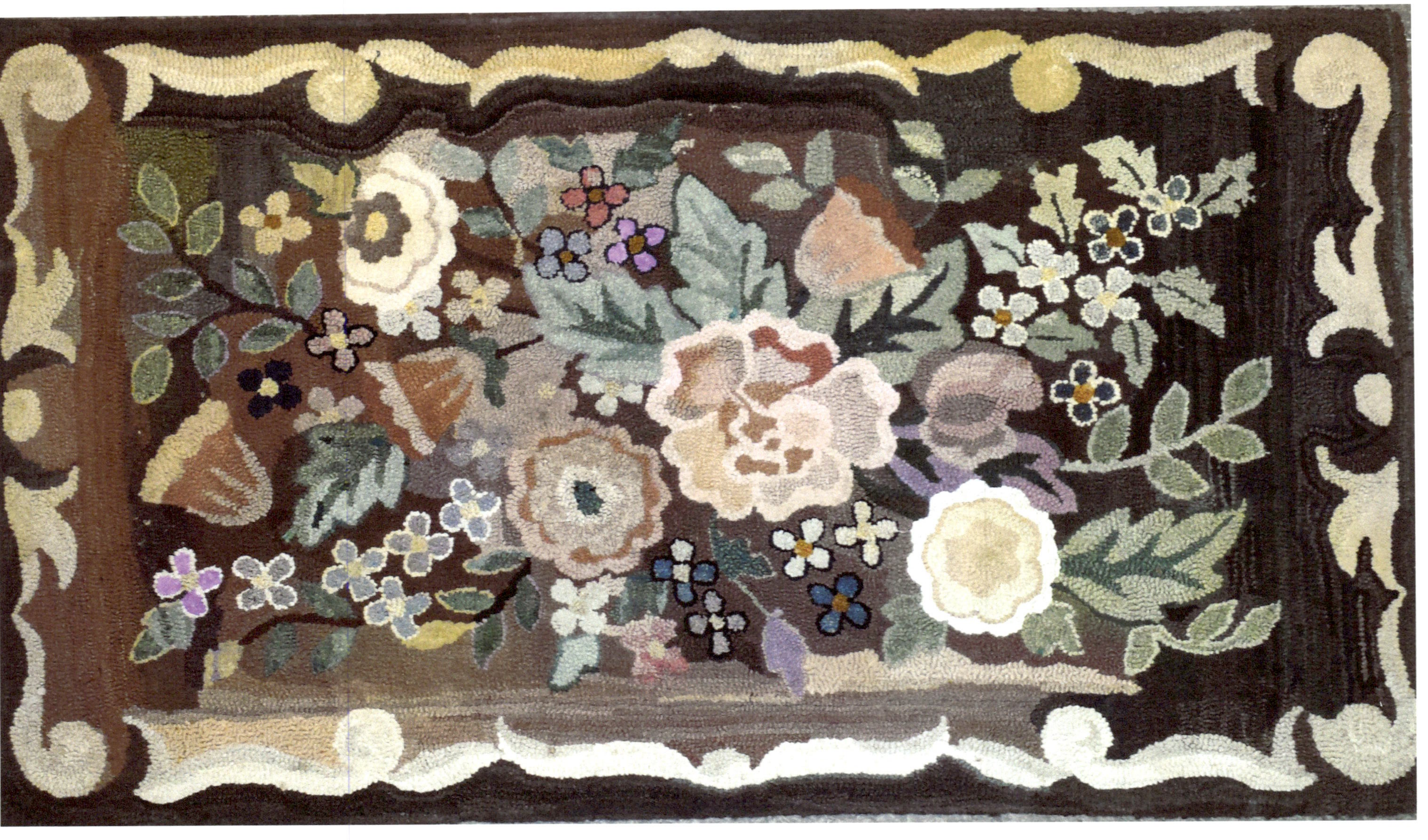

Early 20th Century silk stocking mat, 46"x27"
What I love most about this rug is that not a scrap went to waste. When she ran out of one color, she just started in with another. This rug has served admirably on the floor for many more years than yours truly's been around, and I'd say she's weathered it well!

From Grenfell to Guatemala

1905-1906

The Grenfell Association

For aiding philanthropic work among

The Deep Sea Fishermen of Labrador

Henry van Dyke, President

With best wishes & affec. remembrances
Wilfred Grenfell

A Grenfell Mission flyer, 1905
Photo courtesy of Paula Laverty.

At the end of the 19th century, a British doctor named Wilfred Grenfell (1865-1940) came to North America to serve the medical needs of the people in Newfoundland and Labrador, then part of a British colony. What he found there were scattered communities of hardy residents who depended on fishing and trapping for their survival. These remote areas had no services, no roads, no hospitals, and no economy beyond the fisheries to sustain the people. If the fish didn't run, the people didn't eat.

Many of the illnesses that Grenfell treated were born of poverty. He quickly realized that the efforts he put into improving the health of his patients were futile if they could not also lift their economic status. So he set in motion a plan to promote the handcrafts that were being produced by the community, such as woodworking, embroidery and rug hooking. They called this project The Industrial.

Reindeer Driving, 26.75"x46" Designed by Wilfred Grenfell, in production by 1916, cotton.
Photo courtesy of Paula Laverty.

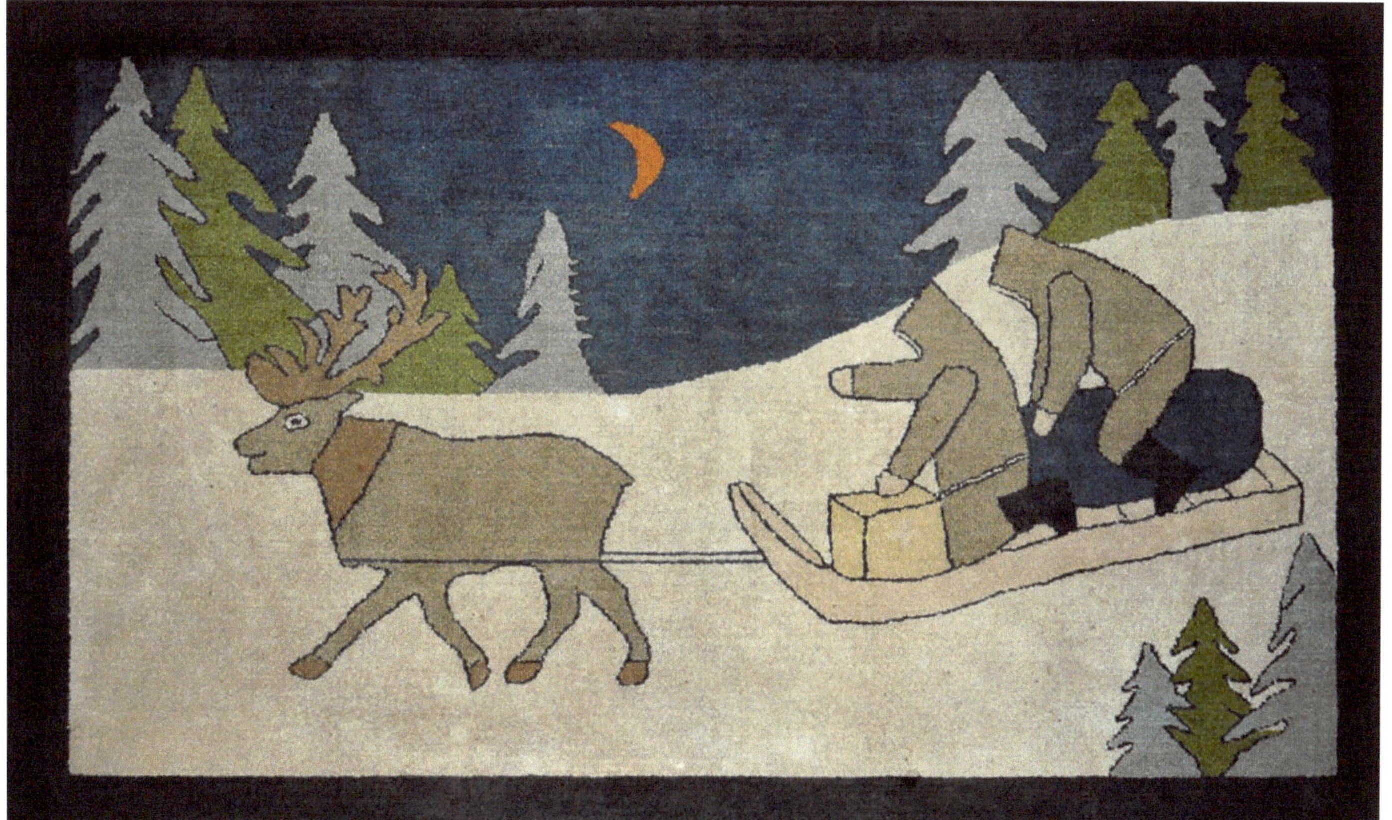

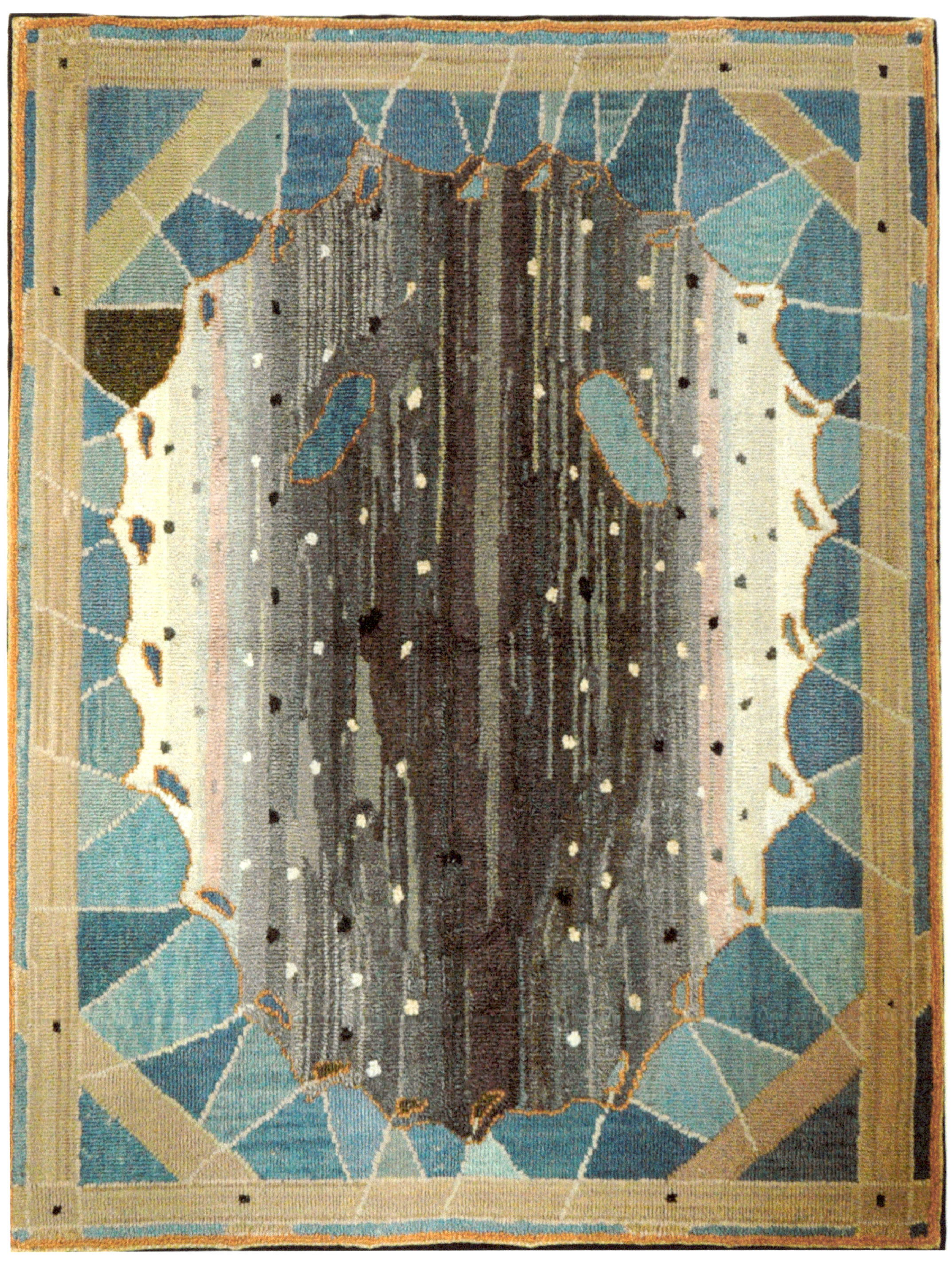

Sealskin Drying, 25"x20" Designed by Rhoda Dawson, in production by 1930-1935, silk, rayon and brin, dyed. Photo courtesy of Paula Laverty.

No little scrap of fabric or yarn went to waste in the charming hooked mats being produced in the area, but in order to market them to the wider world, they needed to find ways to standardize the designs and materials used. In that northern climate, it wasn't practical to raise sheep, so they brought in cotton flannel and occasionally wool, which could be dyed and hooked. Dr. Grenfell himself contributed some eye-catching rug designs, emphasizing images of polar bears and sailing ships unique to the area.

Grenfell hoped that by marketing these crafts in North America and Great Britain, they would bring in needed income to the local families to help them weather hard times. Thanks to Grenfell's tireless promotion, travelling and fundraising all over North America, the response to these handcrafts was positive, and they struggled to keep up with demand for those distinctive hand-hooked mats.

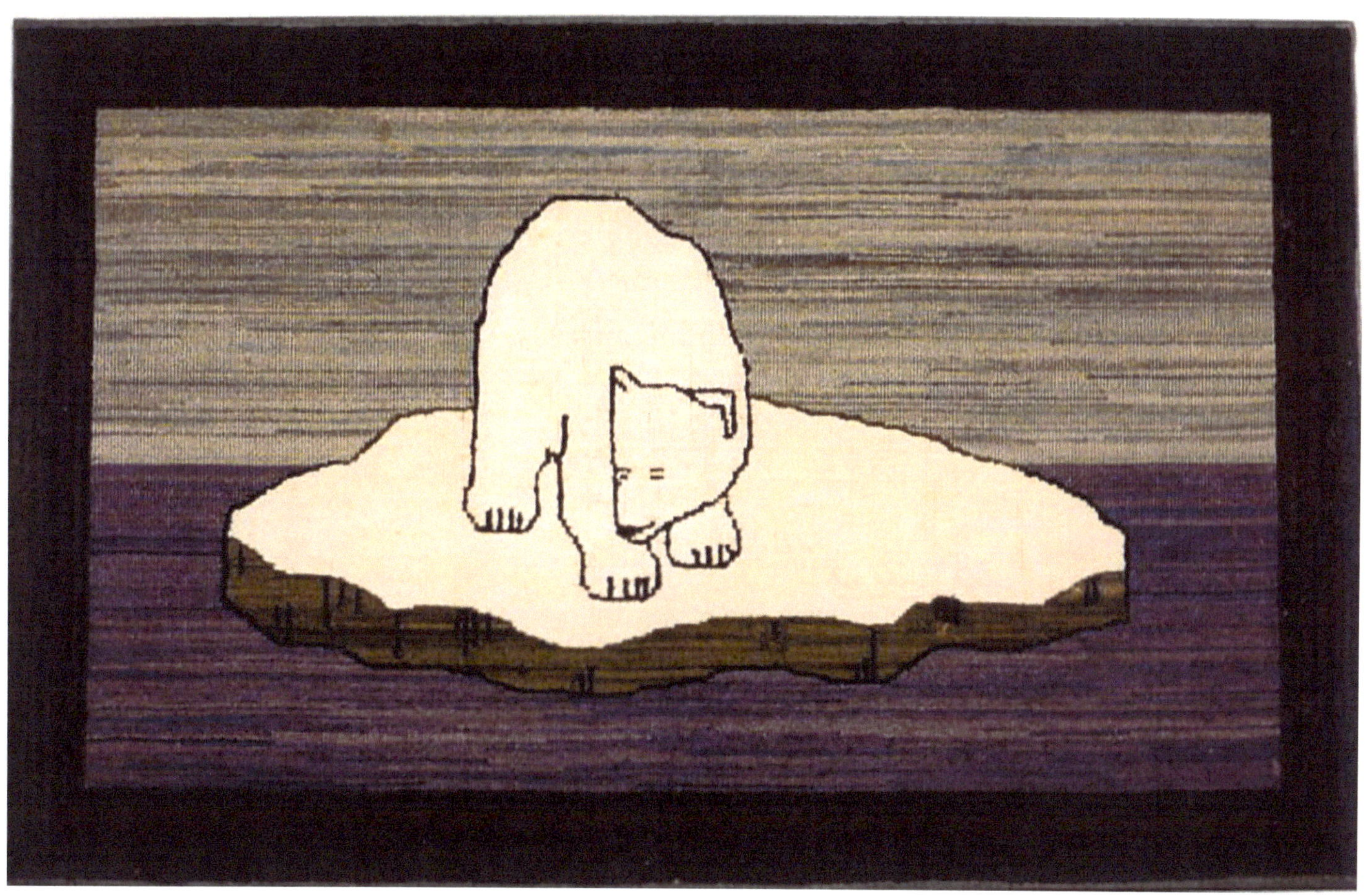

Polar Bear on Growler, 18.5"x30.25" Design in production c. 1928, silk and rayon, dyed.
Photo courtesy of Paula Laverty.

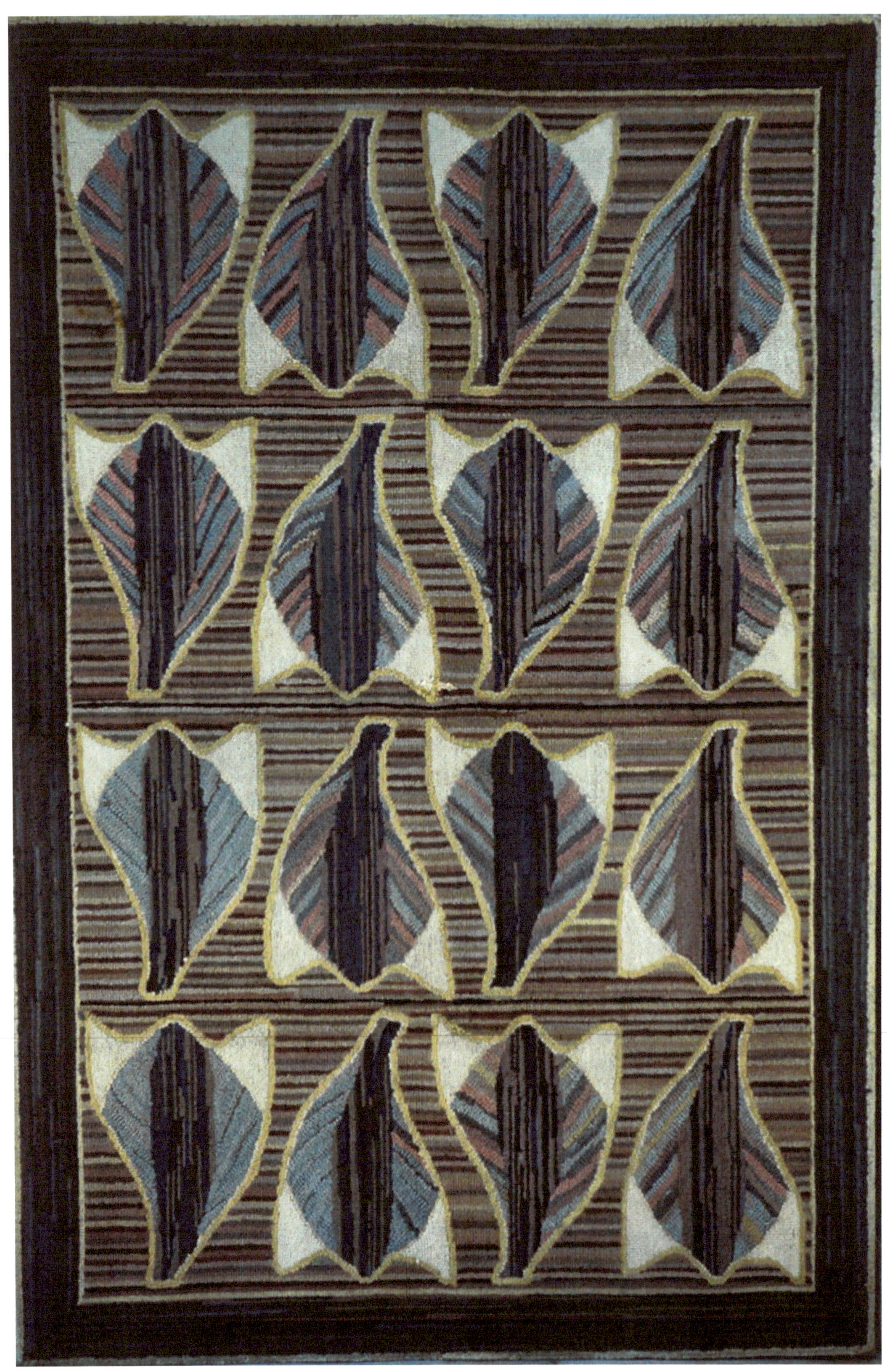

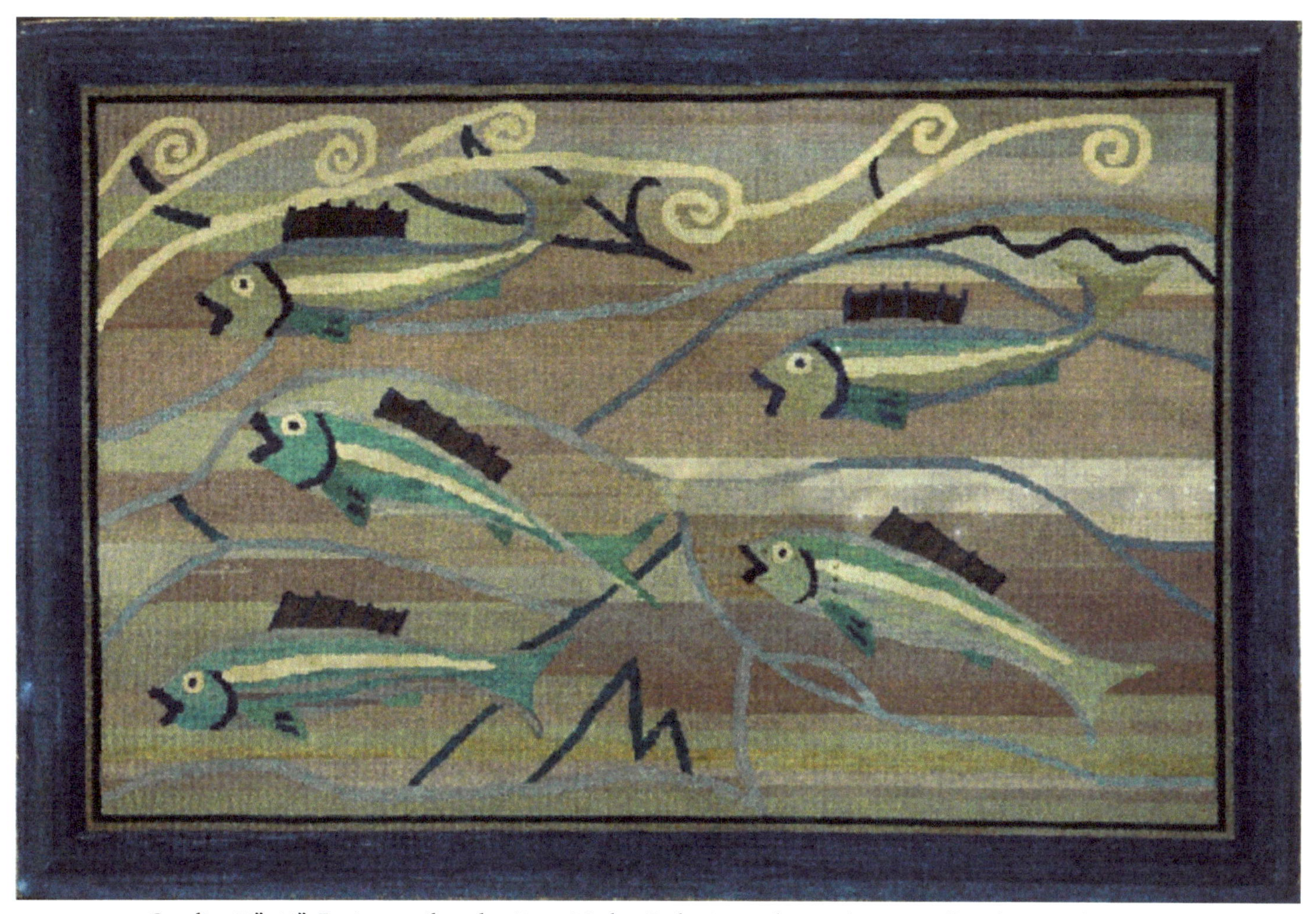

Capelin, 27"x40" Design attributed to Dora Mesher Ricks, in production by 1936, silk and rayon, dyed.
Photo courtesy of Paula Laverty.

By the 1920's, the shorter skirts in ladies' fashion drove the demand for prettier alternatives to drab cotton or woolen leg wear, so silk stockings became all the rage. But to anyone who has ever worn a pair of silk hose, you know how easily they run. When those lovely silk stockings got a snag (or got "laddered"), they were thrown out. A clever rug designer working for The Industrial, Mae Alice Pressley-Smith, began experimenting with cutting up old stockings and hooking them into the rugs. The silk took dye easily and gave a special luster to the surface of the rug. The Industrial began to solicit donations of used silk stockings for rug hooking, and boy, did they get their wish, one year receiving a whopping nine tons of the silken treasures! (*Silk Stocking Mats*, by Paula Laverty, 2005)

Silk stocking Grenfell mats sold like crazy and improved the local economy for many years. But times and fashions change, and after World War II, nylon stockings (which didn't work for rug hooking) replaced silk. Newfoundland and Labrador were annexed into Canada (1949), and with that came greater development and social services. The Industrial continued for many more years, and while it never regained its former glory, it is credited with saving and strengthening a struggling rural community, as well as producing gorgeous artwork that is still coveted to this day.

(opposite)Fish on Flake, 39"x26" Designed by Rhoda Dawson, in production by 1933, silk and rayon.
Photo courtesy of Paula Laverty.

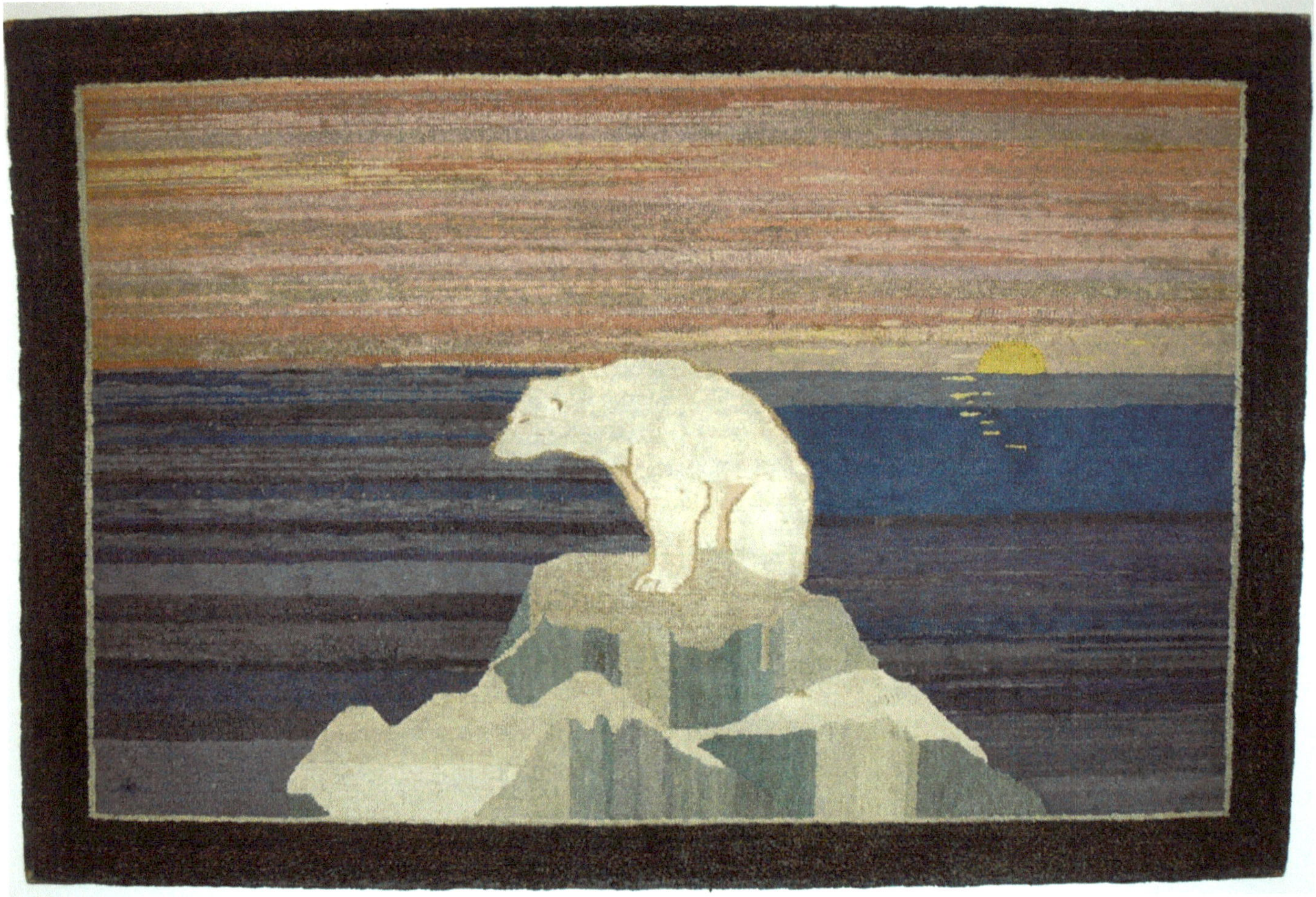

Single Polar Bear on Ice Pan, 26.5"x40.5" Design in production c. 1930, silk or rayon, brin, and cotton, dyed. Photo courtesy of Paula Laverty.

What you have read in this section is just a taste of the fascinating and inspirational story of the Grenfell Mission in Paula Laverty's book, *Silk Stocking Mats, Hooked Mats of the Grenfell Mission,* McGill-Queen's University Press.

This book is a must for any avid rug hooker. Laverty weaves historical fact with local lore, through photographs, letters, articles and interviews which bring this unique story to life.

The book can be purchased at www.grenfellhookedmats.com.

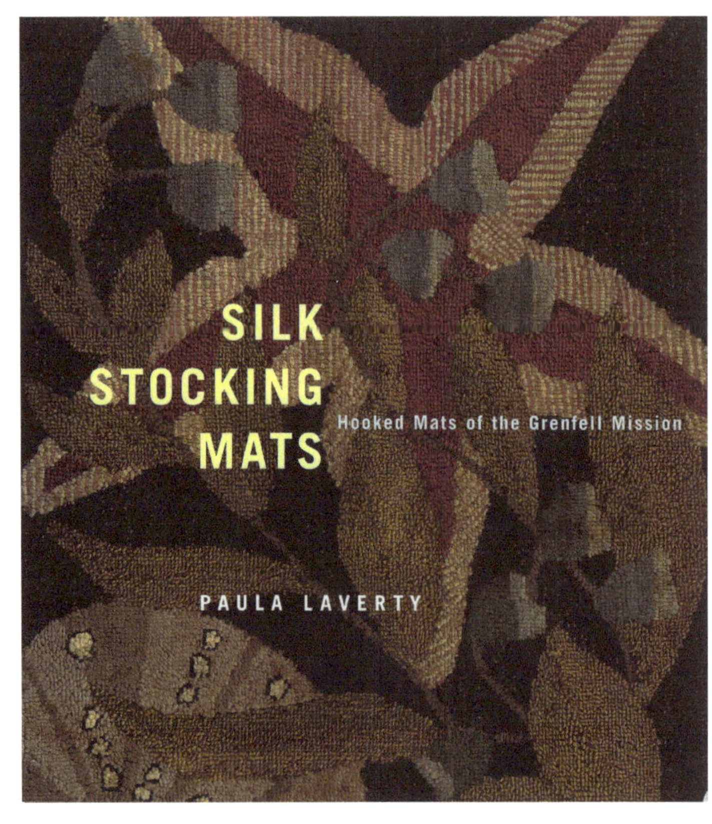

Fast-forward a hundred years or so, and meet Mary Anne Wise and Jody Slocum, renowned fiber artists and teachers who visited Guatemala in 2006. While they were enraptured by the indigenous weaving and embroidery in its riot of joyous color, they couldn't help but contrast that creative ebullience with the extreme poverty in the villages they visited. Especially moving was their visit to a village that had recently suffered a mudslide that claimed 1,400 lives.

A typical tourist might understandably feel distress to observe such suffering while on vacation, but then their memories would likely fade once they returned to their everyday lives. Not Mary Anne and Jody. They promptly mounted fundraisers to benefit the mudslide victims (raising some $150K), but even that didn't seem like enough.

Surely there was more that two such talented fiber artists could do to improve the lives of the struggling female artisans they so admired.

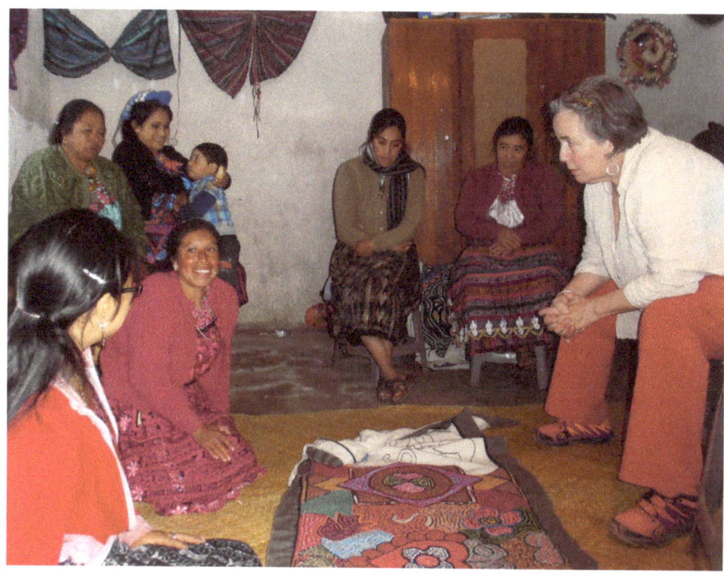

Mary Anne Wise and the Chirijquaic Rug Hooking Group. Photo by Multicolores.

They returned to Guatemala, offering classes in rug hooking to local women. The success of the first class in June 2009 led to a further seven workshops (between 2009-2012) in which Mary Anne and Jody taught their Guatemalan students more advanced drawing and design techniques. This required innovative thinking when confronted with the challenge of teaching, for example, proportion and scale, to women with few years of schooling. But what their students may have lacked in formal education, they more than made up for in their innate appreciation of color in their weaving and embroidery, and so they took to the rug hooking instruction readily. Wool yarn or fabric would have been much too expensive to make rug hooking accessible to the local artists, but used clothing was cheap and plentiful, in bright colors that wouldn't need to be dyed before hooking, so that's what Mary Anne and Jody taught their students to utilize.

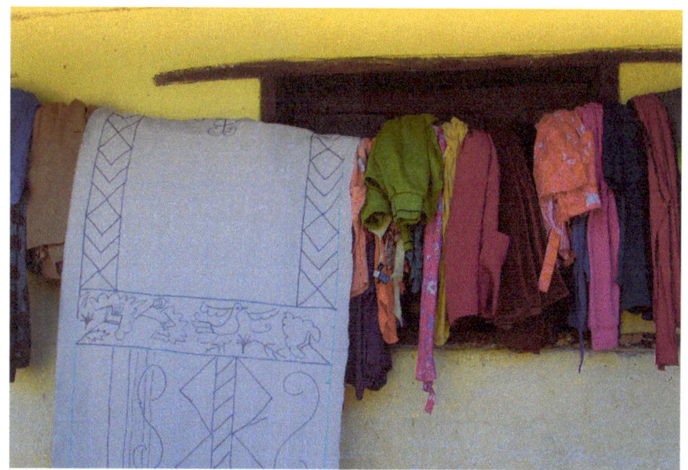

Second-hand clothing plus a design ready to be hooked. Photo by Multicolores.

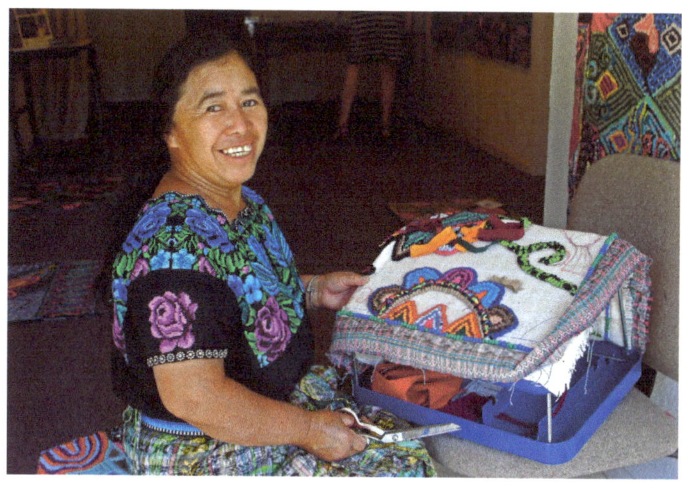

Carmen Maldonado rug hooking. Photo by Cheryl Walsh Bellville.

When some of those first rugs were sold, they didn't just bring in money, they changed lives. Women living in poverty that had felt isolated and hopeless about their future and the lives of their children suddenly began to feel hope that, with the craft of rug hooking, they could substantially change life for themselves and their families.

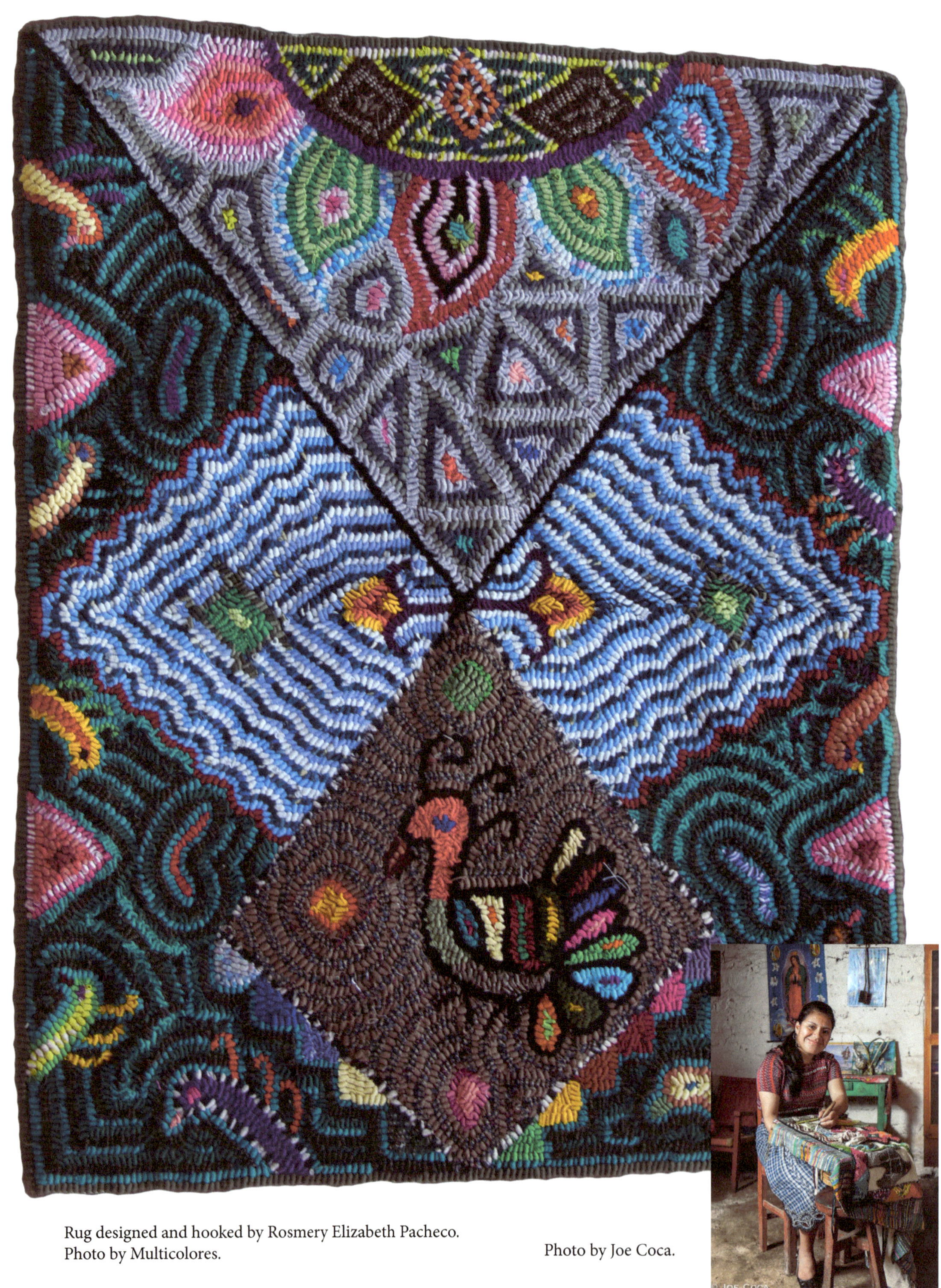

Rug designed and hooked by Rosmery Elizabeth Pacheco.
Photo by Multicolores.

Photo by Joe Coca.

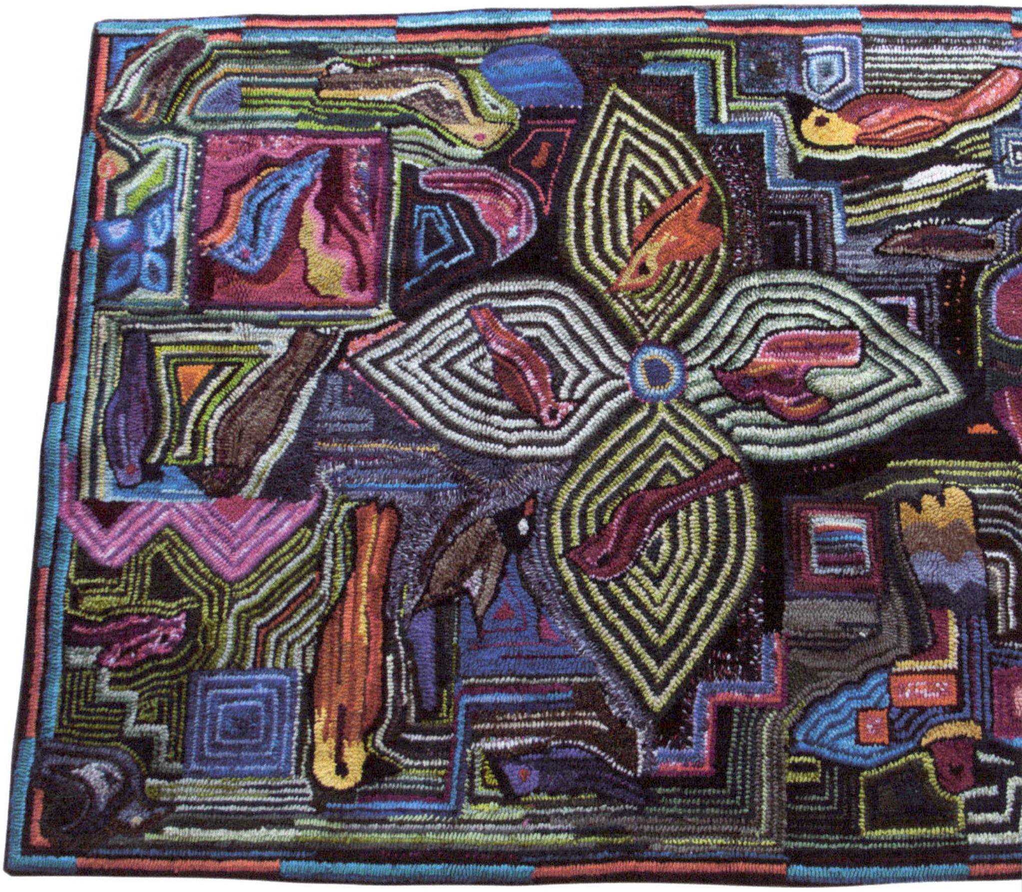

Rug designed and hooked by Yolanda Sebastiana Calgua Morales.
Photo by Multicolores.

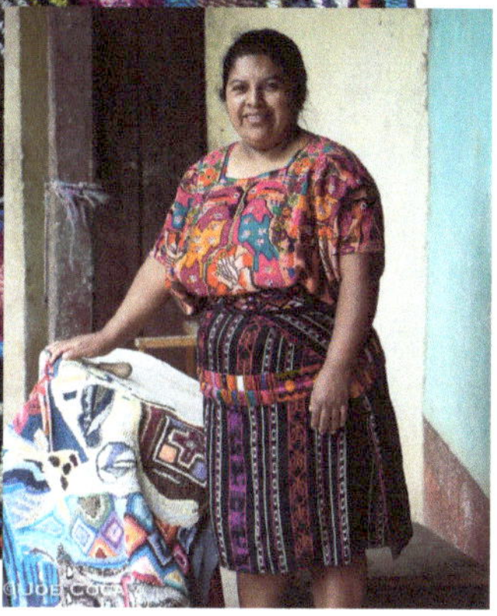

Photo by Joe Coca.

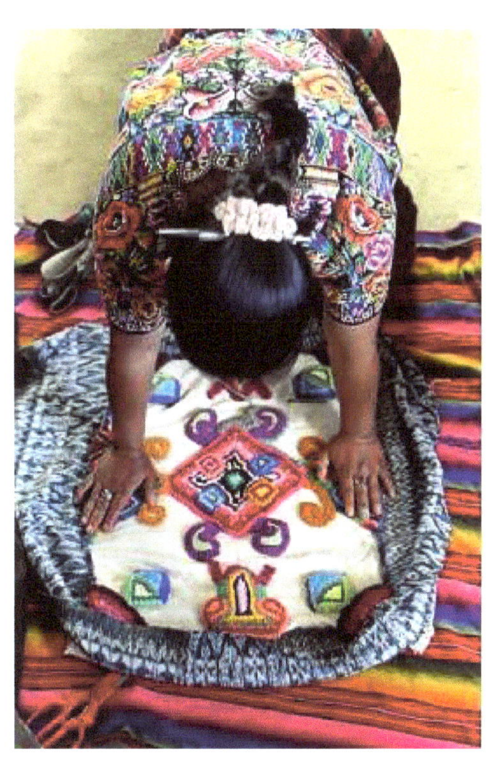

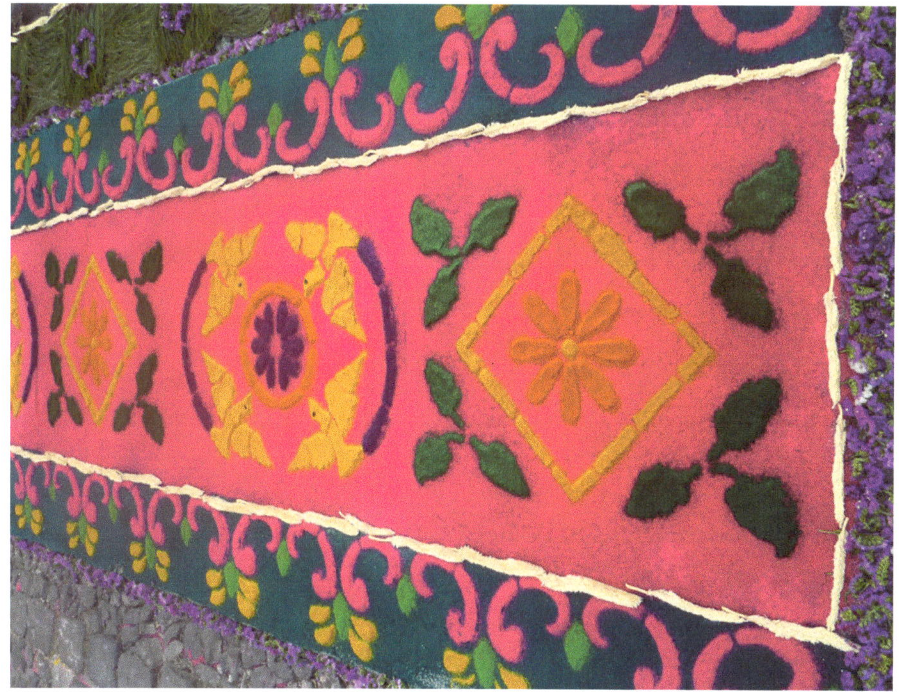

Inspiration for the designs come from the colorful huipils (blouses) the Guatemalan women wear (photo left by Joe Coca), as well as the colorful street carpets (alfombras) which decorate the streets during Semana Santa (holy week), made from sand and colored sawdust, decorated with plants and flowers (photo above by Multicolores).

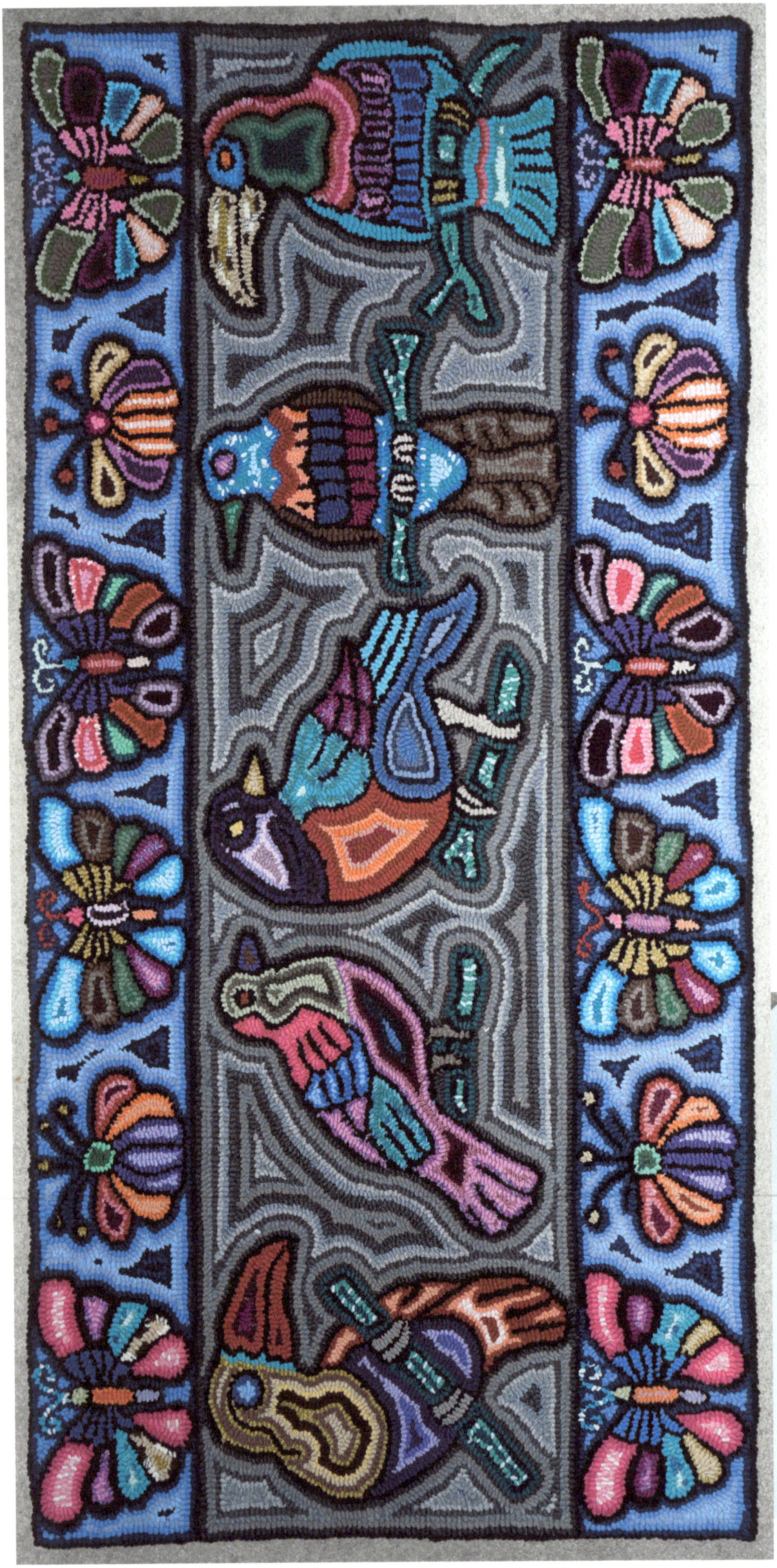

Rug designed and hooked by Irma Raquel Churunel.

Photos by Nancy Huntington.

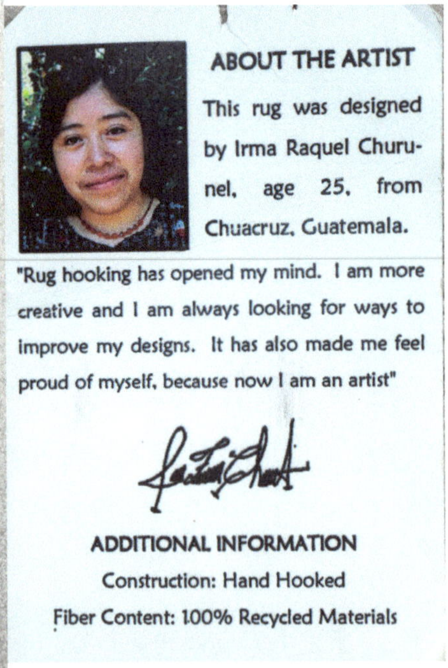

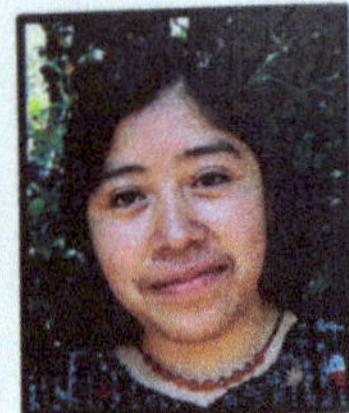

ABOUT THE ARTIST

This rug was designed by Irma Raquel Churunel, age 25, from Chuacruz, Guatemala.

"Rug hooking has opened my mind. I am more creative and I am always looking for ways to improve my designs. It has also made me feel proud of myself, because now I am an artist"

ADDITIONAL INFORMATION

Construction: Hand Hooked

Fiber Content: 100% Recycled Materials

With each new year, Mary Anne and Jody offered more workshops, encouraging greater technical skill. The yearly tours they hosted brought visitors to Guatemala from all over North America, creating a cross-cultural appreciation of the art of rug hooking. A new initiative, Teach the Teachers, empowered Mayan women to branch out and teach rug hooking in their own communities, so the craft could be ensured a good foundation for the future.

Rug hooking was taking off; women were beginning to produce more and bigger rugs, with a deepening understanding of style and construction. The next step was to figure out how to market these unique rugs to the wider world.

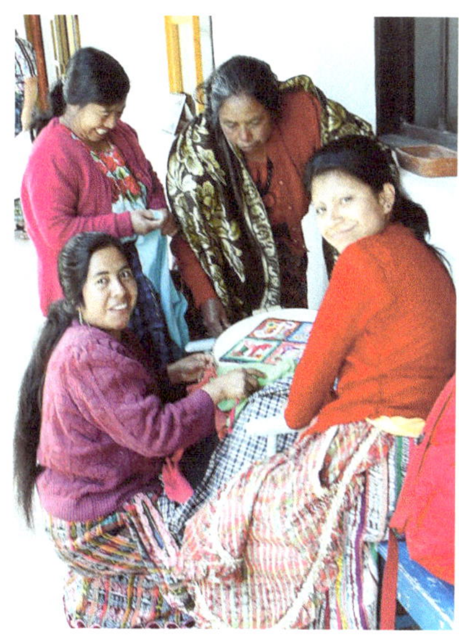

Teach the Teachers Class 2012 - Carmen Maldonado, back (r) Maria Sacalxot, front (l) Ramona Tzunun, front (r) Rosmery Pacheco. Photo by Multicolores.

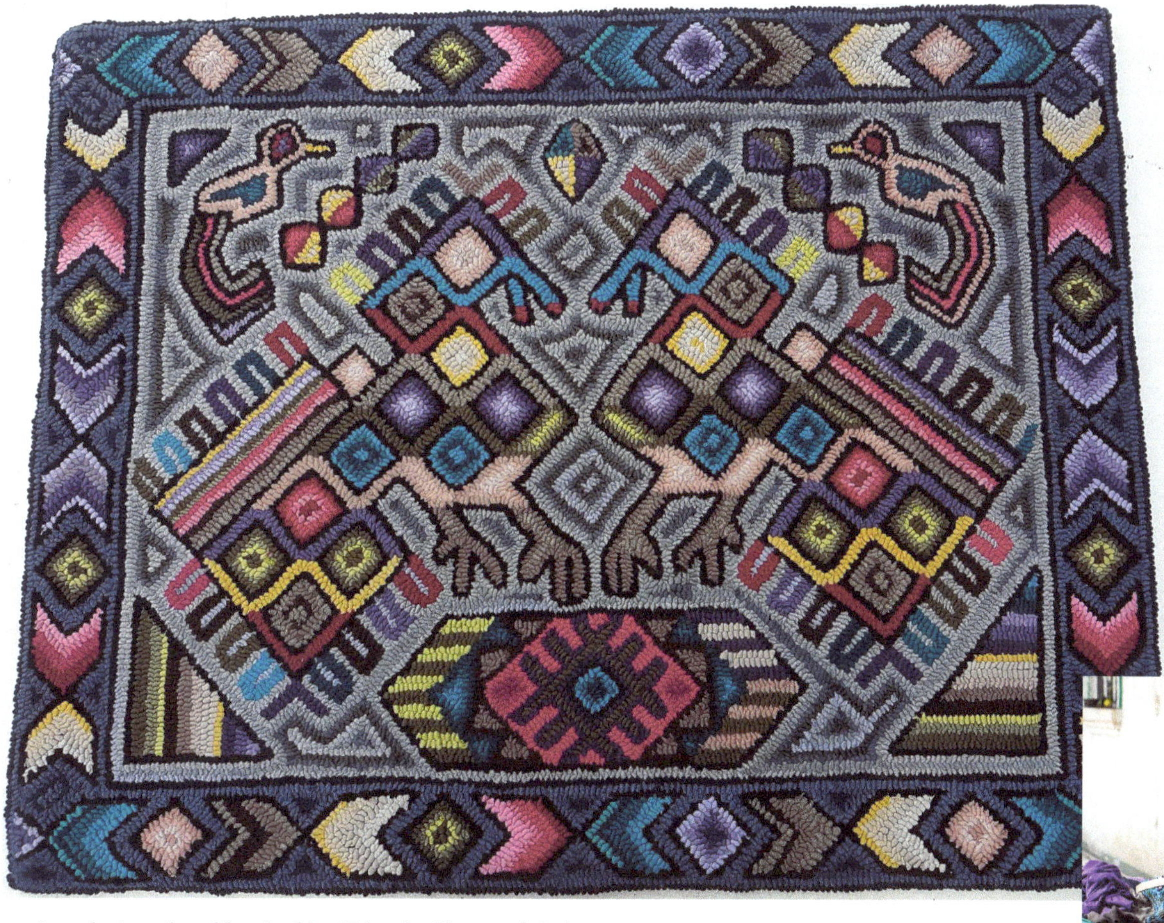

Rug designed and hooked by Yolanda Churunel Ajú. Photo by Multicolores.

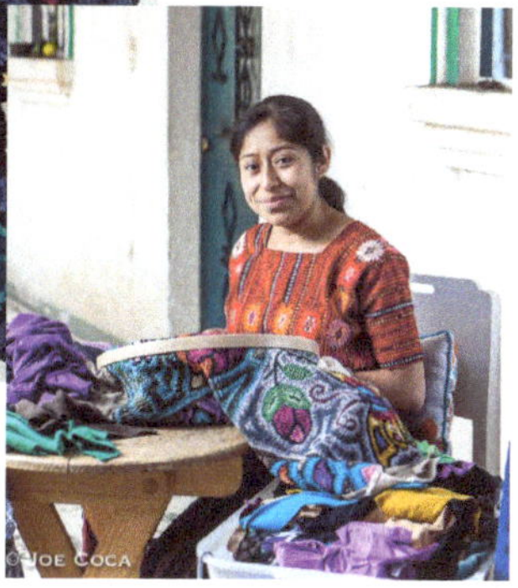

Photo by Joe Coca.

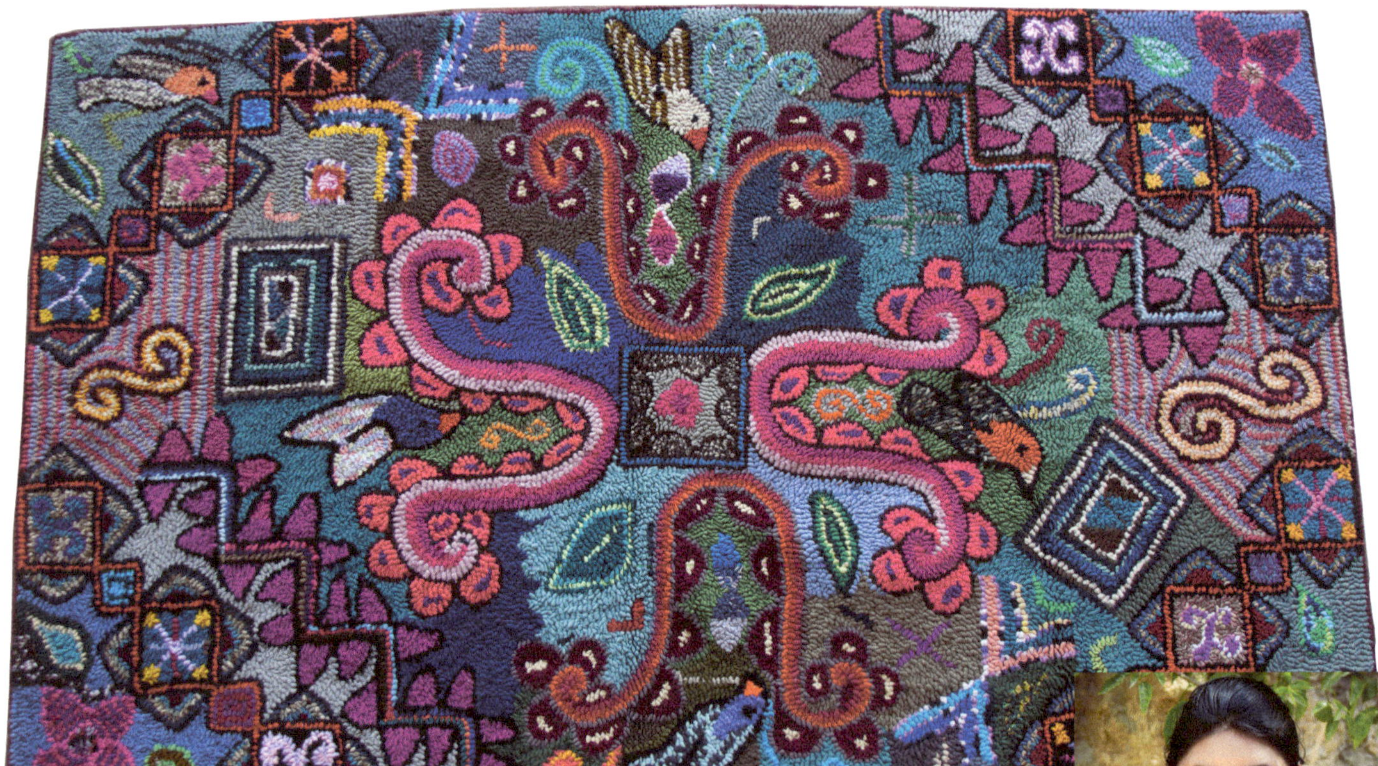

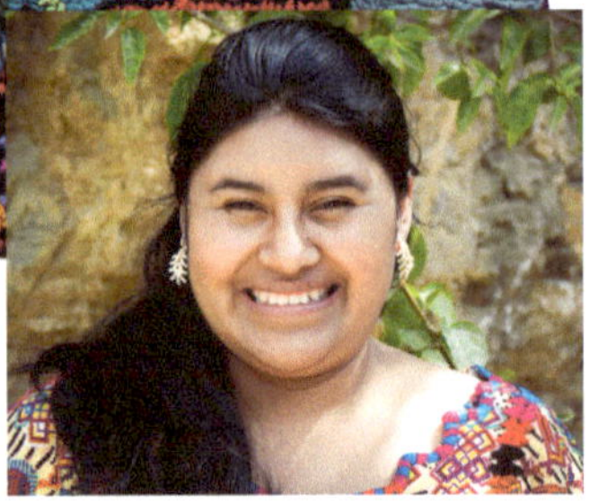

Rug designed and hooked by Zoila Calgua Morales.
Photos by Multicolores.

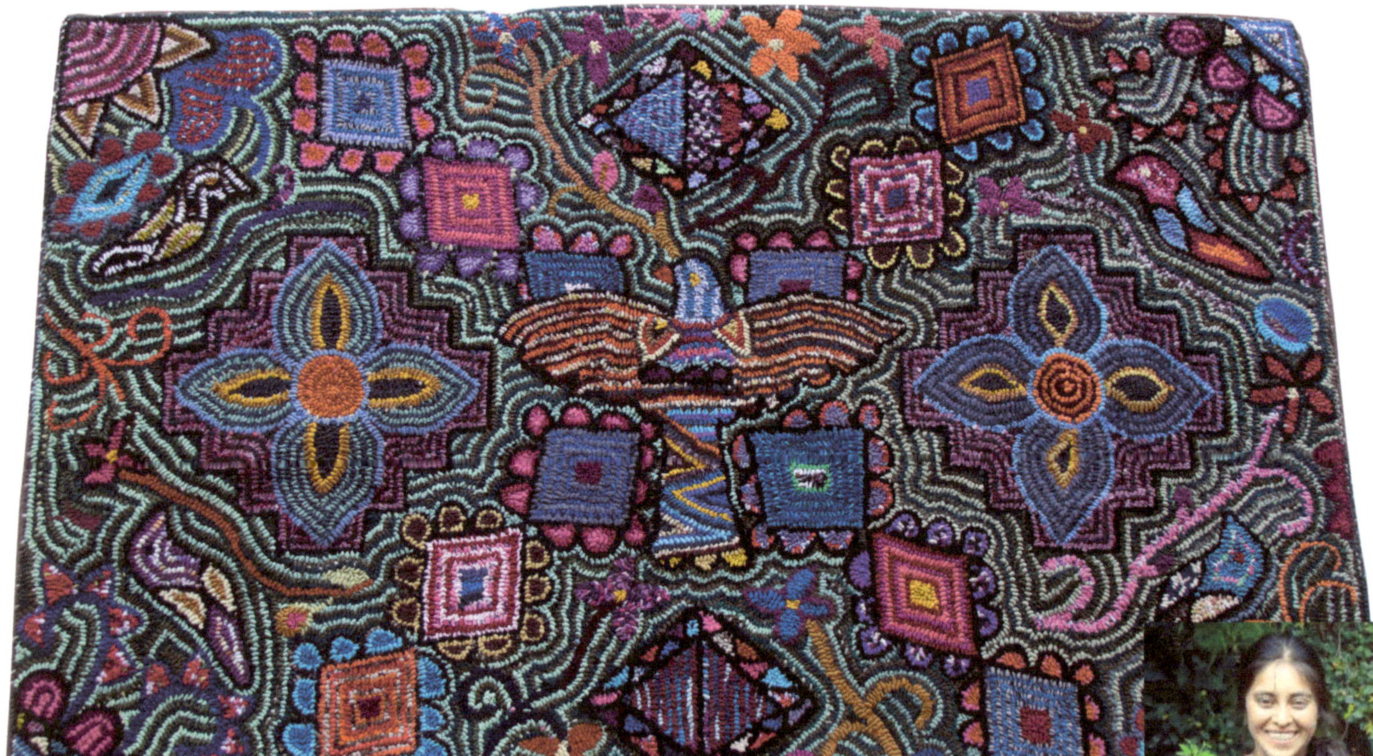

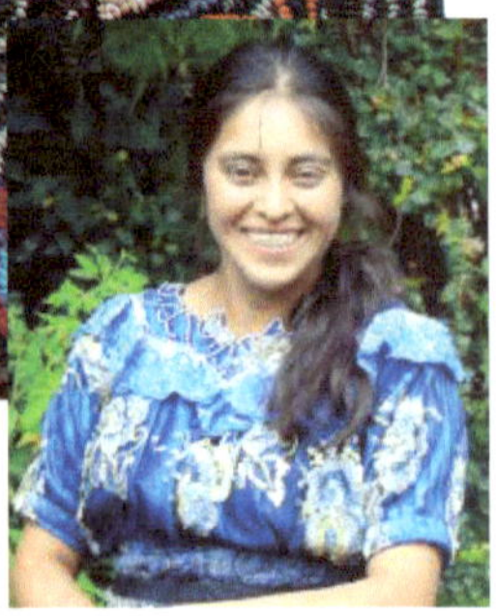

Rug designed and hooked by María Estela Az Tamayac.
Photos by Multicolores.

The work of the Mayan rug hookers has been internationally recognized. The Mayan Women's Rug Hooking Cooperative was formed in 2013, representing 60 artists in seven communities in Guatemala. By March 2014, the Cooperative had evolved into the non-profit Multicolores, enabling them to offer opportunities to other artisan crafts. Currently Multicolores' rug hookers are joined by embroiderers, in training, from 4 communities. Mary Anne and Jody are co-founders of Multicolores and sit on its board, as do two of the local rug hookers.

In 2017, in addition to ongoing artisan training, Multicolores introduced programs to support the well-being of the artists in the belief that Multicolores should have a social and economic mission. These included establishing better working conditions for the artists at home, health and nutrition programs, eye tests, talks on preventing injuries to hands and shoulders from rug hooking, and a three-year leadership program.

2014 was the first year they brought their rugs to the Santa Fe International Folk Art Market, to stunning success. Of the 252 rugs they brought to the festival that year, only two were left unsold!

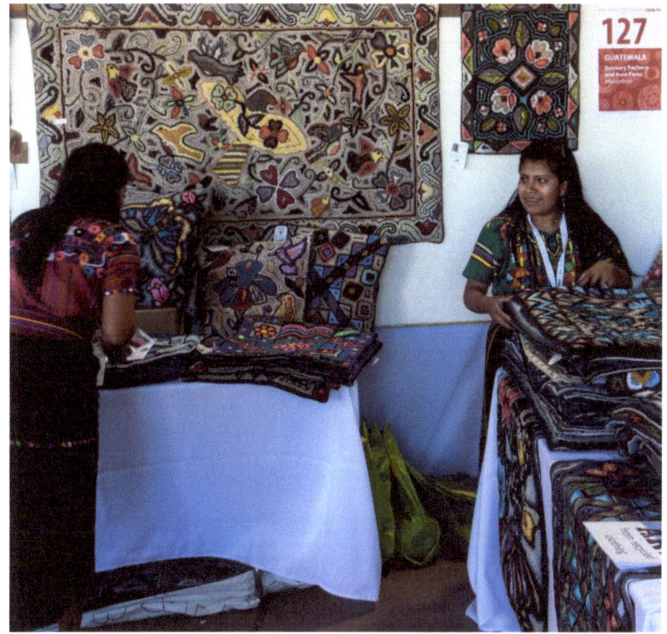

Aura Perez Can (l) - Multicolores' Social Services Coordinator; Rosmery Pacheco (r) - artists' representative 2018.

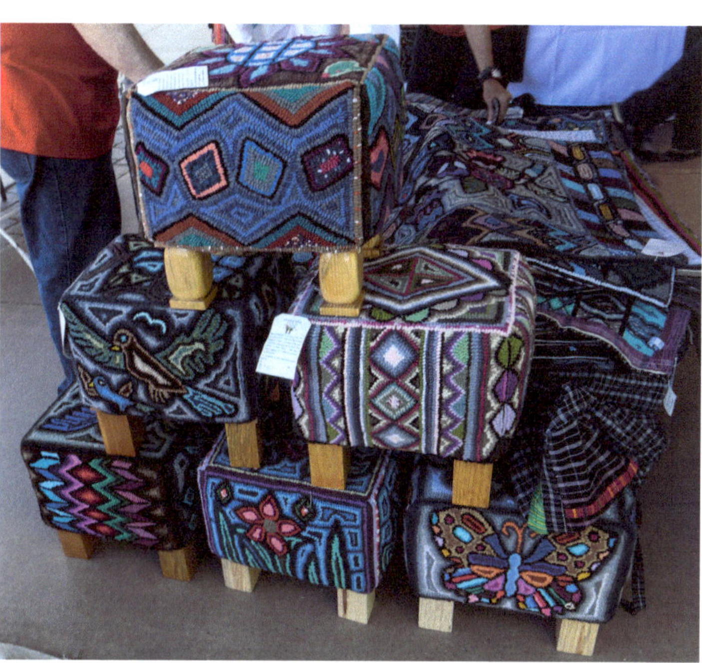

Footstools and rugs from their booth.
Above images provided by Nancy Huntington.

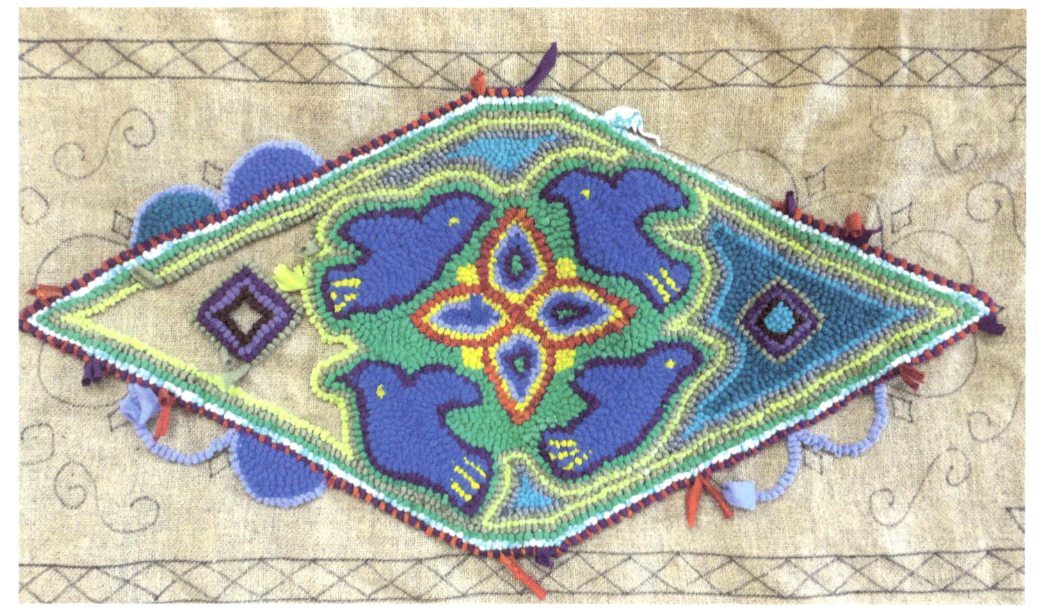

Did you know that you can buy Multicolores patterns exclusively from Honey Bee Hive (https://rughook.com)?

This pattern (left) was designed by Rosario Guiterrez Pacheco (MC-05).

Catherine Kelly is hooking the pattern shown here, and she kindly provided the photograph.

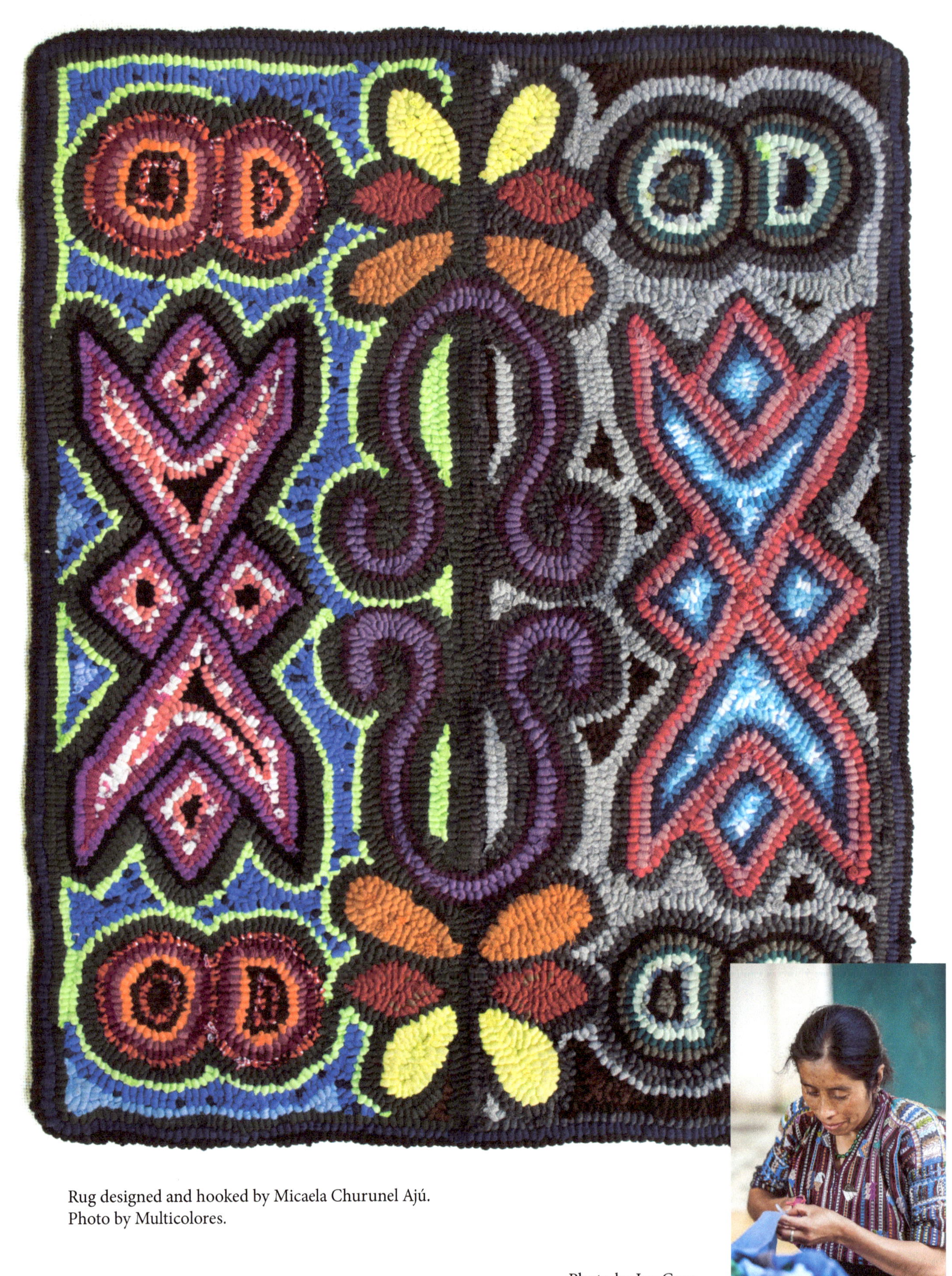

Rug designed and hooked by Micaela Churunel Ajú.
Photo by Multicolores.

Photo by Joe Coca.

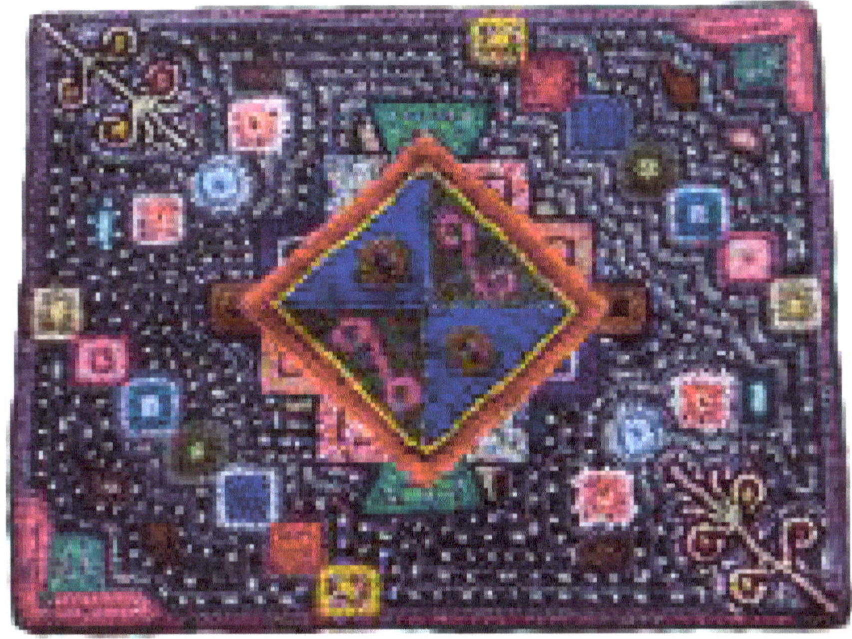

Rug designed and hooked by Hilda Raquel García Tzunun.
Photo by Multicolores.

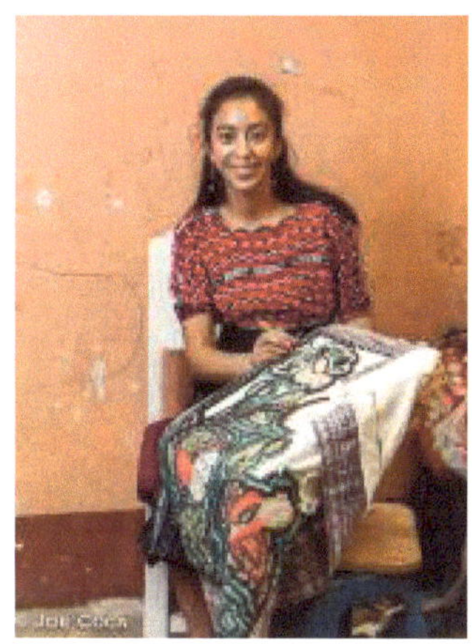

Photo by Joe Coca.

In 2011, Mary Anne and Jody started Cultural Cloth, a brick and mortar (and online) store in Maiden Rock, WI, which imported not only rugs and other art from Guatemala, but textiles, jewelry and pottery made by women and men from some 25 countries. Mary Anne and Jody work hand in hand with these talented artists. They don't dictate designs to their artisans, but they do offer advice on projects that might appeal to Cultural Cloth customers.

The changes that were brought about in these women's lives is nothing short of remarkable. Income from rug hooking has made it possible for their children to remain in school, to put better food on the table, to provide for more advanced medical care, and to bring in needed improvements to their living conditions. In many cases, money from rug hooking has doubled the family income. And the benefits haven't been just economic, either. Making money doing something you love, making a living through artistic expression, has brought about a renaissance in these artists' sense of well-being and hope for the future, where before there was little.

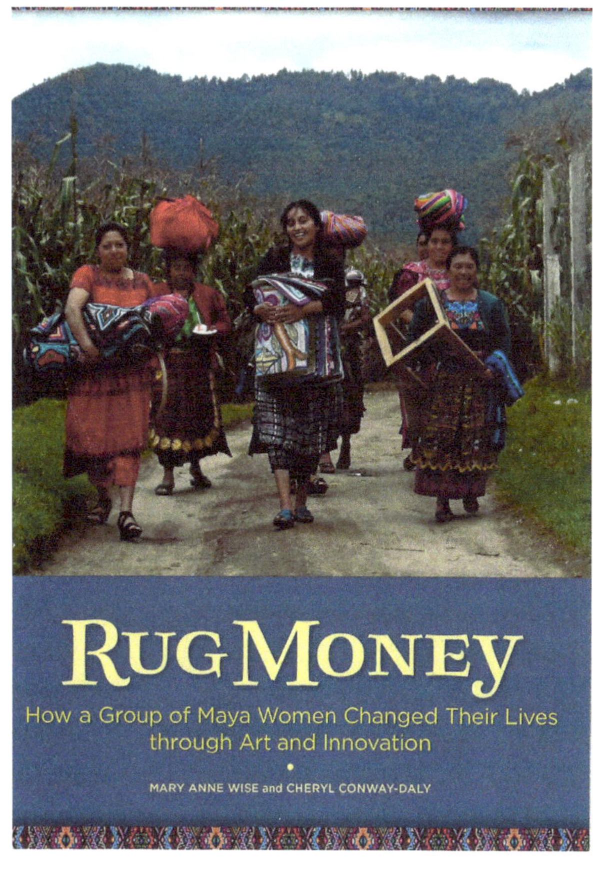

You can purchase hand-hooked rugs and other crafts, as well as their wonderful book, *Rug Money, How A Group of Maya Women Changed Their Lives Through Art and Innovation* at www.culturalcloth.com.

Please support Multicolores (www.multicolores.org), a non-profit organization which accepts tax-deductible contributions.

The photographs in this section by Multicolores, Joe Coca and Cheryl Walsh Bellville are from *Rug Money* and were provided courtesy of Thrums Books.

Gallery

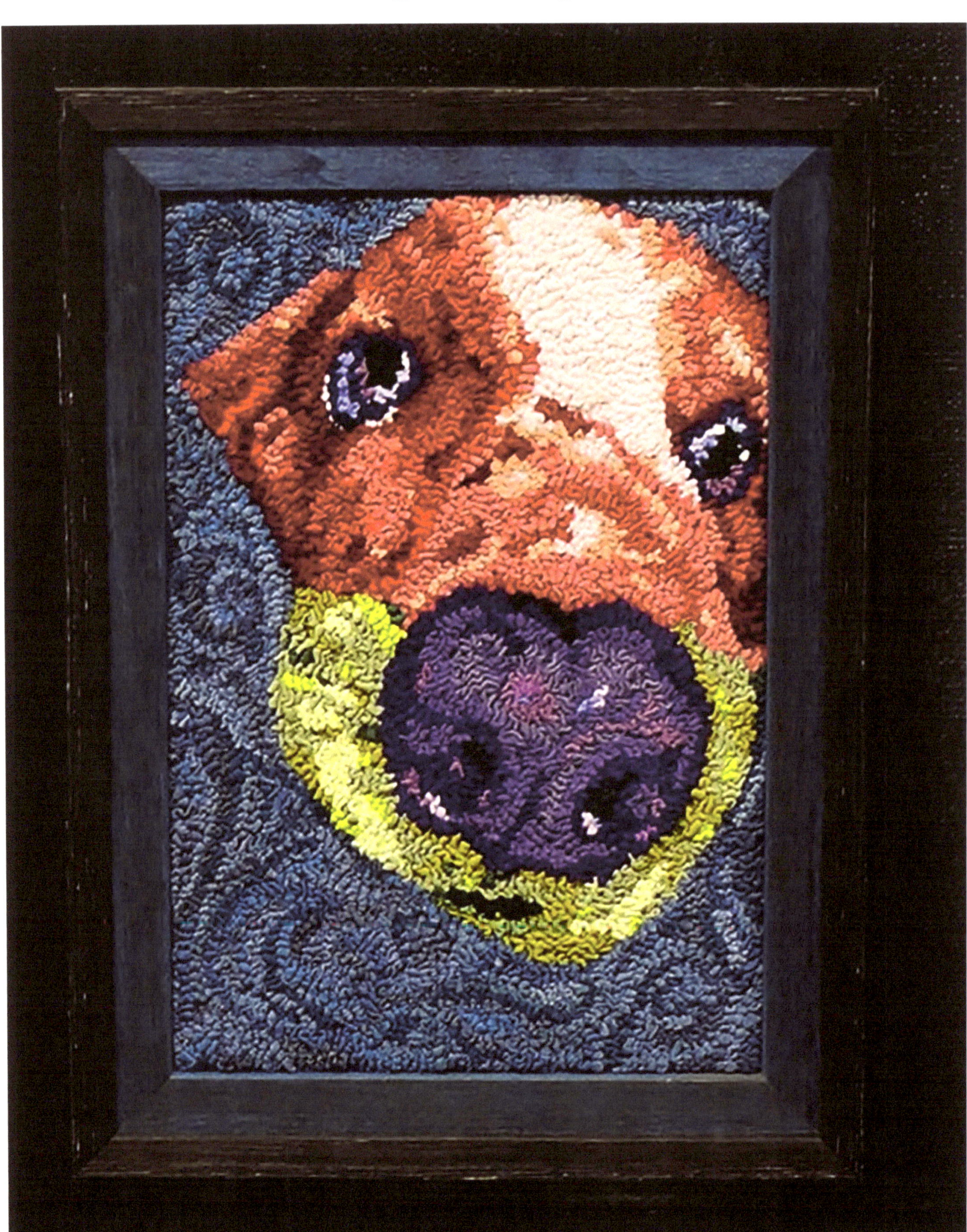

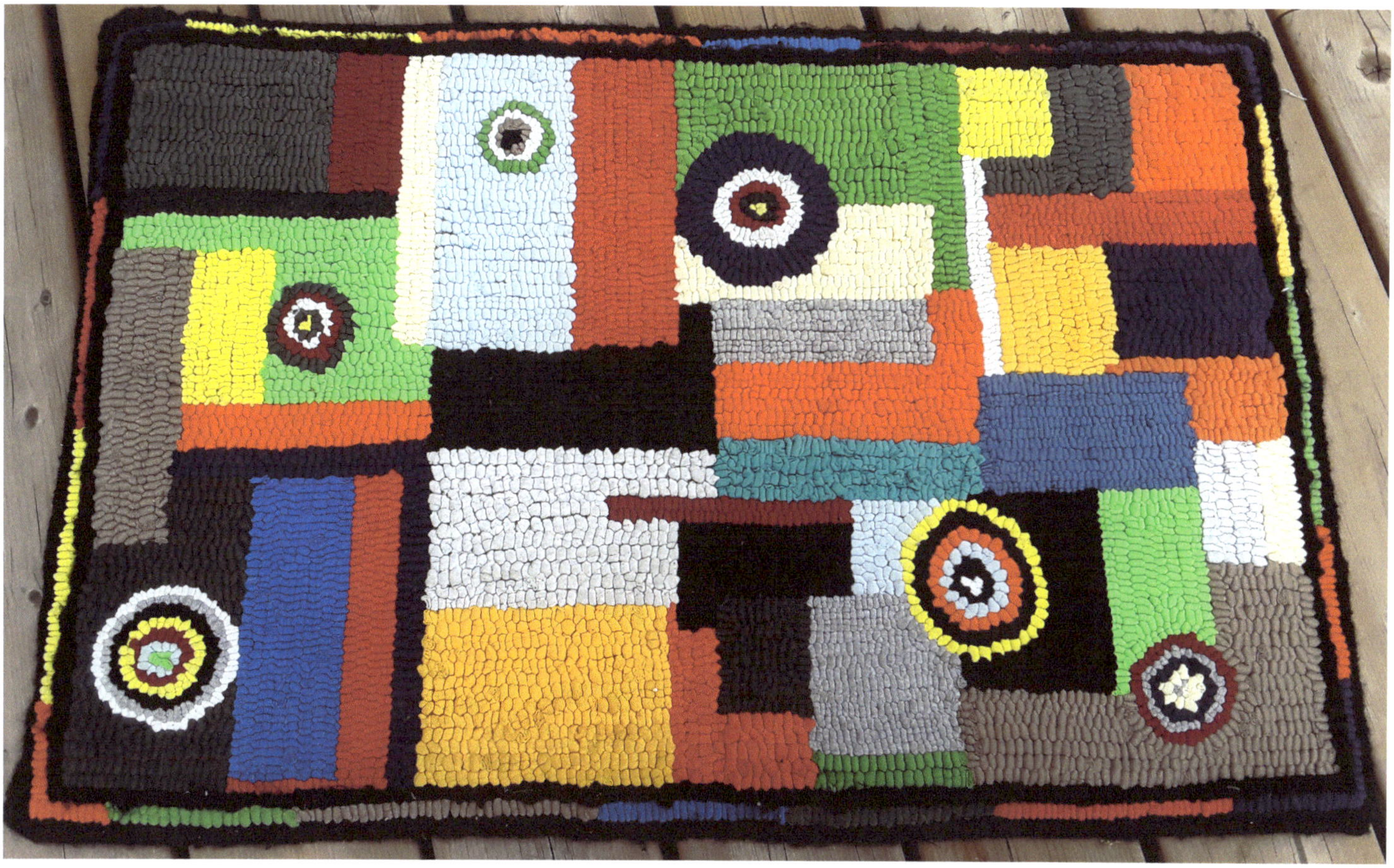

Pete's Rug, 22"x33" Designed and hooked with T-shirts by Linda DeVillers.
Photo by Linda DeVillers.

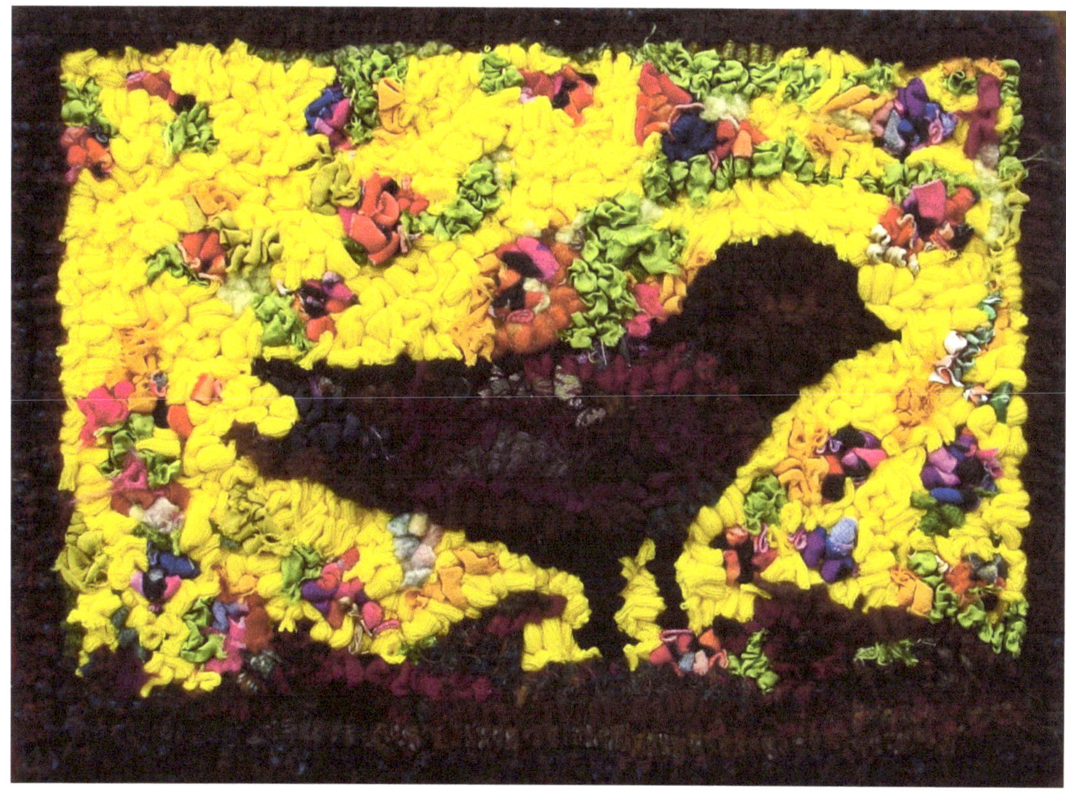

(opposite) Tynan, 15"x10"
Designed and hooked with T-shirts by Laura Salamy.
Photo by Laura Salamy.

Into the Field, 9"x6.5" Designed and hooked with woven wool and cotton, sweater, woven silk, a variety of synthetic knits and dried plant fiber by Jane Sittnick.
Photo by Jane Sittnick.

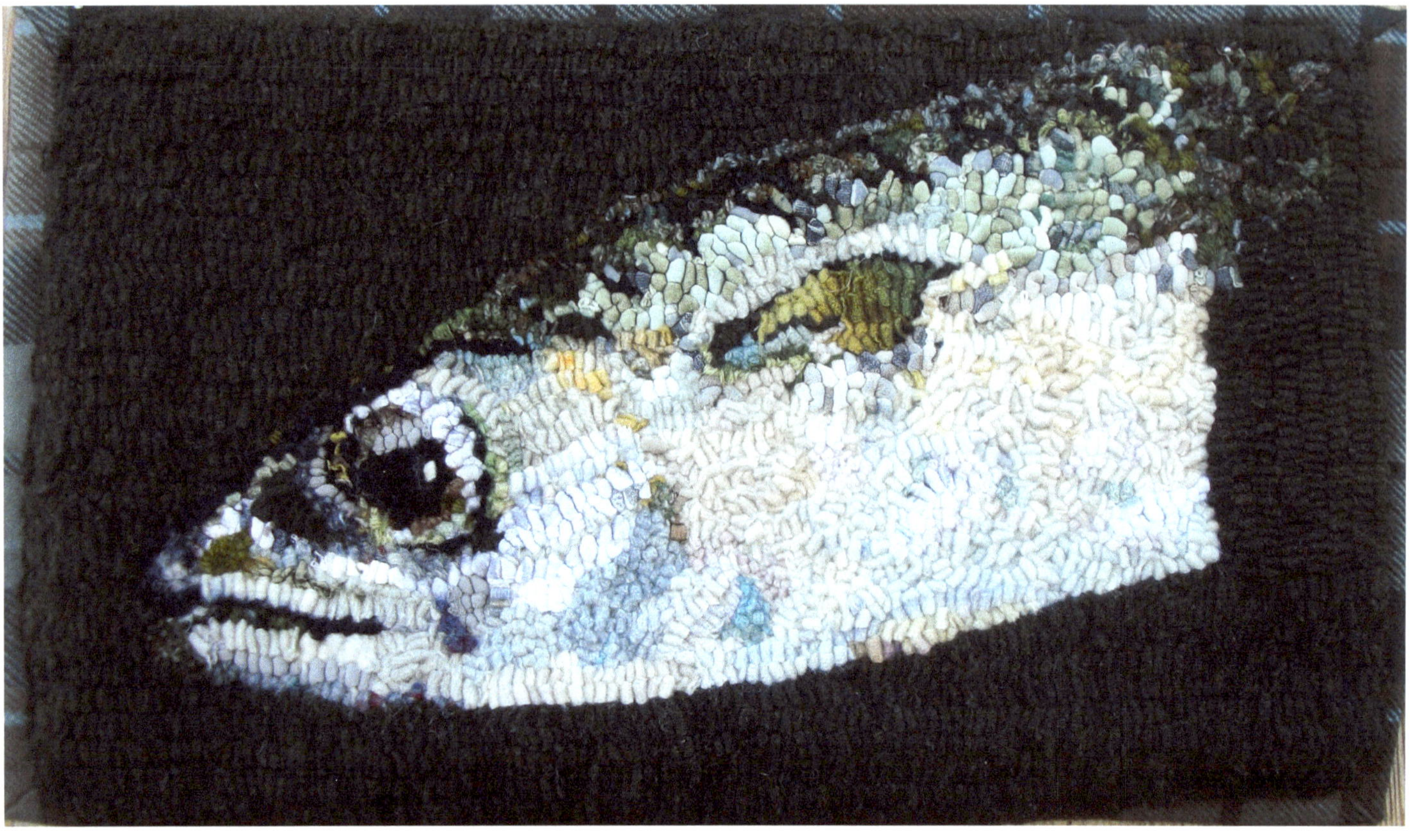

Mackerel, 15"x11" Designed and hooked with wools, yarns and synthetic knits by Jane Sittnick.

North Atlantic, 12"x11" Designed and hooked with wool: woven and knitted, yarns, stockings, and velvet by Jane Sittnick.

Photos by Jane Sittnick.

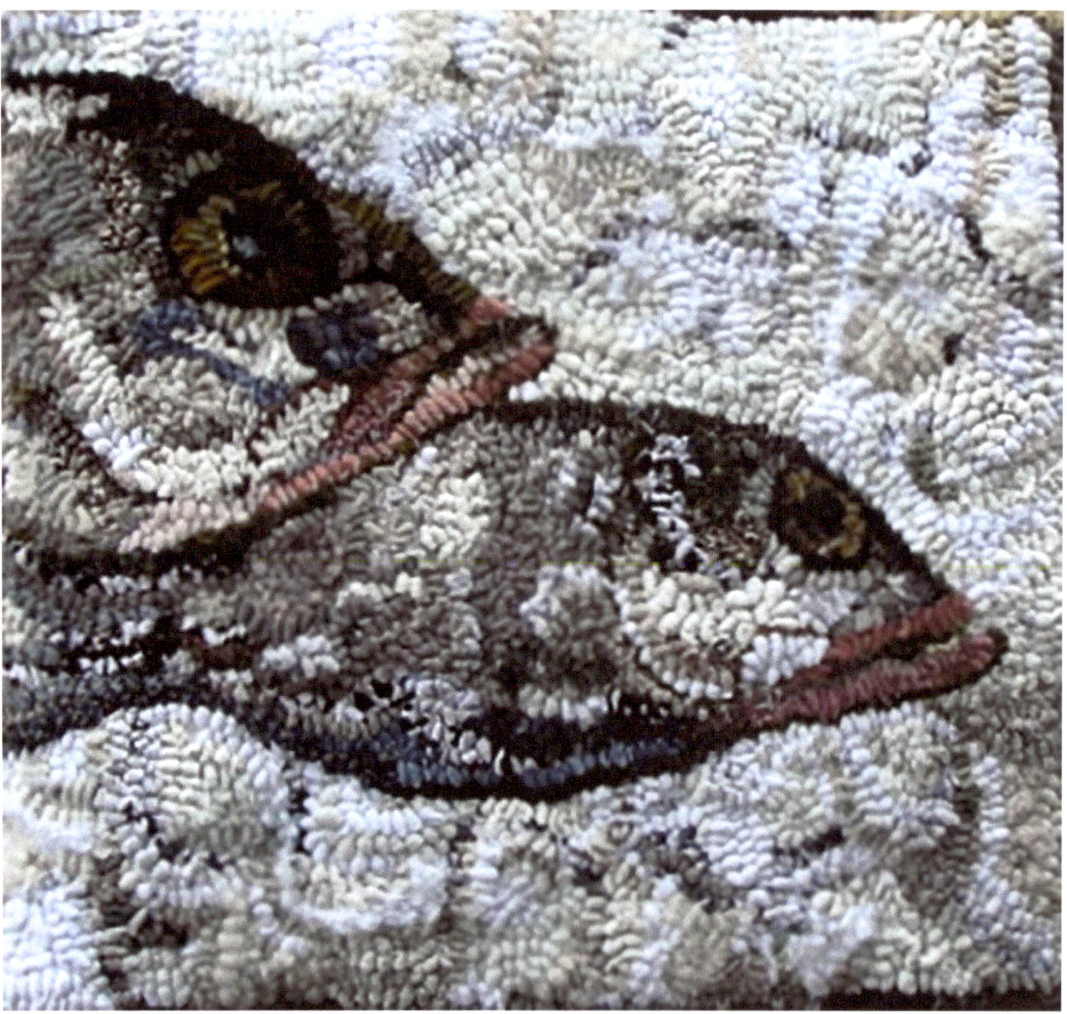

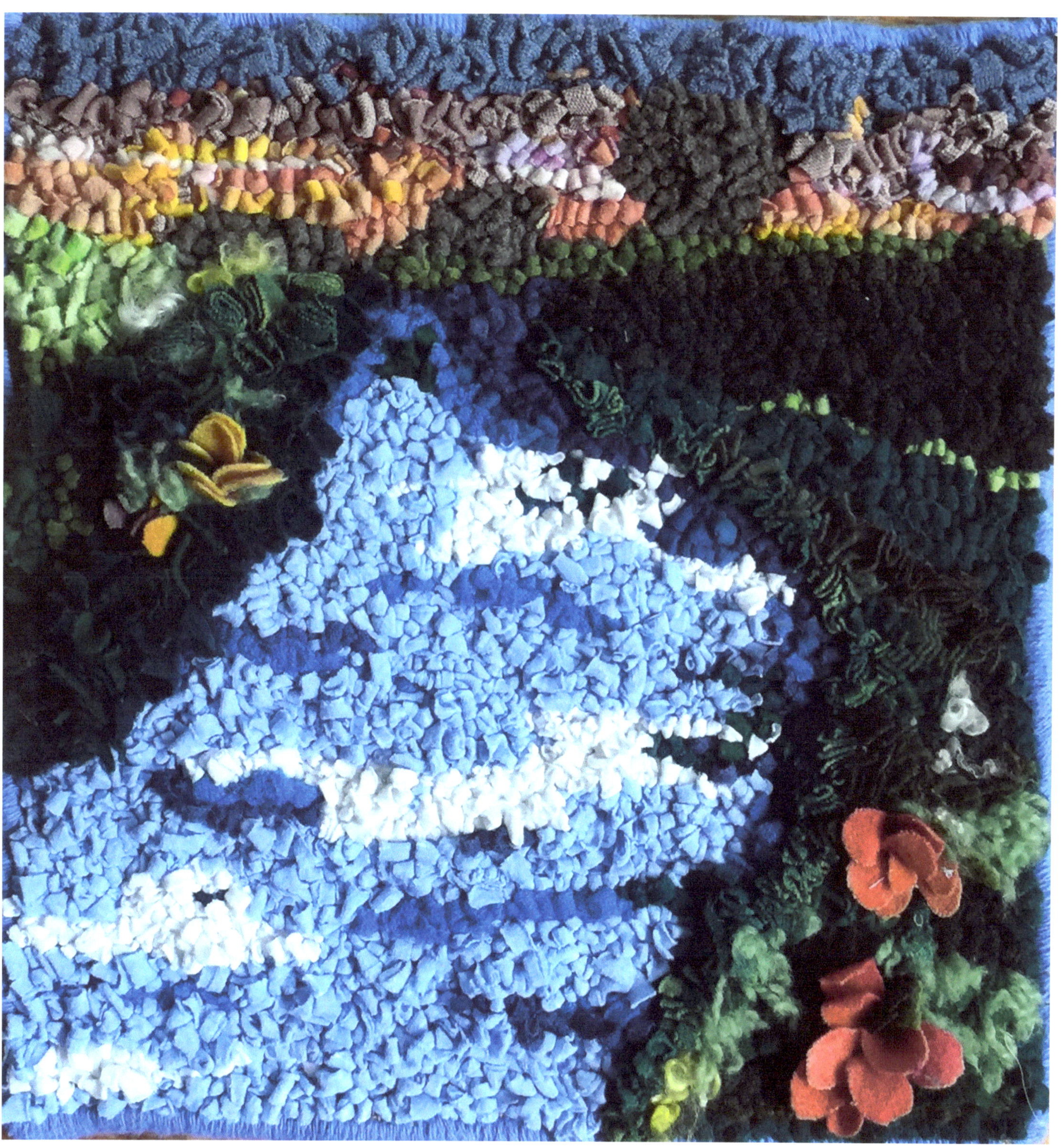

River Scene, 14"x14" Designed and hooked with T-shirts, wool fabric and yarn by Stephanie Krasney. Photo by Stephanie Krasney.

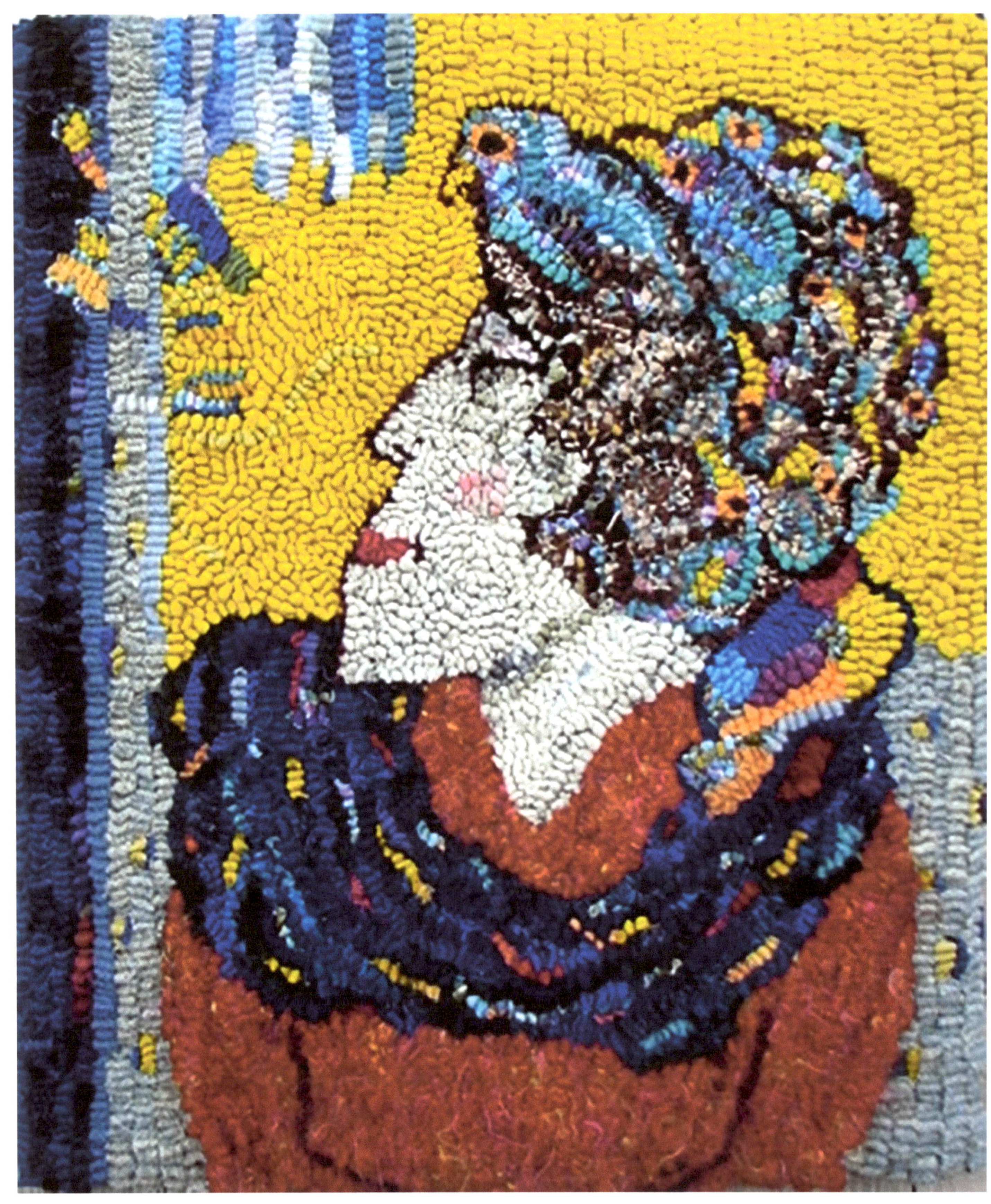

Madame 12"x14" Designed and hooked with woven wools, synthetics and silk, knit synthetics and cottons, yarns, and a cut sweater by Jane Sittnick.

Photo by Jane Sittnick.

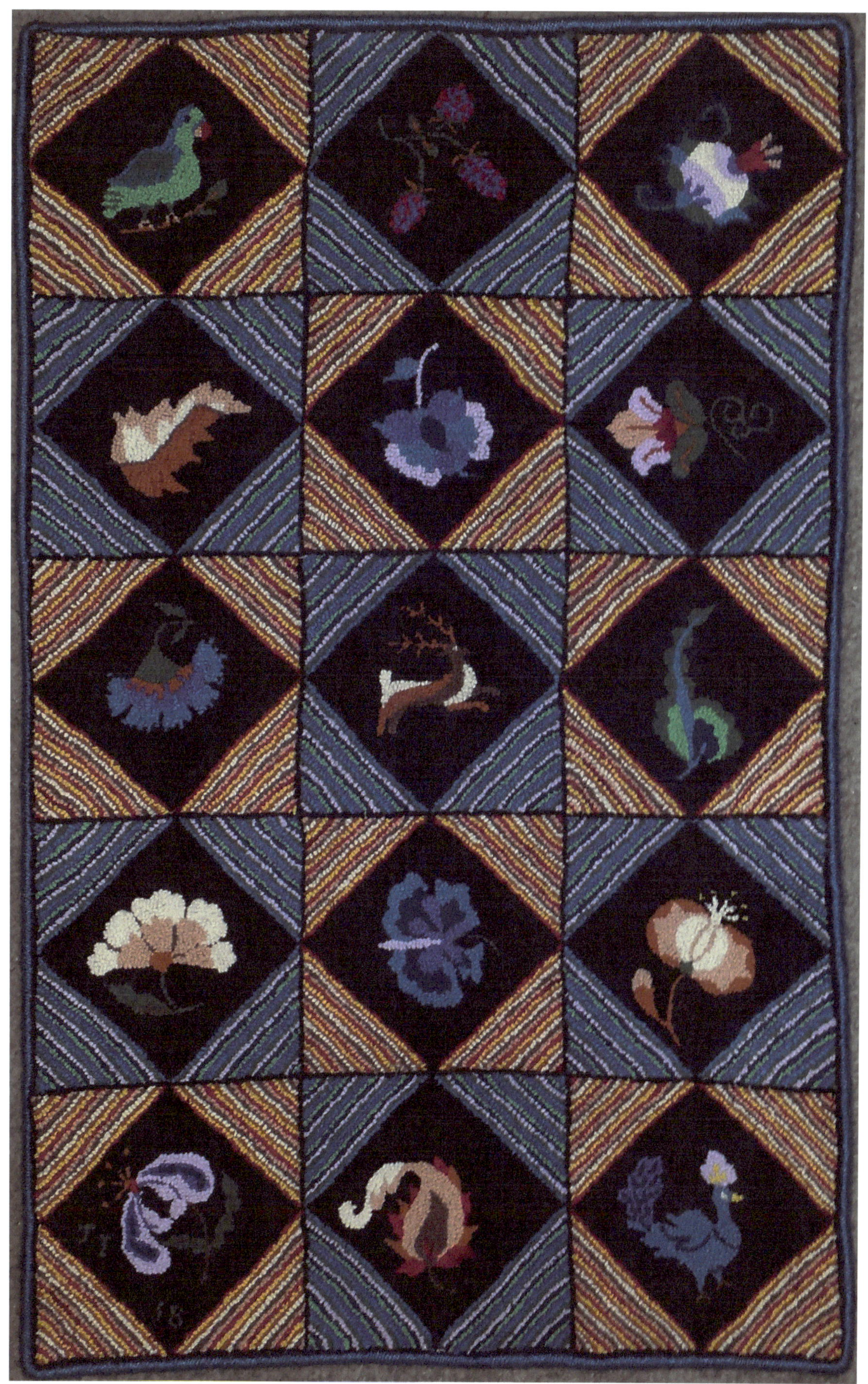

Demelza 24.5"x39" Designed and hooked with T-shirts by Judy Taylor
To hook the black background, I cut up three T-shirts; one bright black, and two which were slightly faded for a variegated effect. So using this technique, I can create any size background, and still get that lovely variegated effect that I get with yarn.

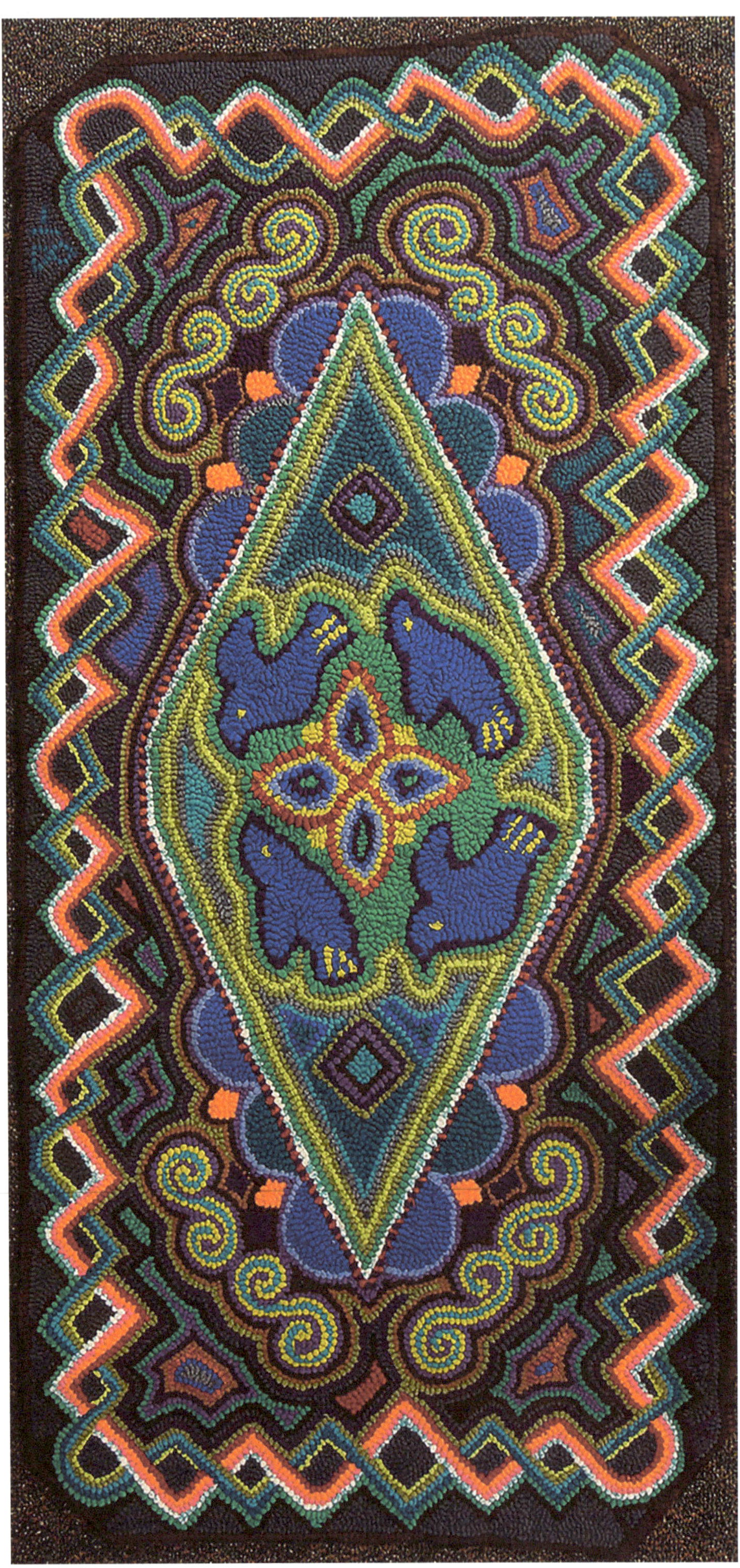

Frida y Multicolores Conmigo, 22"x47"
A Multicolores pattern designed by Rosario Guiterrez Pacheco, (Honey Bee Hive pattern number MC-05) hooked with T-shirts by Catherine Kelly

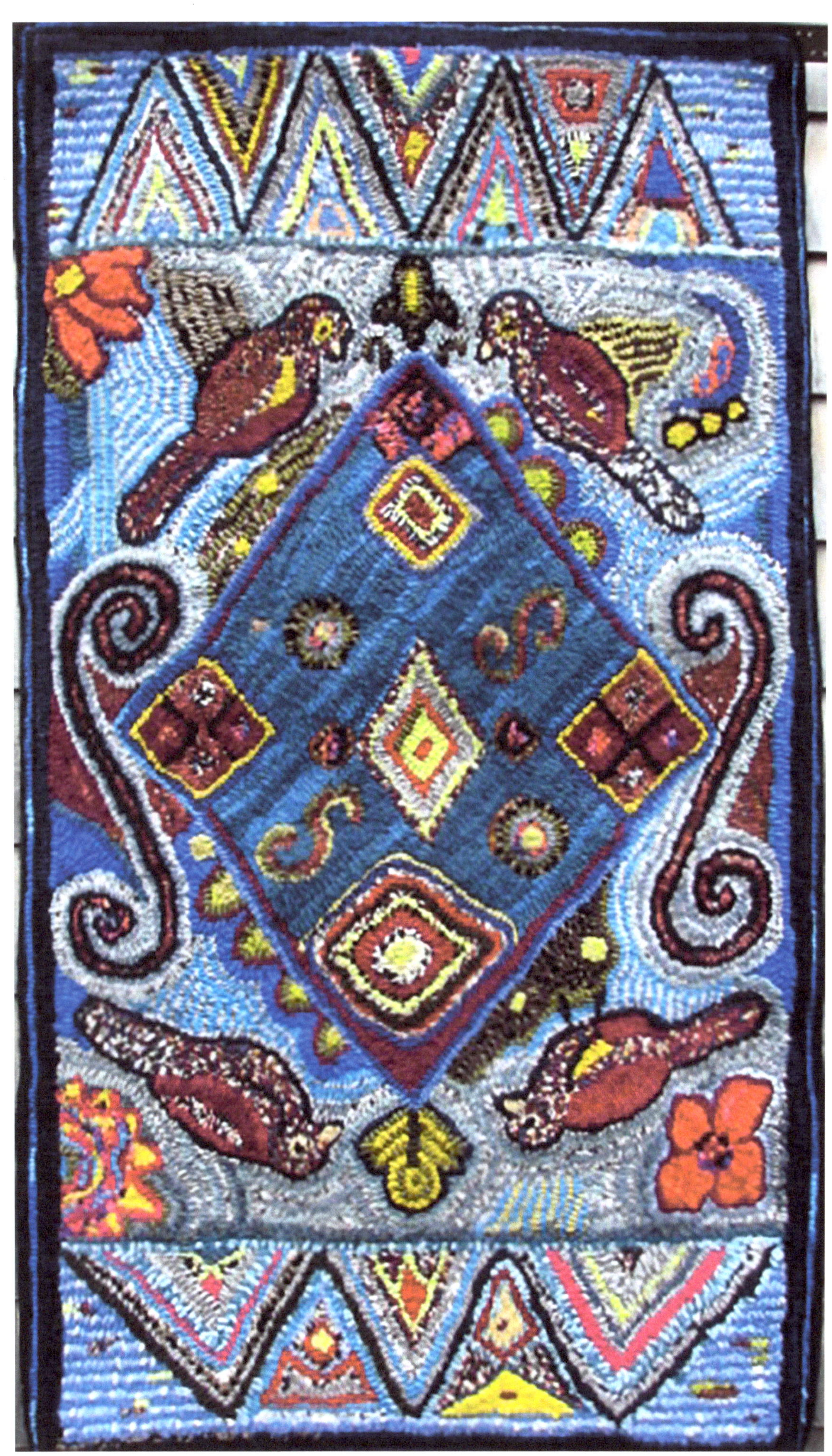

During Jane's stay in Guatemala, she partnered with Nicolosa Pacay Baran, a Mayan rug hooking teacher, to design and select fibers for her rug. Once she returned home she completed hooking the rug, all the while reminiscing about her experiences there and the memorable people she met.

Jane's Guatemalan Rug, 39"x22.5"
Designed by Nicolasa Pacay Baran. Hooked by Jane Sittnick from recycled clothing.

Photo by Jane Sittnick

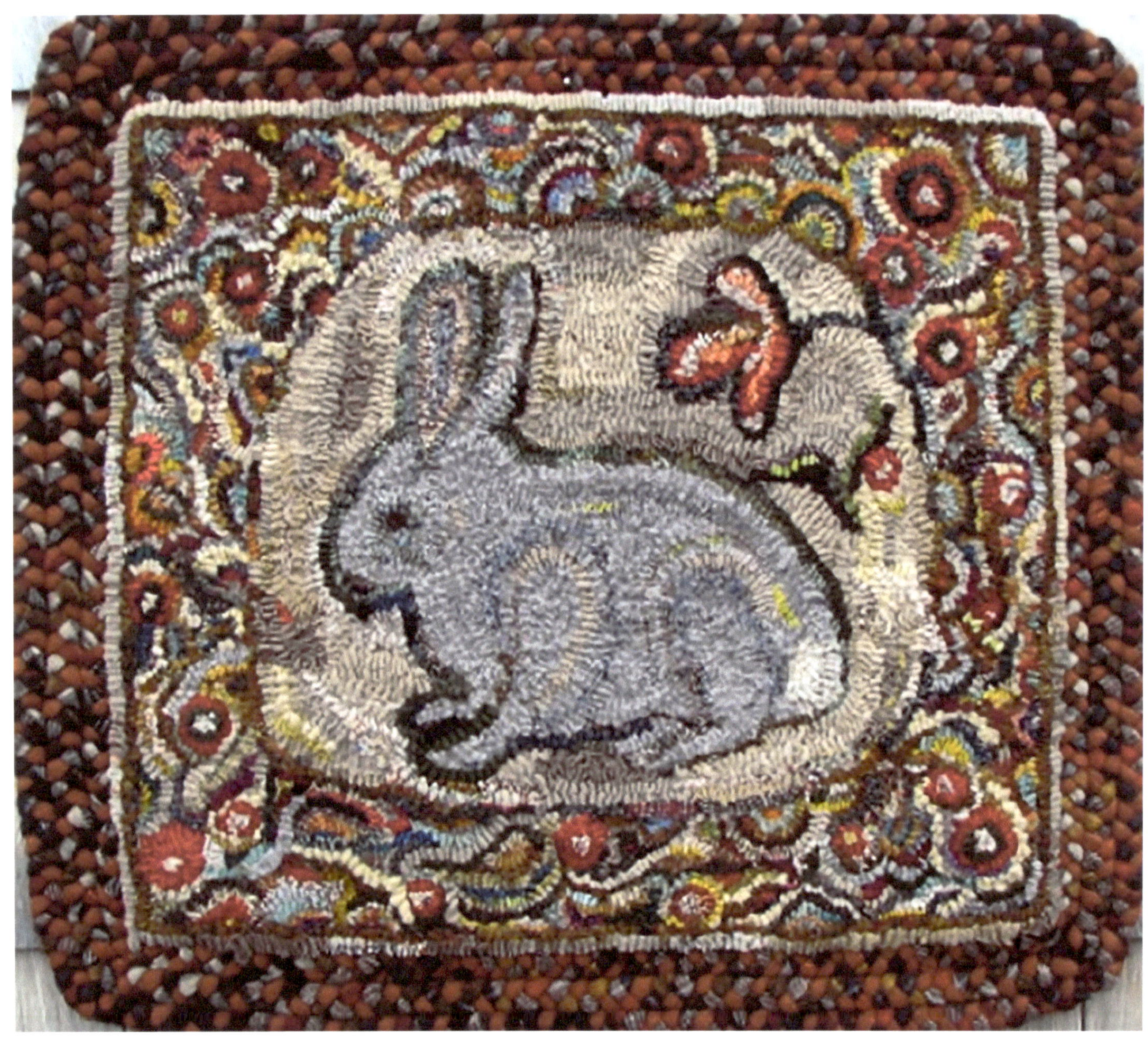

Miscou Rabbit, 20"x22" Designed and hooked with woven wool, cotton, rayon,and silk, cut mohair and cashmere sweaters by Jane Sittnick.

Photo by Jane Sittnick

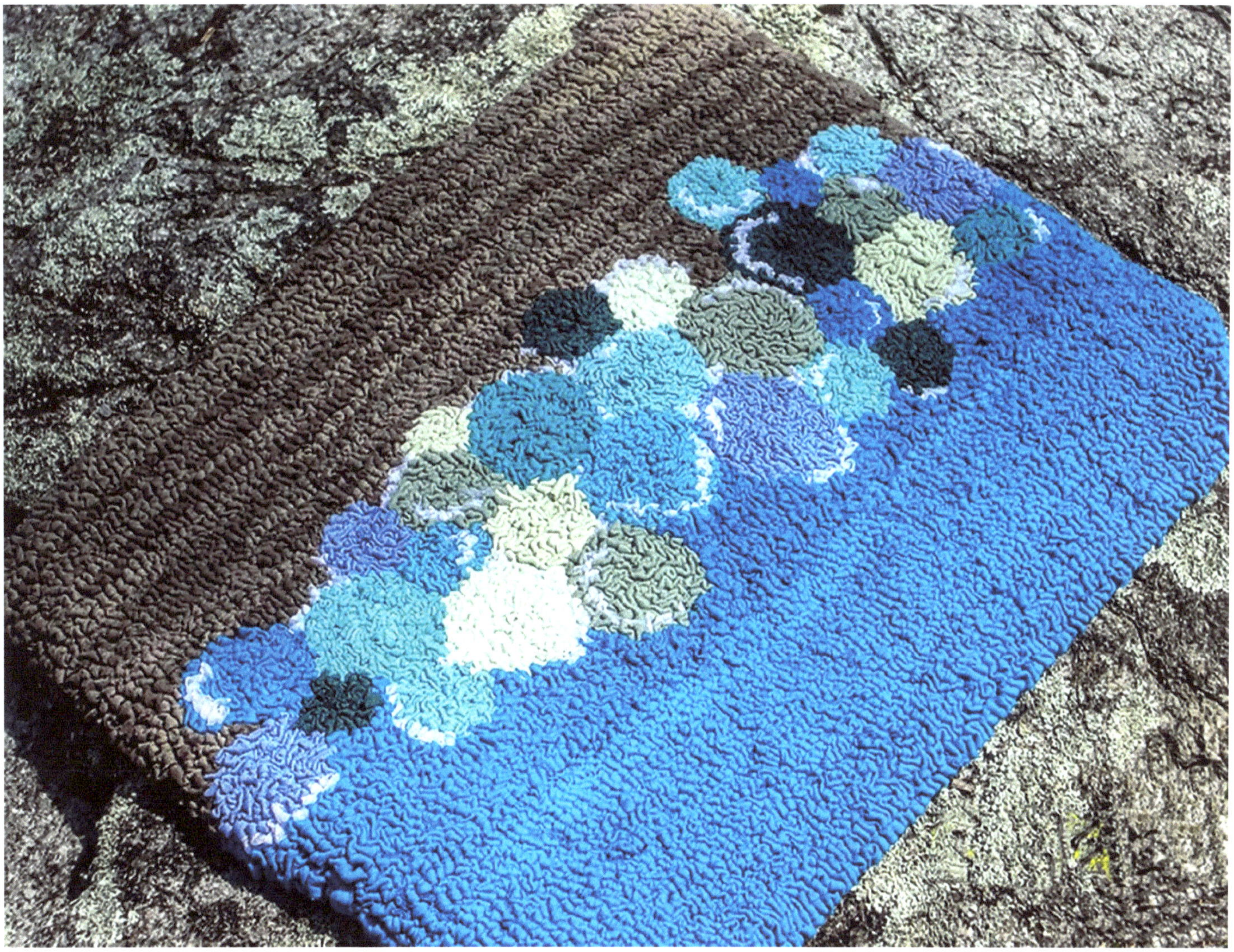

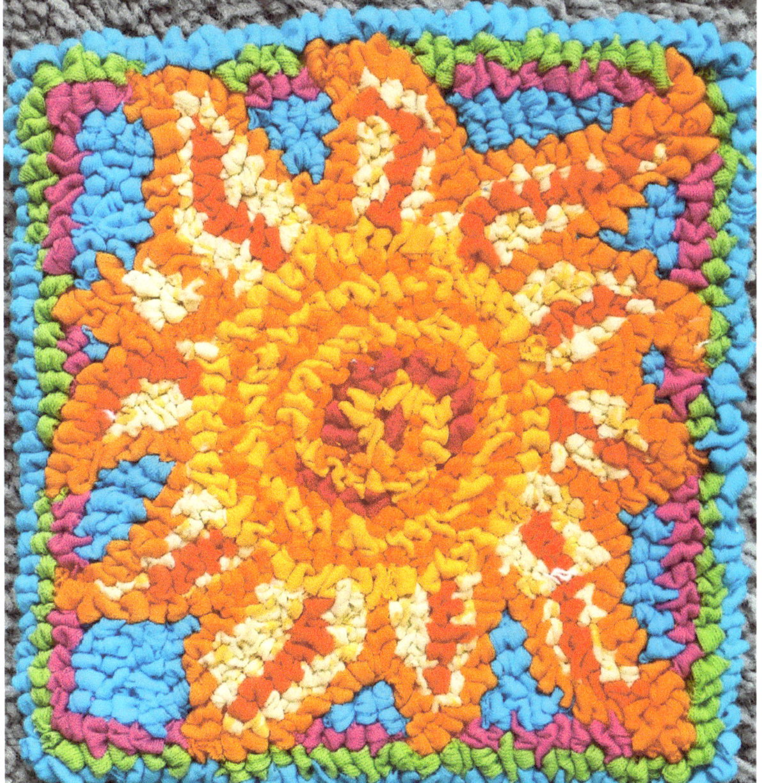

Beach Bubbles 17"x13"
Designed and hooked with T-shirts and ribbon by Laura Salamy.

Key West Mug Rug, 6"x6" Designed and hooked with T-shirts by Laura Salamy.

Photos by Laura Salamy.

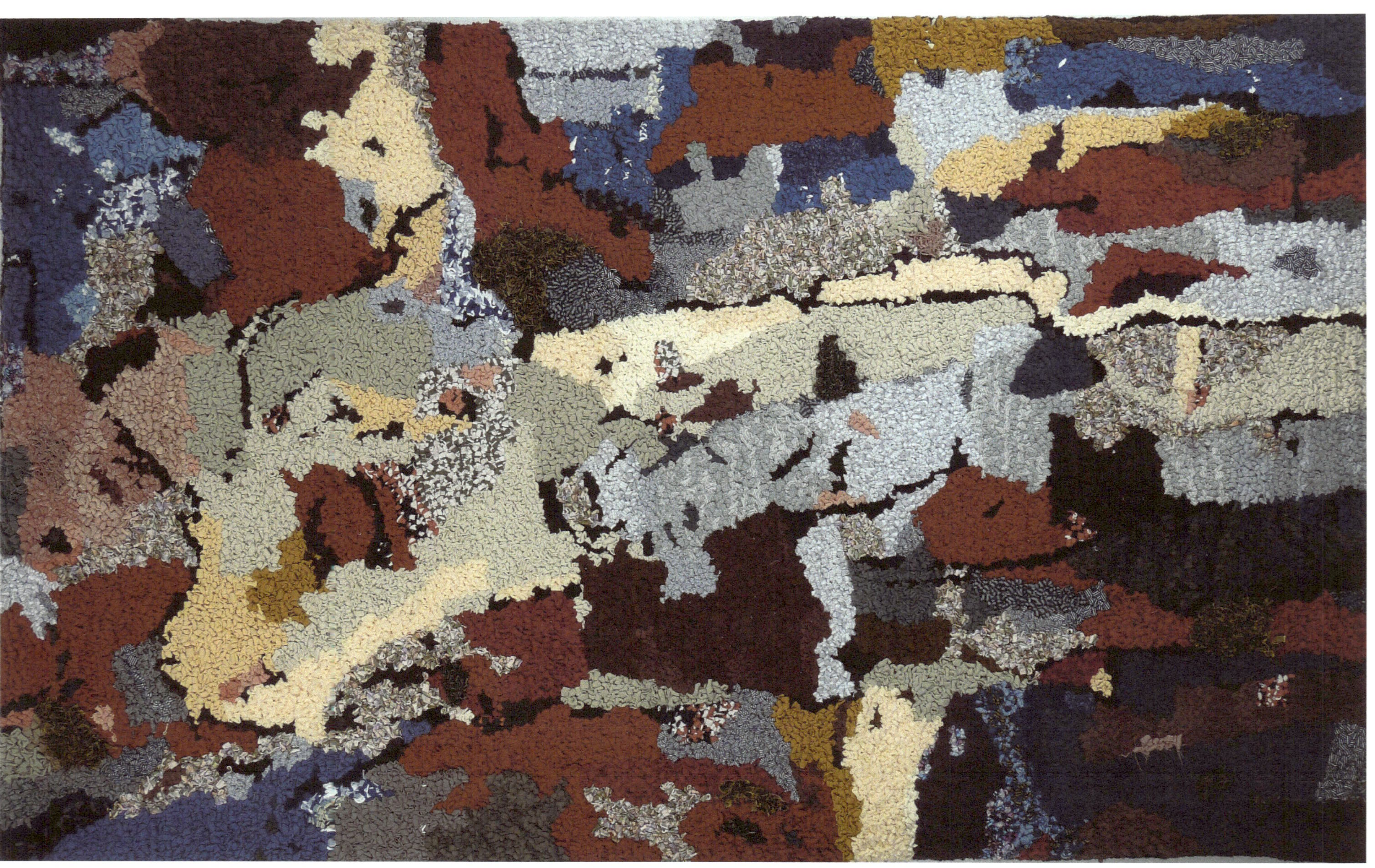

Mystery Bay, 52”x34” Designed and hooked with new and recycled stretch knit fabric, largely recycled T-shirts by Gail Nichols. Photo by Gail Nichols.

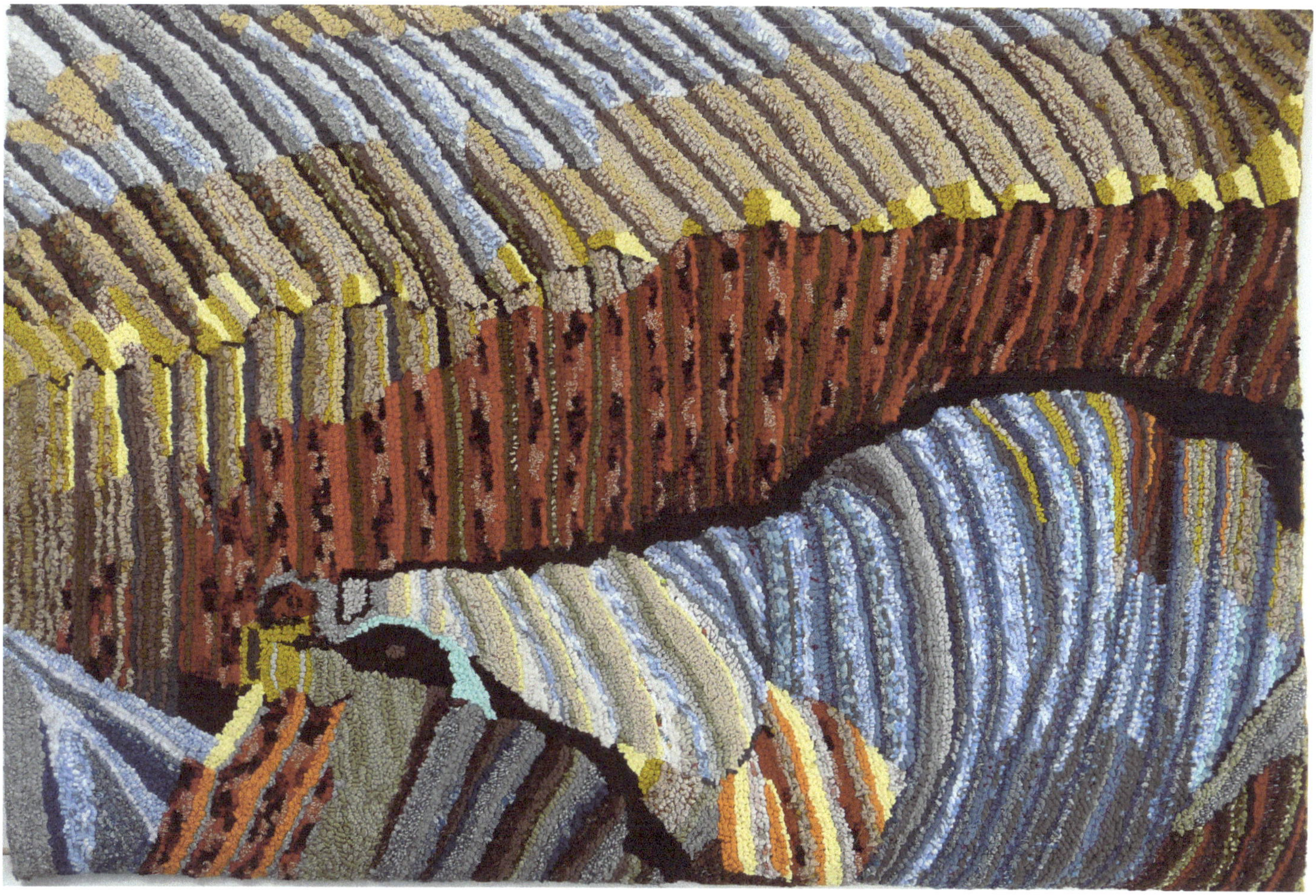

Bob's Creek Culvert, 37"x55" Designed and hooked with recycled stretch knit fabric, predominantly recycled T-shirts by Gail Nichols.

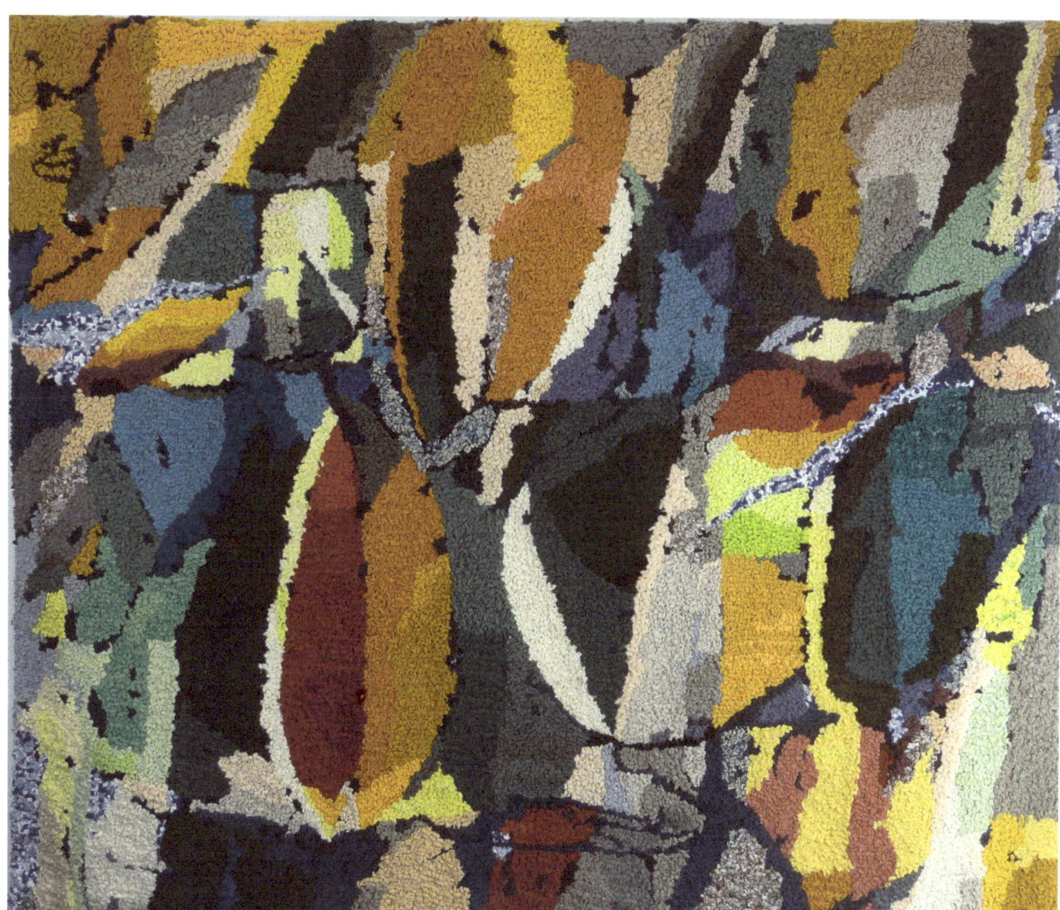

Autumn Leaves, 48.8"x56.6" Designed and hooked with new and recycled fabric, mostly stretch knits including recycled T-shirts by Gail Nichols.

Photos by Gail Nichols.

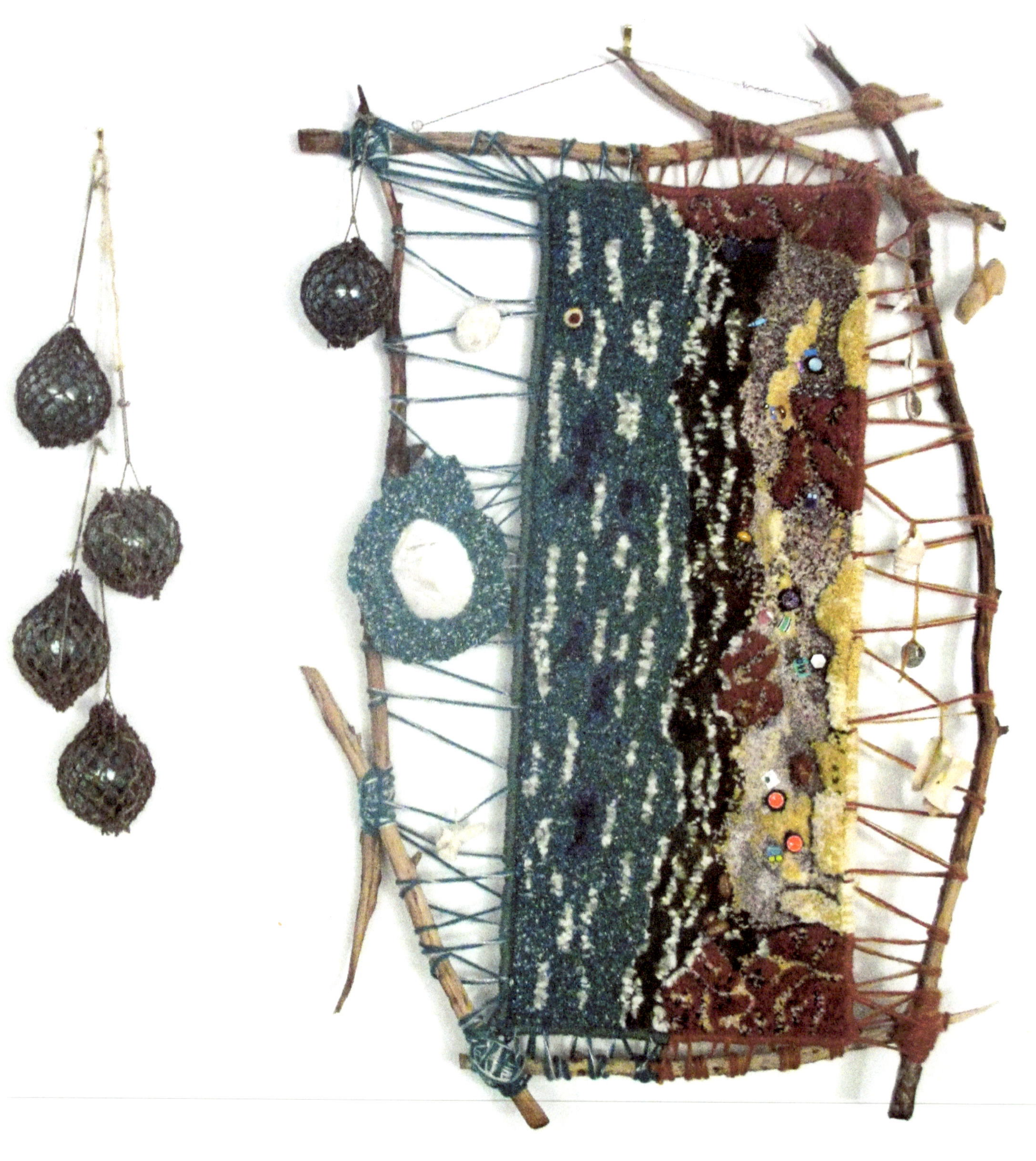

Migration, 16"x38" (hooked area) Designed and hooked with recycled wool blankets & knitting yarns, t-shirt cotton, and embellished by Judi Tompkins.
Photo by Judi Tompkins.

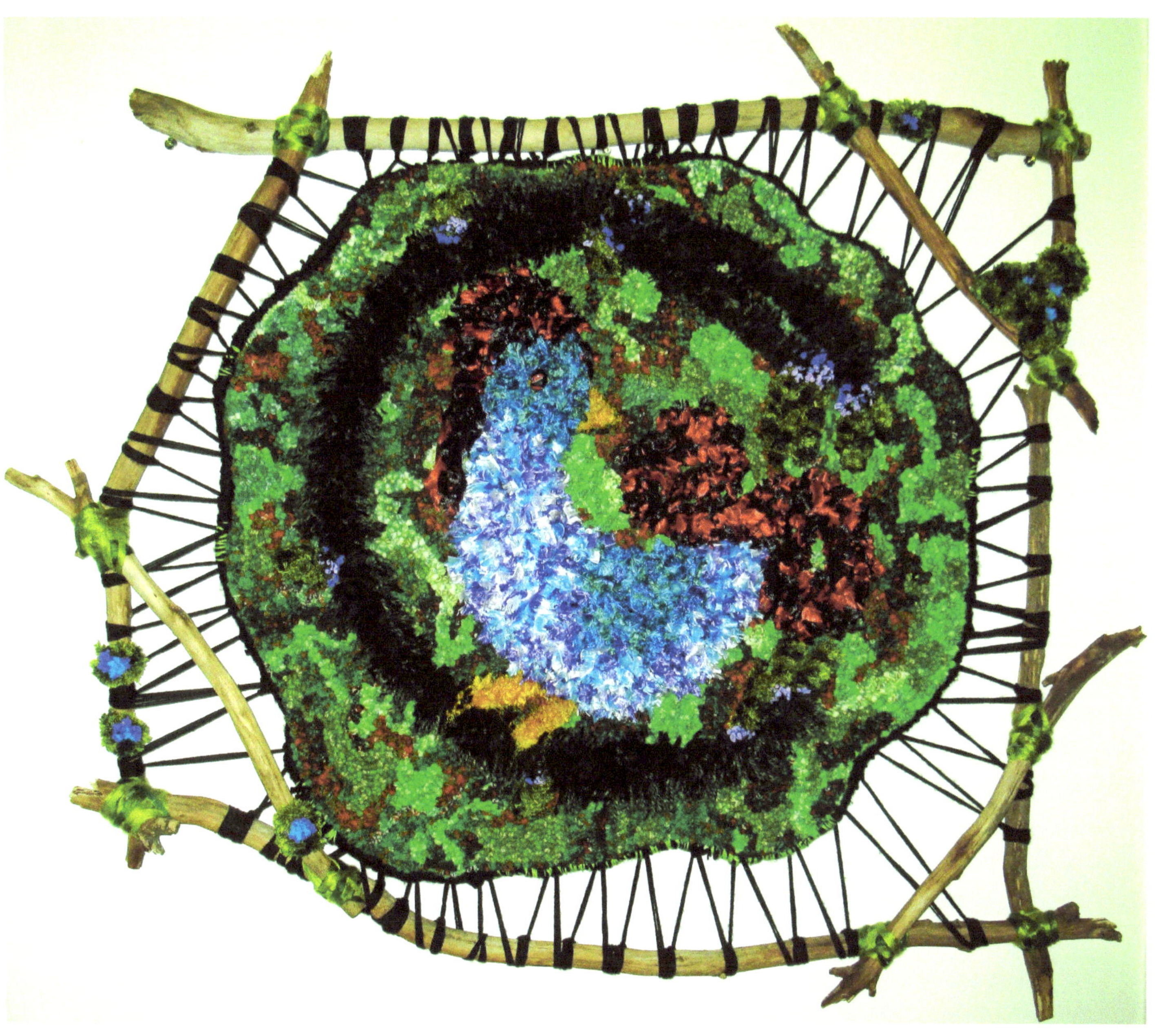

Pretty Bird, 31”x30” (hooked area) Designed and hooked with recycled wool blankets, Lycra, wool and novelty yarns by Judi Tompkins.
Photo by Judi Tompkins.

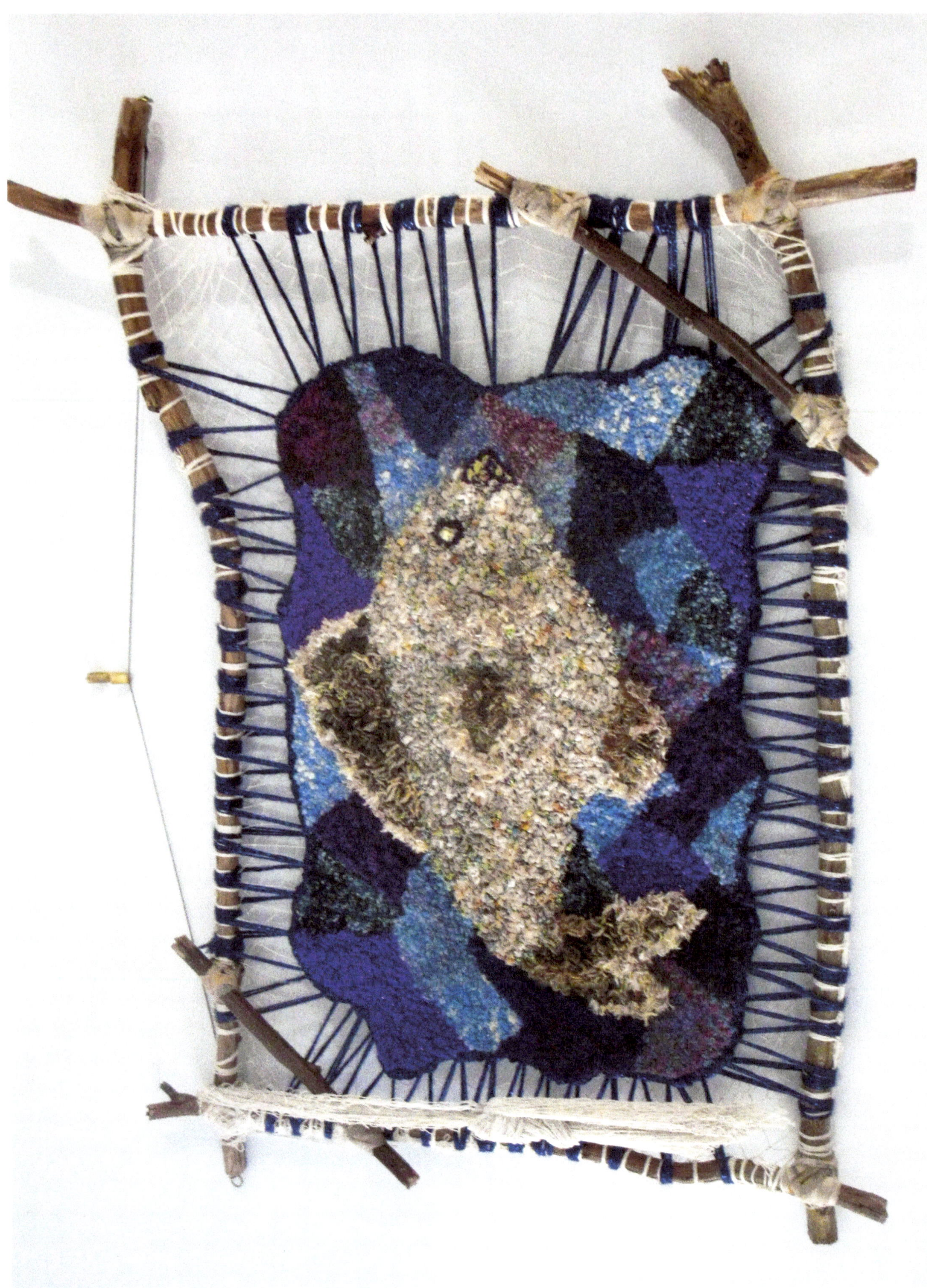

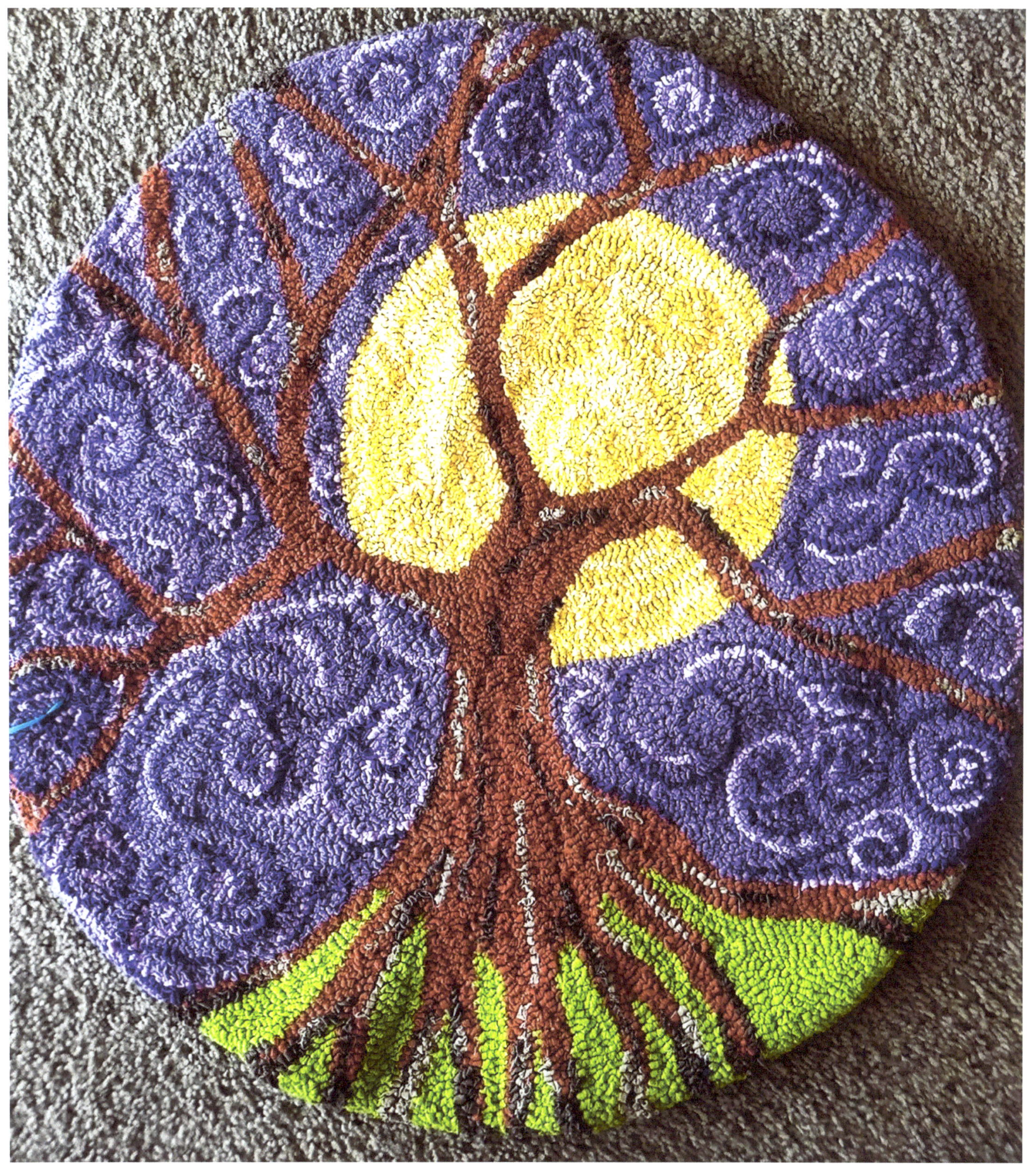

Tree of Life, 28" diameter Designed and hooked with T-shirts by Laura Salamy.
Photo by Laura Salamy.

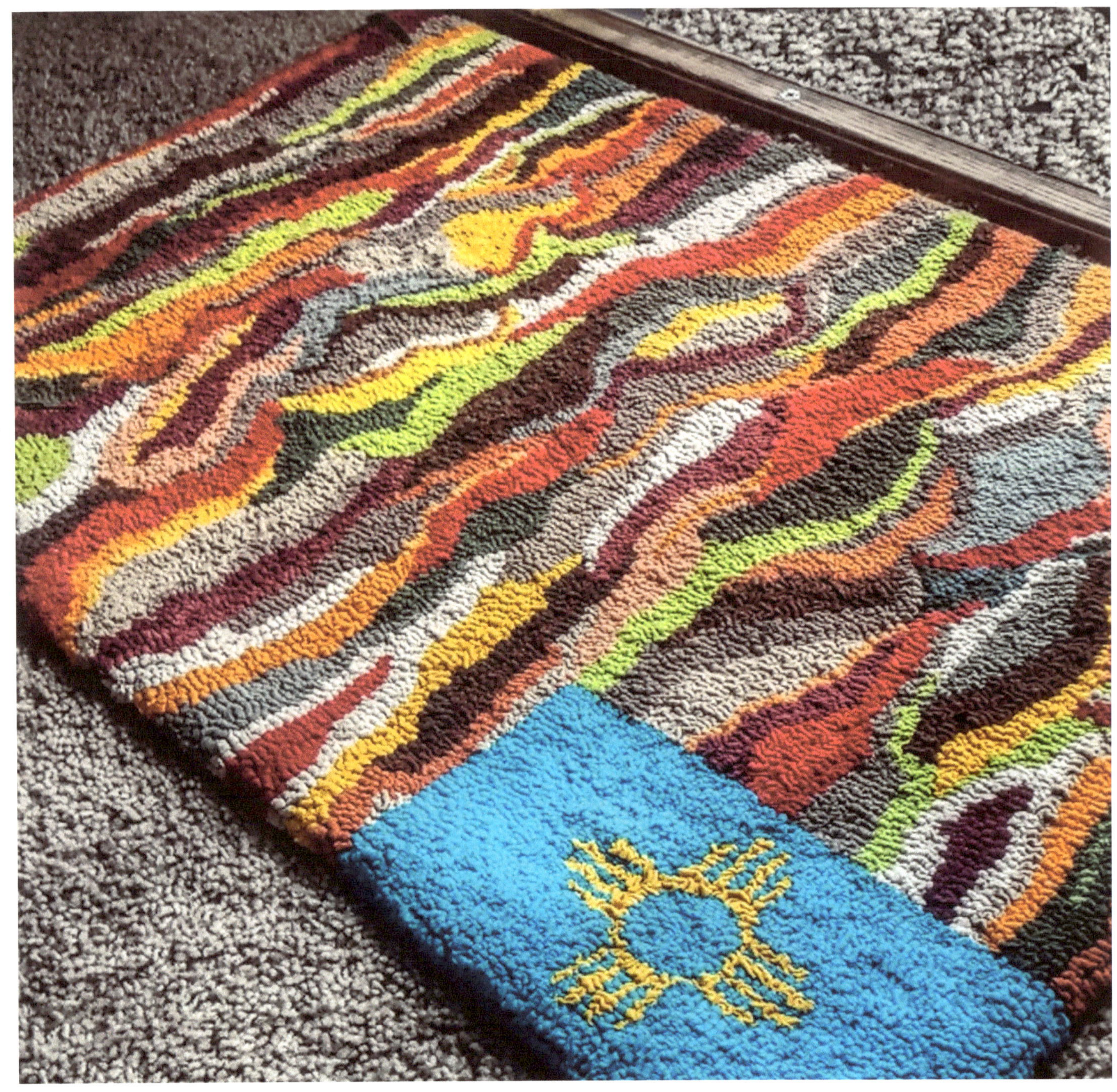

Welcome to New Mexico, 29.5”x20” Designed and hooked with T-shirts by Laura Salamy.
Photo by Laura Salamy.

Moveable Feast, 8 hooked cubes 4"x4" on each side.

Designed and hooked with wool and T-shirts by Judi Tompkins.

Photos by Judi Tompkins.

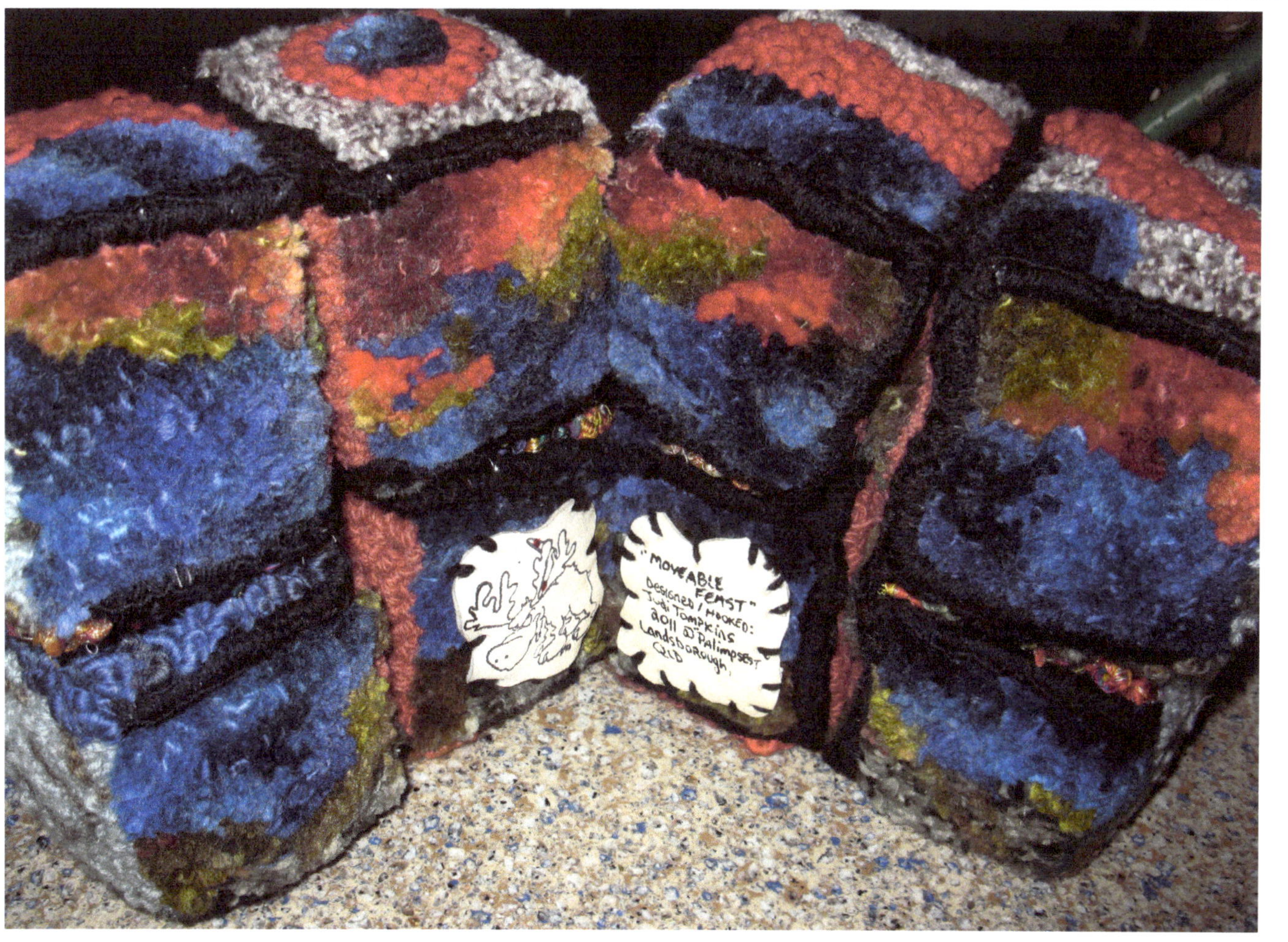

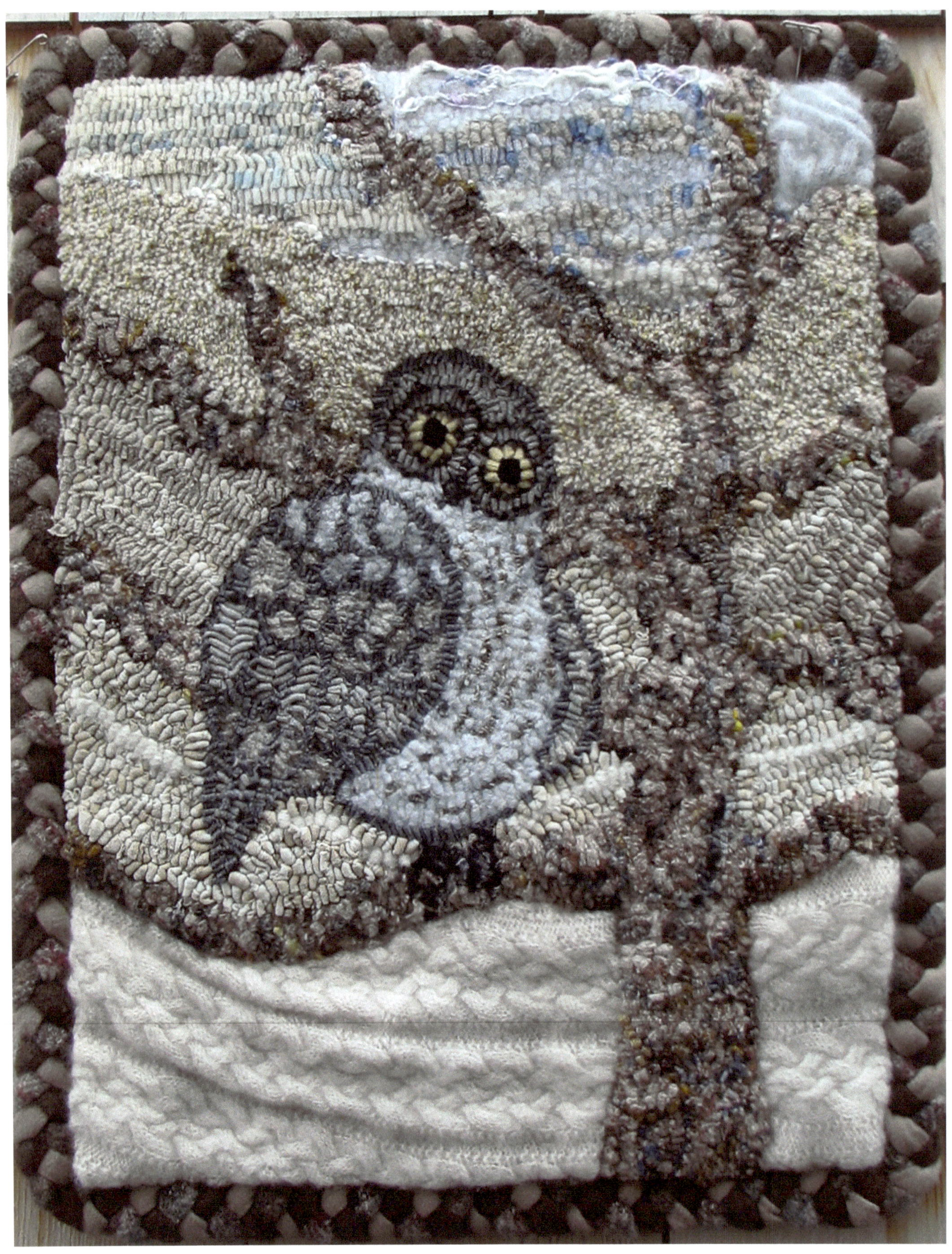

Passing Winter Storm in the Dunes, 17.5"x14" Designed by Wanda Kerr, hooked and embellished with woven wool, cut cashmere and wool sweaters, yarns, and knitted synthetic fibers by Jane Sittnick
Photo by Jane Sittnick

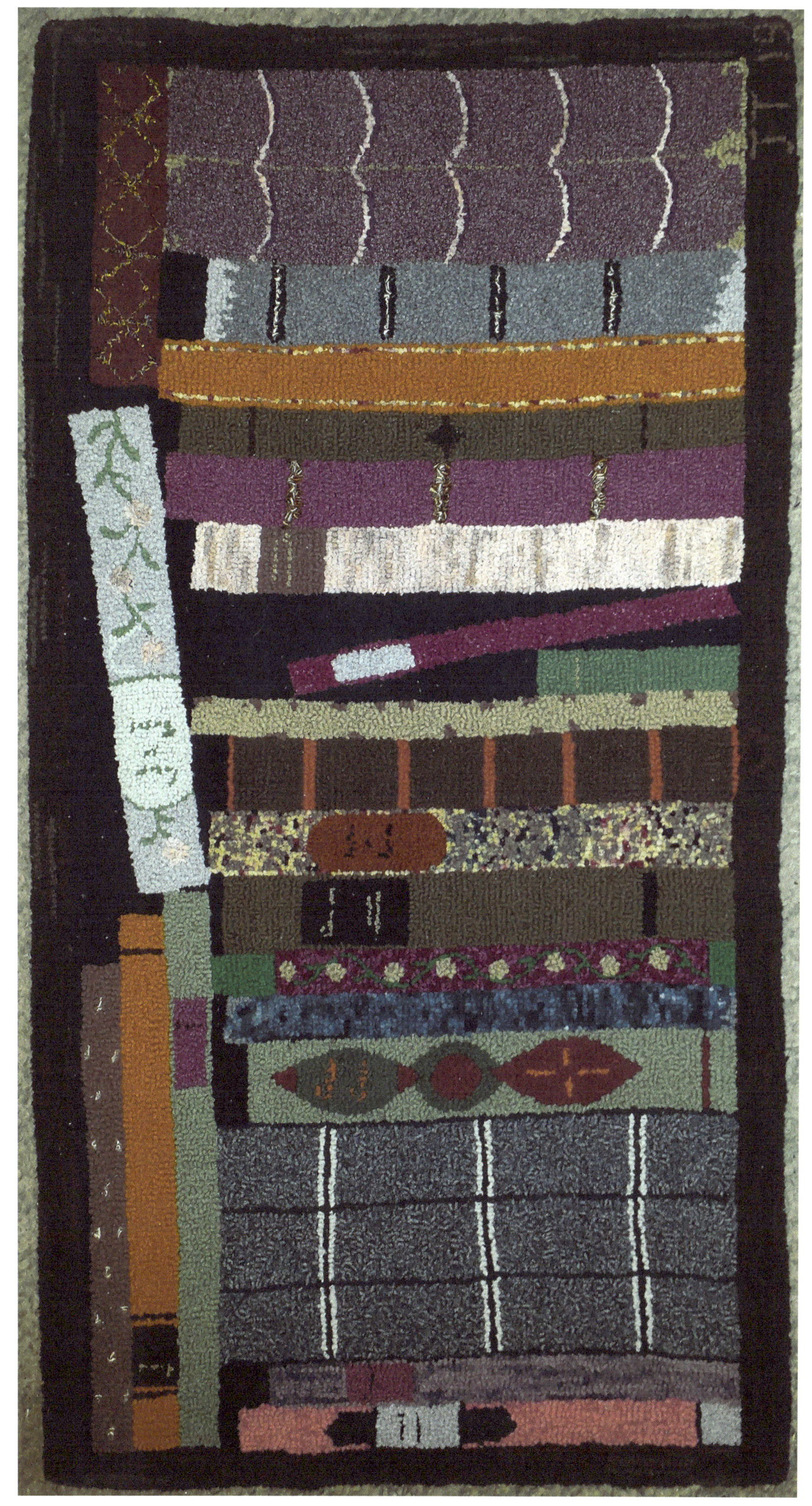

Old Books, 17"x32" Designed and hooked with T-shirts by Judy Taylor

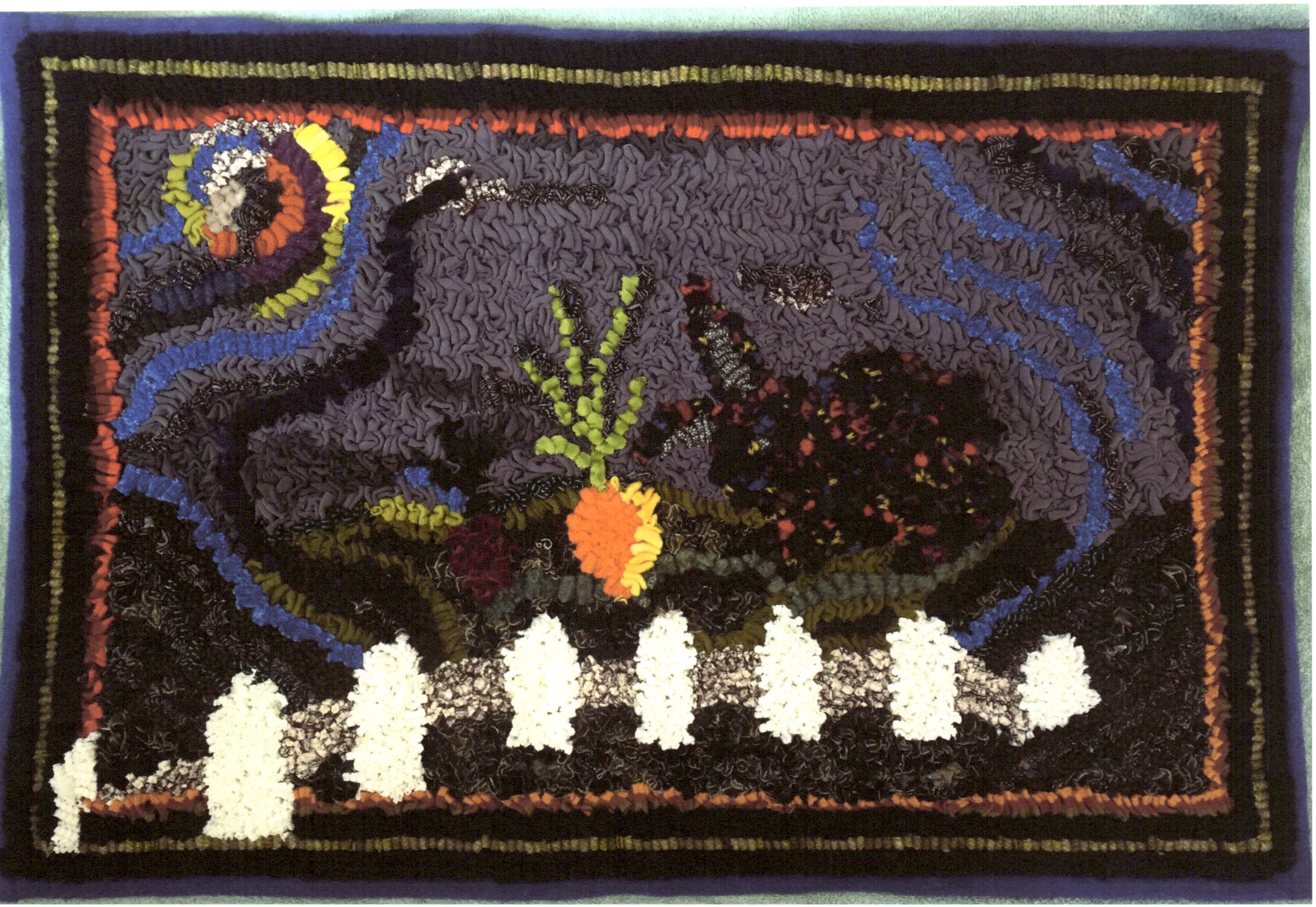

Midnight Bunny in the Garden of Eatin' 29"x20.5" Adapted from a pattern by Connie Hughes and hooked with T-shirts, felted sweaters, cut velvet stretchy pants, polyester blouses, velvet velours and knit metallic by Catherine Kelly

Making Your Own DeLovely Frame

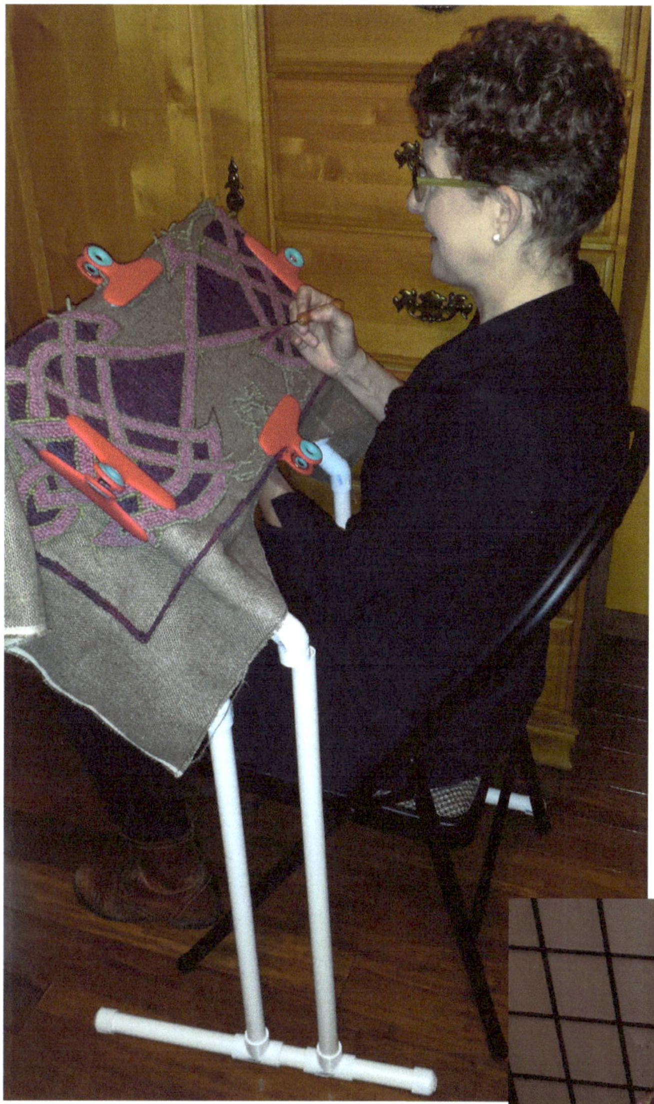

For many people, wrapping the rug around your legs is perfectly fine, but there are some limitations. You can't change position with the rug wrapped around your legs, and it can be proibitive to wrap yourself up with a rug in the hot weather! So it's great to know that you can make your own frame, specially designed for rug hooking.

This frame design will allow you to use it as a lap frame (for sitting on a couch) and a floor frame, for sitting in a folding chair. At the end of these instructions, you will see how you can also add a set of longer legs so you can rug hook standing up! If you're going to spend hours and hours at the craft, it's nice to know you can mix it up a bit, so you don't get stiff or uncomfortable.

Using common materials like PVC pipes, clamps and rubberized material (like you lay in your cupboards), you can easily make my DeLovely frame. Before you glue your cut pipes together, it's a good idea to slip them together to make sure it's a good fit for you. This way, if you want to adjust the length or width, you can customize the pipe lengths to suit you.

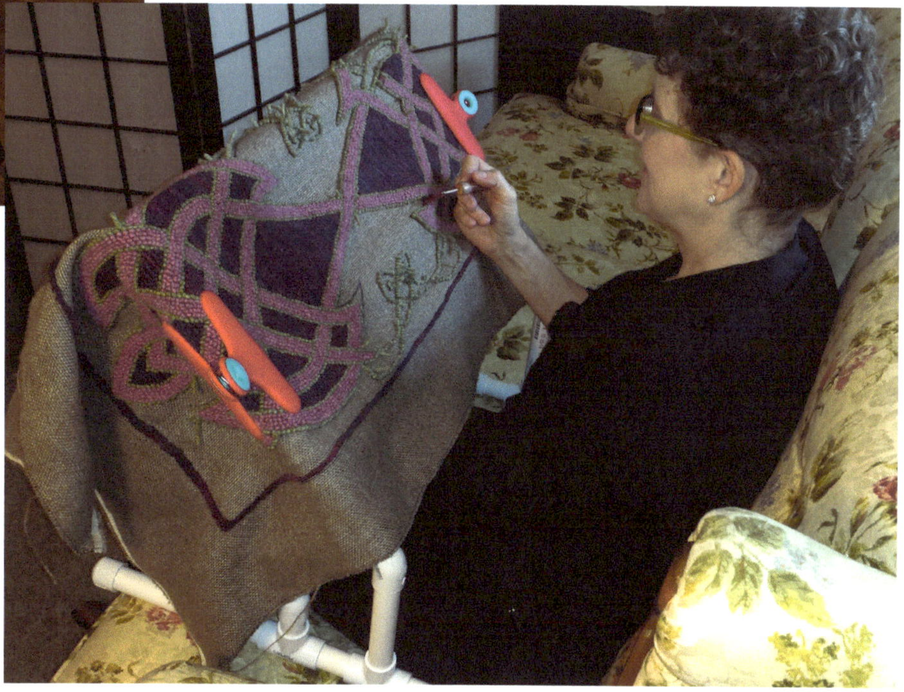

Floor frame (above), showing the use of an extra set of clamps.

Lap frame (right) shows me working with a single set of clamps. It's a matter of personal preference. I would suggest starting with one set, and add another if you find you like a tighter working surface.

These instructions are for you to make a frame for personal use, not for sale.

You will need:
(A) 3-10' long 3/4" PVC pipes, 200 PSI
(B) 4-3/4" Dia 45 degree PVC Sch 40 slip elbows
(C) 4-3/4" Dia 90 degree PVC Sch 40 side outlet elbows (slip)
(D) 12-3/4" Dia PVC Sch 40 tees (slip)
(E) 4-3/4" Dia PVC Sch 40 caps (slip)
(F) 2 (or 4) OXO Large Kitchen Clamps
(G) Goop Glue
(H) Rubber shelf liner, cut into 2-3.5"x7" and 2- 3.5"x18" pieces

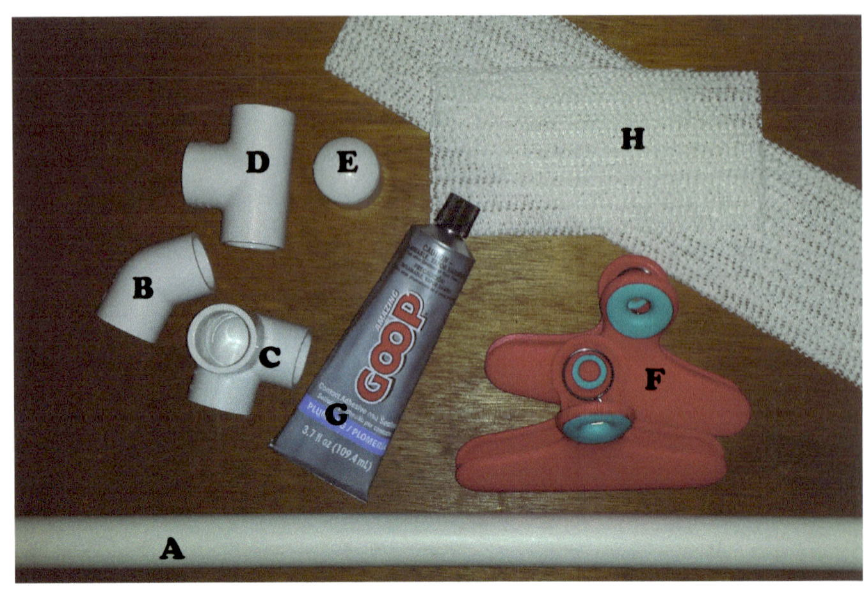

Cut your PVC pipes into the following lengths:

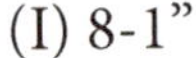

(I) 8-1"
(J) 2-1.5"
(K) 2-2.5"
(L) 6-4"
(M)2-5.5"
(N) 6-8"
(O) 4-20"
(P) 2-22.5"
(Q) 2-26.5"

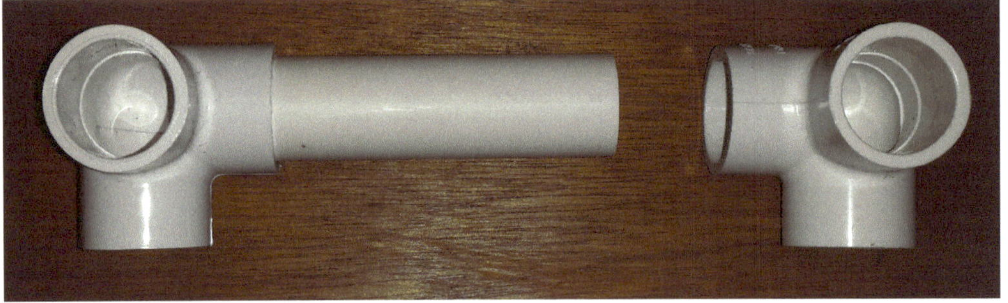

Step 1: Making the first side section. Using a toothpick, slather Goop glue into one end of (C) (the 3-way corner bits) and insert one 4" pipe. Put glue in another (C) and stick it on the other end.

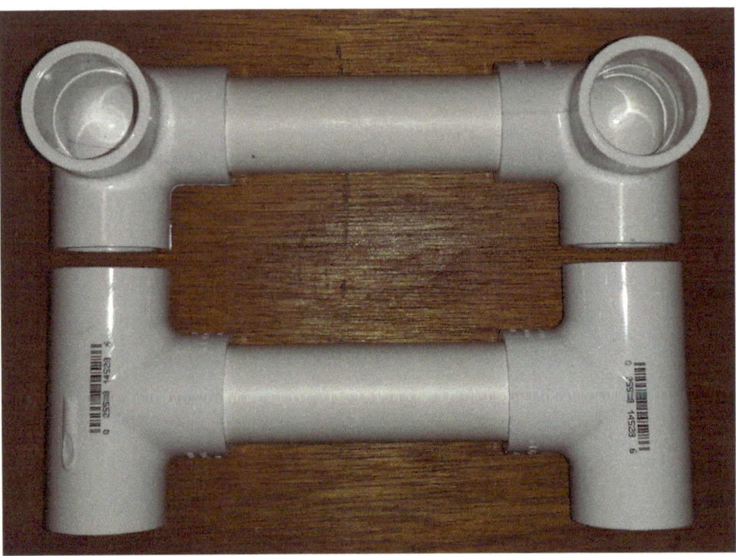

Step 2: Slather glue into the middle collar of a Tee (D) and insert one 4" pipe. Slather glue into the middle collar of another Tee and stick it onto the 4" pipe. Then line this section up so it is the same length as in Step 1. (Goop glue doesn't dry instantly, so you have a little time to adjust all of your angles, then when you've completed all the steps, you will let the frame dry for 24 hours.)

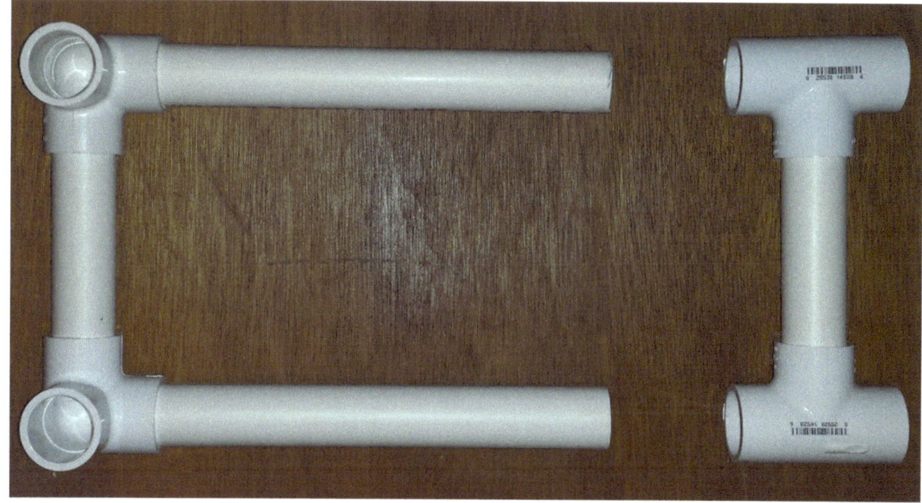

Step 3: Now the view is sideways, adding to the two pieces you made in Steps 1 and 2. Slather glue in the bottom of both (C) units, and insert an 8” pipe in each.

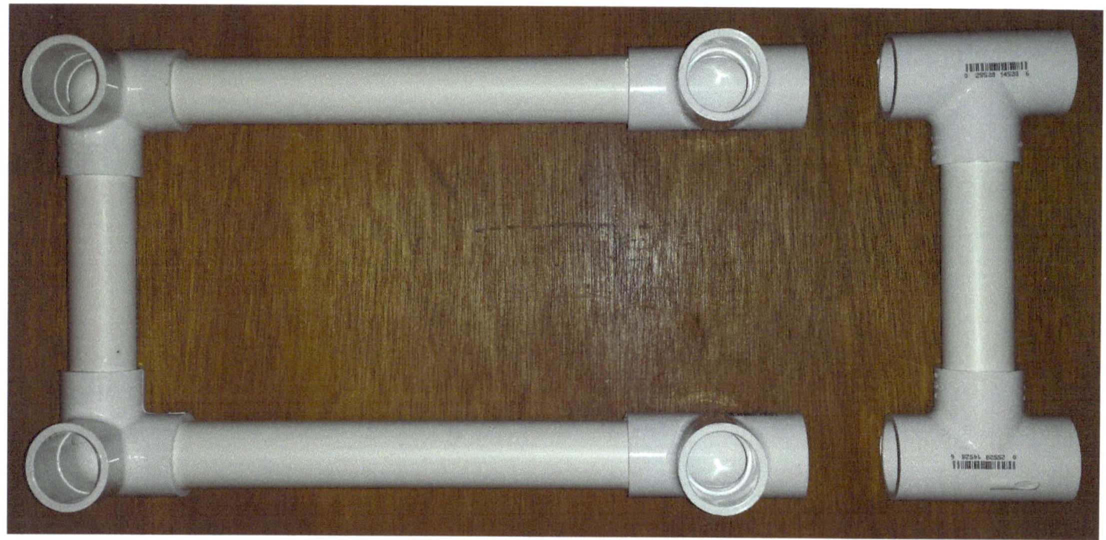

Step 4: Slather glue into the end of a Tee (D) and stick it on the 8” pipe. Repeat for the other 8” pipe. Line the middle collar holes of the Tees so they point up like the open C elbows on the top corners.

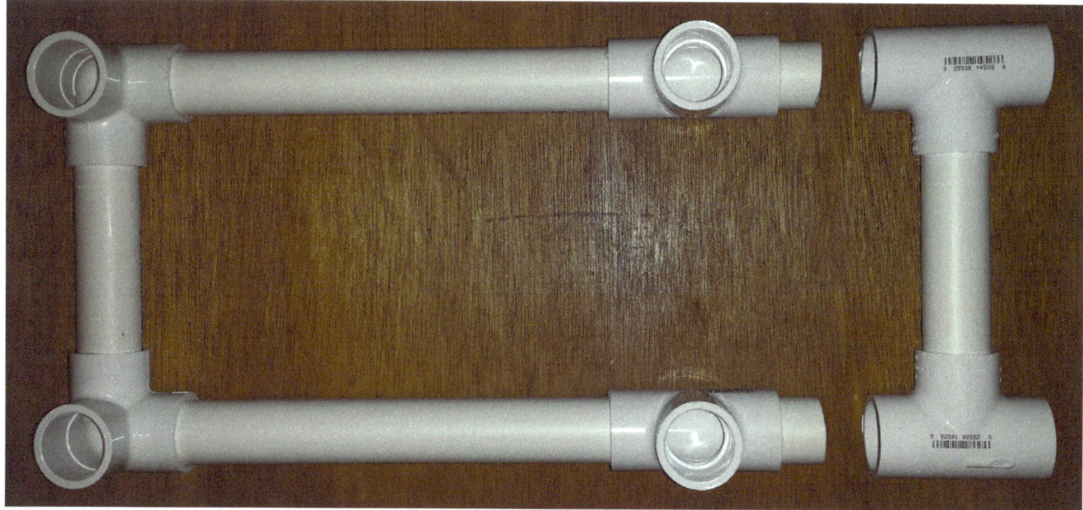

Step 5: Slather glue into the other end of the Tee in Step 4, and insert a 1” pipe. Repeat this for the other 8” pipe side.

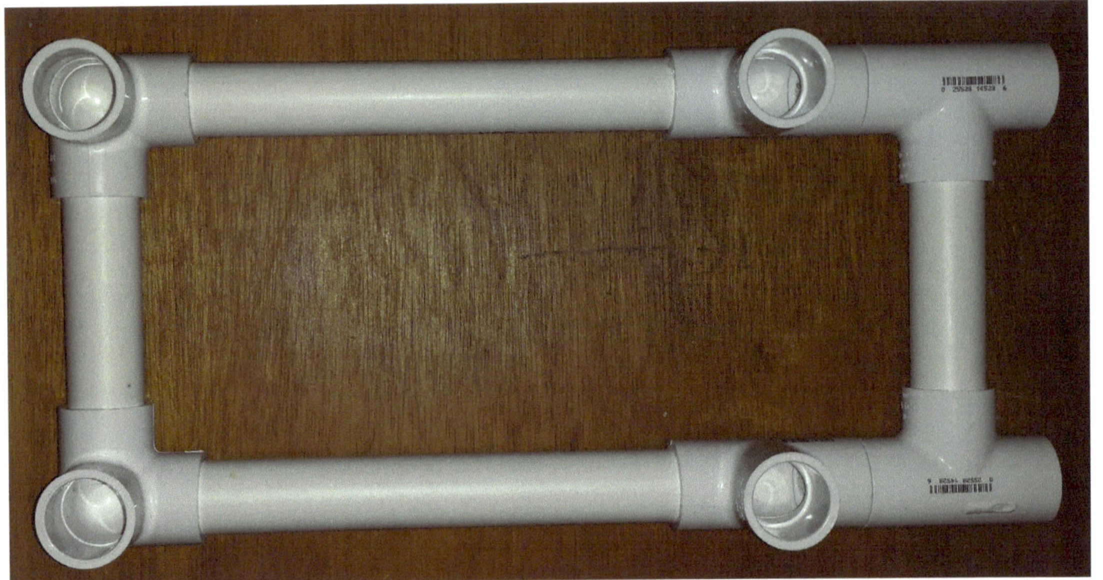

Step 6: Slather glue into the end of the Tee to connect the bottom of the side section to the top. Repeat this for the other Tee on the bottom. Repeat Steps 1-6 to create the other side section.

Step 7: Lay the side sections together (but do *not* glue), and adjust the angles so the openings line up and everything seems square.

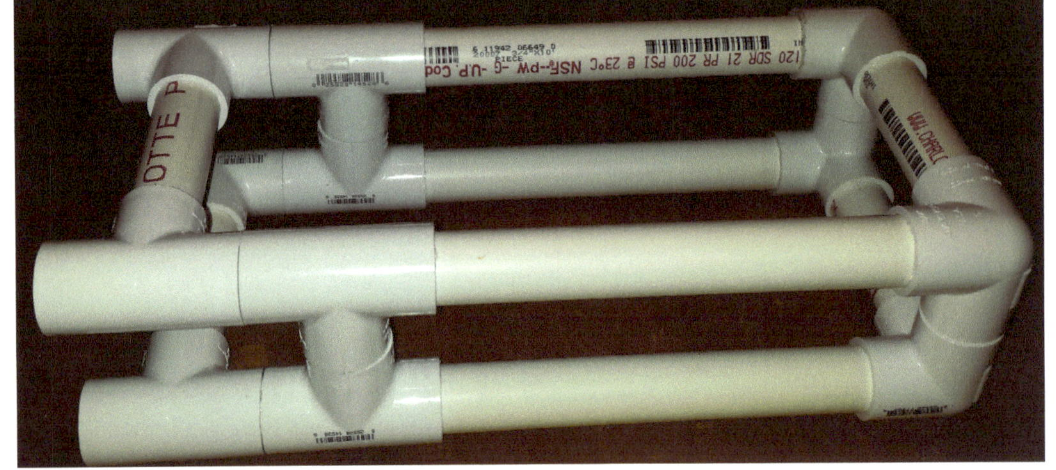

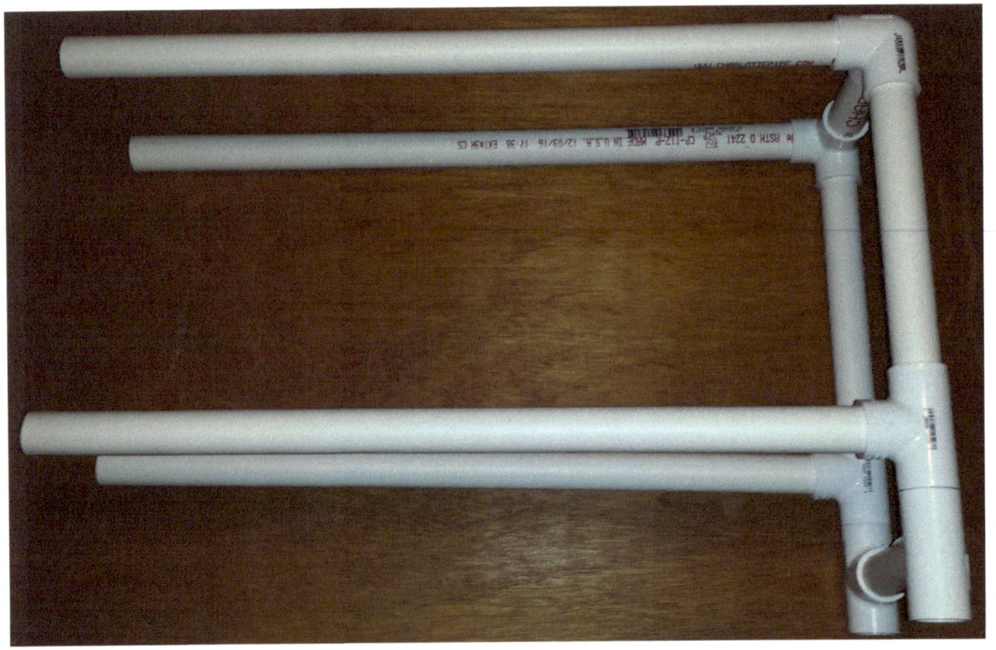

Step 8: Insert your cross-bars (20" pipe) into one of the side sections. NOTE: DO NOT GLUE THE CROSS-BARS. Just slip them into place. This way, the frame is collapsible and can fit into your rug hooking bag.

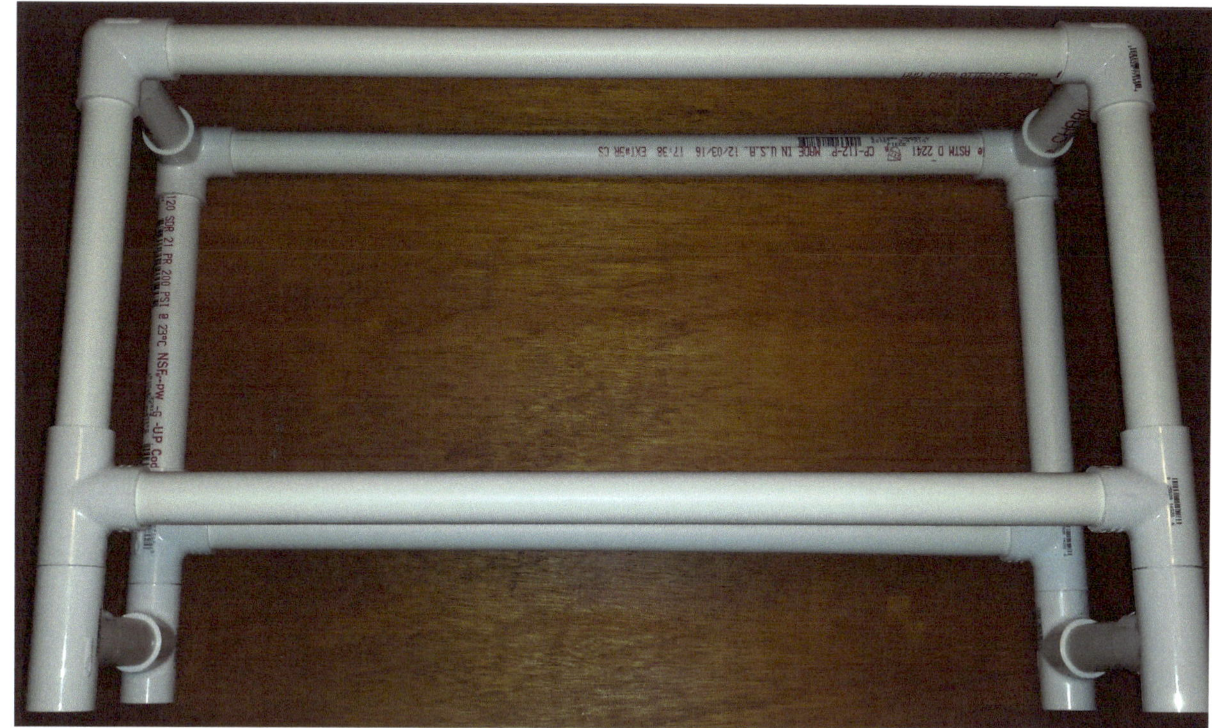

Step 9: Slip the other side section onto the other end of the cross-bars. Flip the frame so the open Tees are on the top.

Step 10: Slather glue into one of the open Tees and insert a 1” pipe. Repeat this for the other three open Tees. (In the photo on the right, the Tee in front has the 1” pipe, the one in the back doesn’t.)

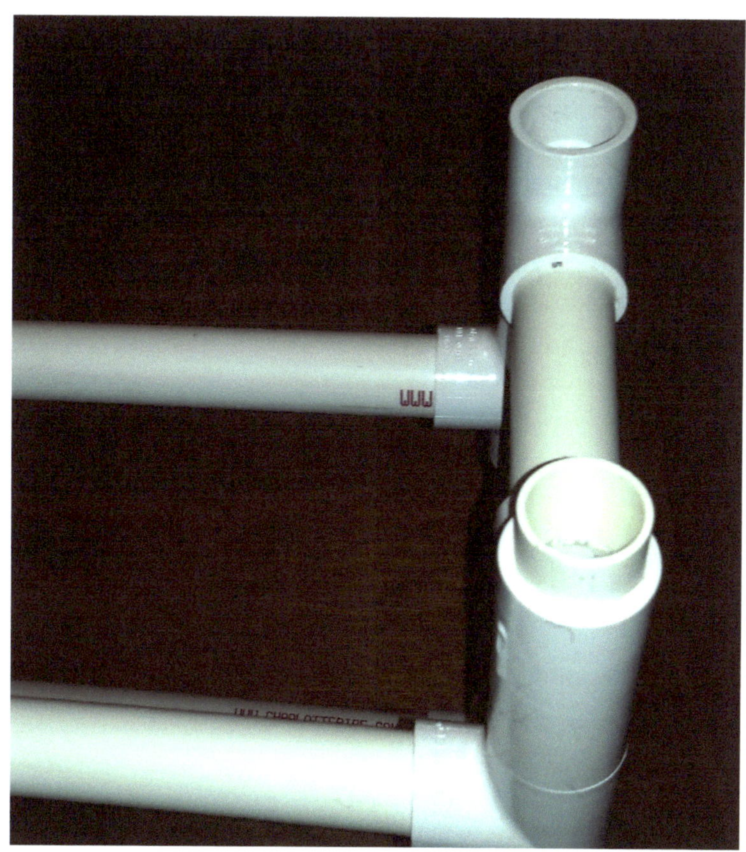

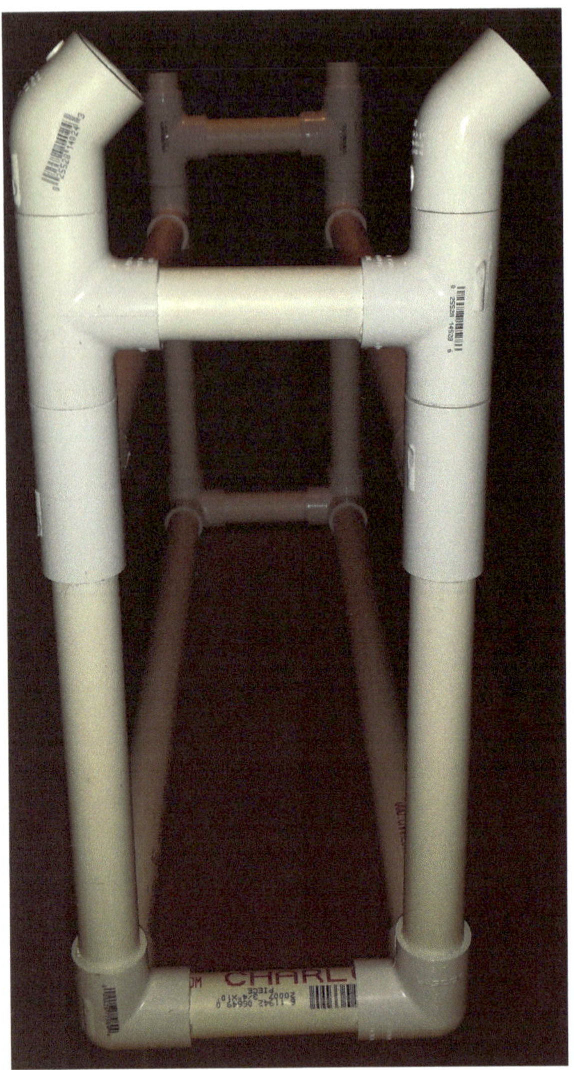

Step 11: Slather glue into one of the 45 degree elbows and put it onto one of the 1" pipes, facing toward the back. Repeat this step for the other three 1" pipes, facing all the elbows toward the back. (In the photo to the left, two of the elbows in the foreground have been added, in the back of the picture, you see the 1" pipes where the elbows will be added next.)

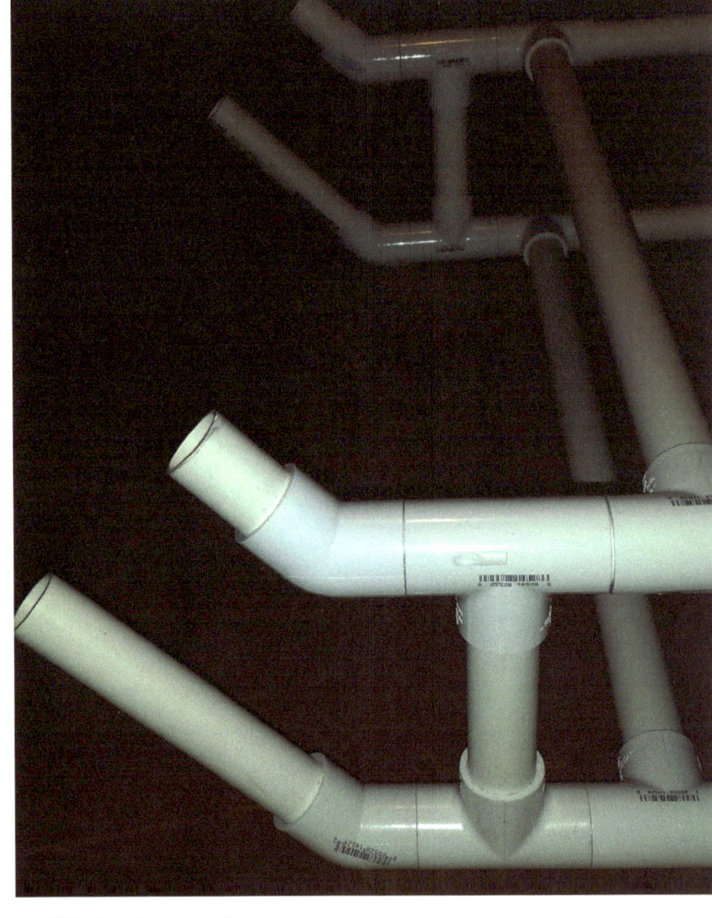

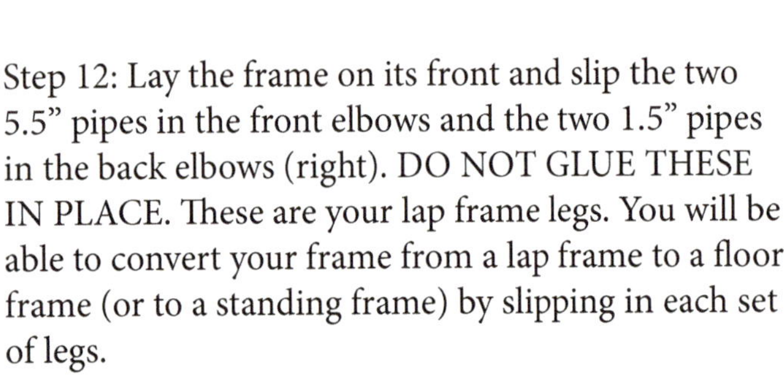

Step 12: Lay the frame on its front and slip the two 5.5" pipes in the front elbows and the two 1.5" pipes in the back elbows (right). DO NOT GLUE THESE IN PLACE. These are your lap frame legs. You will be able to convert your frame from a lap frame to a floor frame (or to a standing frame) by slipping in each set of legs.

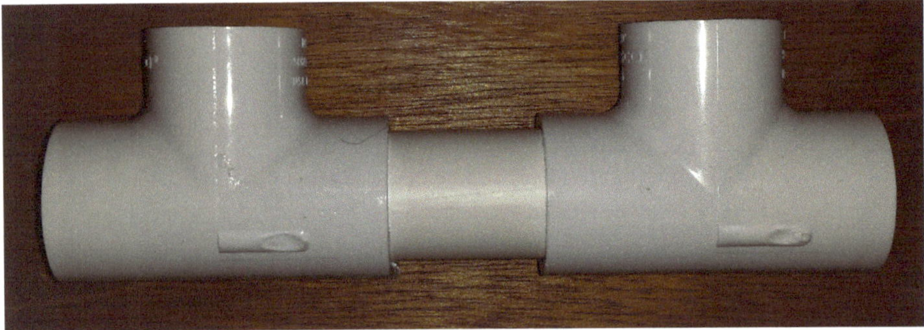

Step 13: Making the feet. Slather glue into one of the ends of a Tee, and insert a 2.5" pipe. Repeat for the other Tee and connect to the 2.5" pipe.

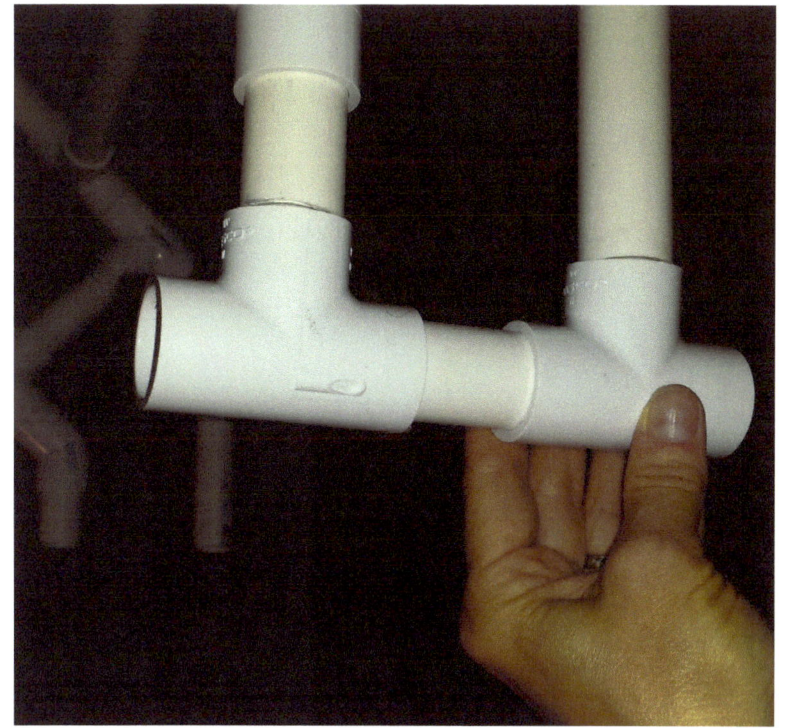

Step 14: Hold the piece you made in Step 13 up to the lap frame legs, and adjust the length so the Tee's middle collar holes line up with the legs.

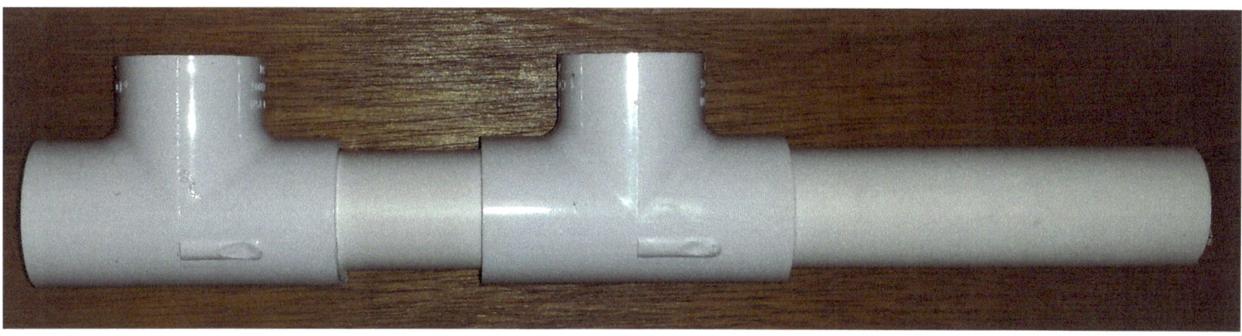

Step 15: Slather glue into one of the Tee ends, and insert a 4" pipe.

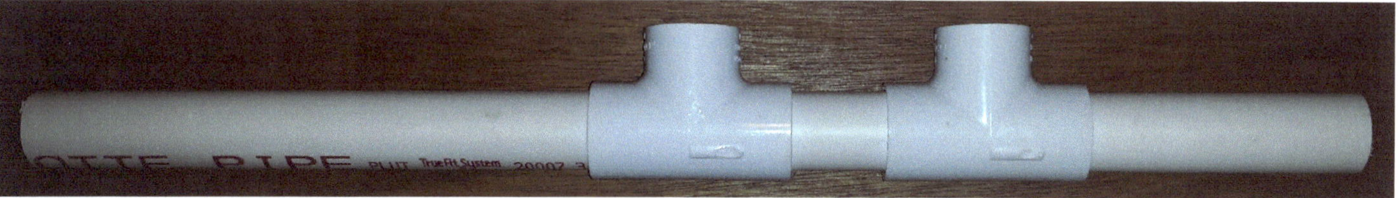

Step 16: Slather glue into the other Tee end, and insert an 8" pipe.

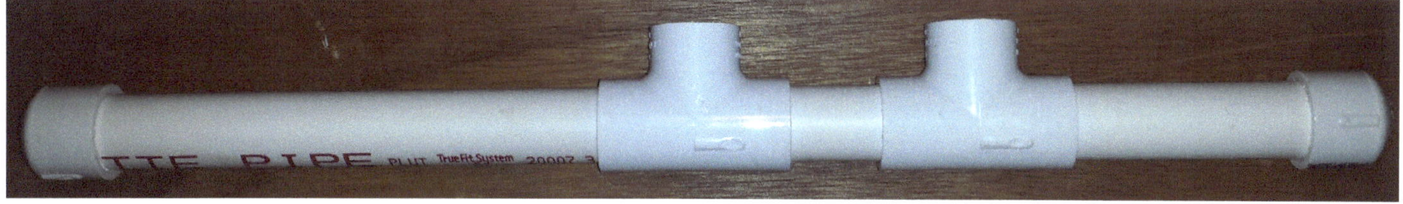

Step 17: Slather glue into one of the end caps and insert the 4" pipe. Repeat for the 8" pipe. Repeat Steps 13-17 to create the other foot section.

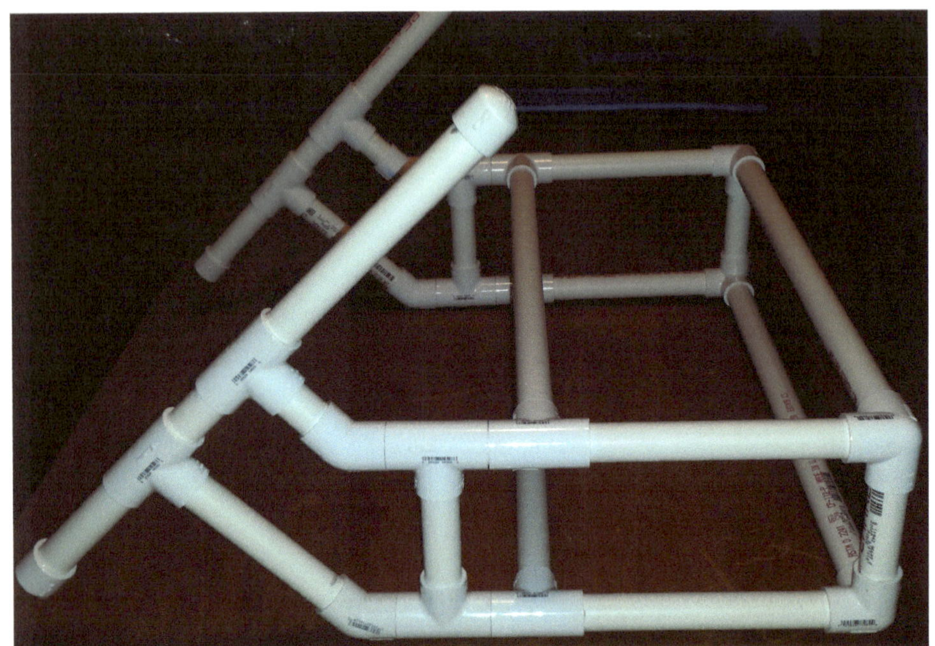

Step 18: Slip the feet onto the lap frame legs, with the shorter section (4" pipe) toward the front (left). DO NOT GLUE.

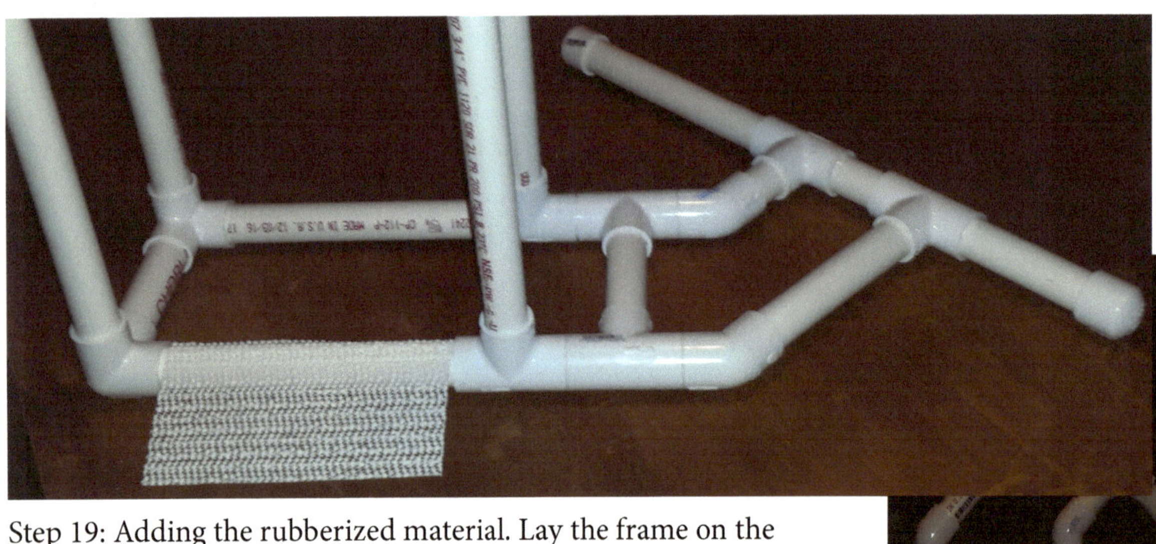

Step 19: Adding the rubberized material. Lay the frame on the side. Slather glue along one of the 8" pipes. Lay the material on the glue, and turn the frame to add more glue all around the pipe, and wrap the rubberized material around (above). This is a good time to check that the legs and feet are lying nicely flat on the table, so everything dries square. Repeat this step for the other 8" pipe on the front side of the frame.

Step 20: Lay the frame on its top. Slather glue on the 20" cross-bar in the front (the same side as the 8" pipe with the rubberized material). Lay the rubberized material on the pipe, then turn the frame so you can slather glue all around the pipe (right). Wrap the rubberized material around.

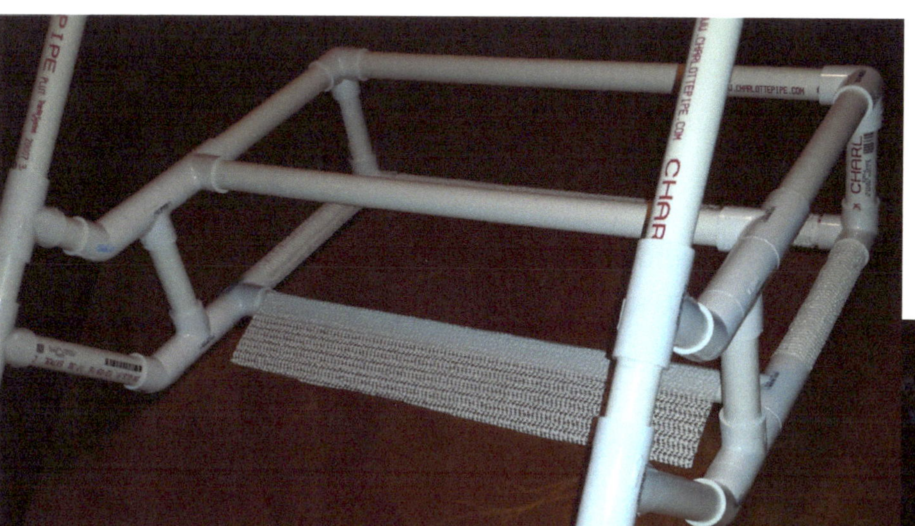

Step 21: Lay the frame on its front. Slather glue on the bottom 20" cross-bar. Lay the rubberized material over the glue. Turn the frame so you can slather glue all around the pipe (left). Wrap the rubberized material all around.

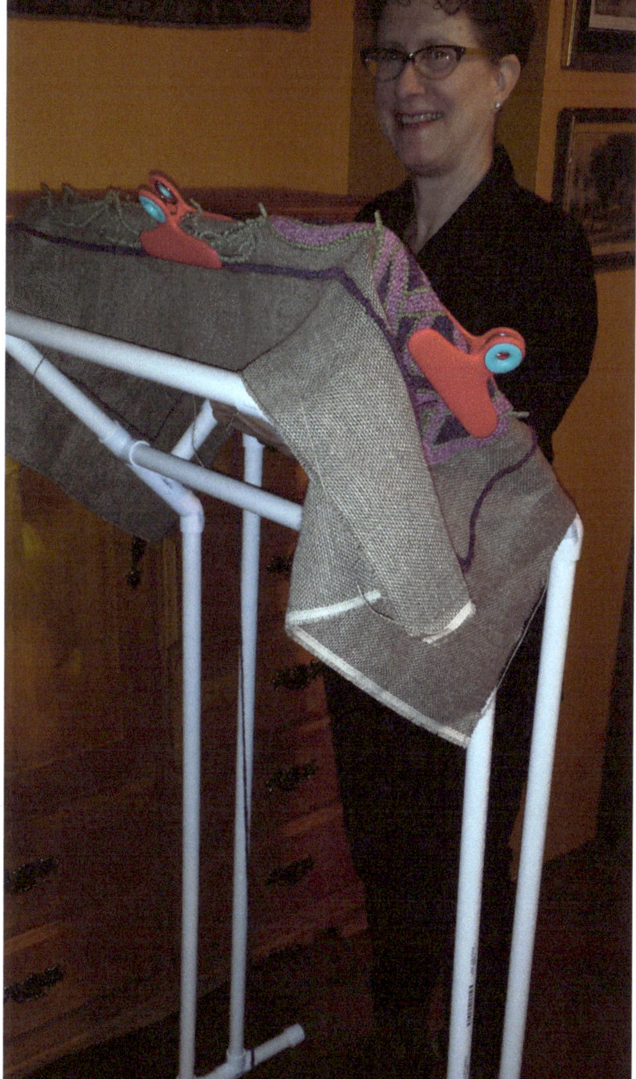

Let the frame dry in this configuration (above). This is a good time to check once again that all of your angles are correct and the frame looks square.

It's totally optional, but it's a really good idea to cut longer legs for a standing frame. Rug hooking is a sedentary activity, and sometimes it's good to get up off that chair. If you want to do this, you can cut a longer set of legs. I am 5'5", so for my height, I cut two 43.25" pipes for the front and two 39.75" pipes for the back. I especially appreciate this option when I'm in my booth at a show, rug hooking for 8-10 hours a day.

To change the legs from the lap frame to the floor frame (or the standing frame), you don't need to remove the rug. Just lay the frame face down and pull out the current legs, slip in the new ones, and stick the feet on.

One of the nice things about this frame design is that it holds the rug so it's facing you, avoiding neck strain from looking down at your lap for long periods.

To begin hooking on the frame, lay the backing over it (design side up) and clamp down one side. Then tug the backing over the other side and clamp it.

Phew! You did it!

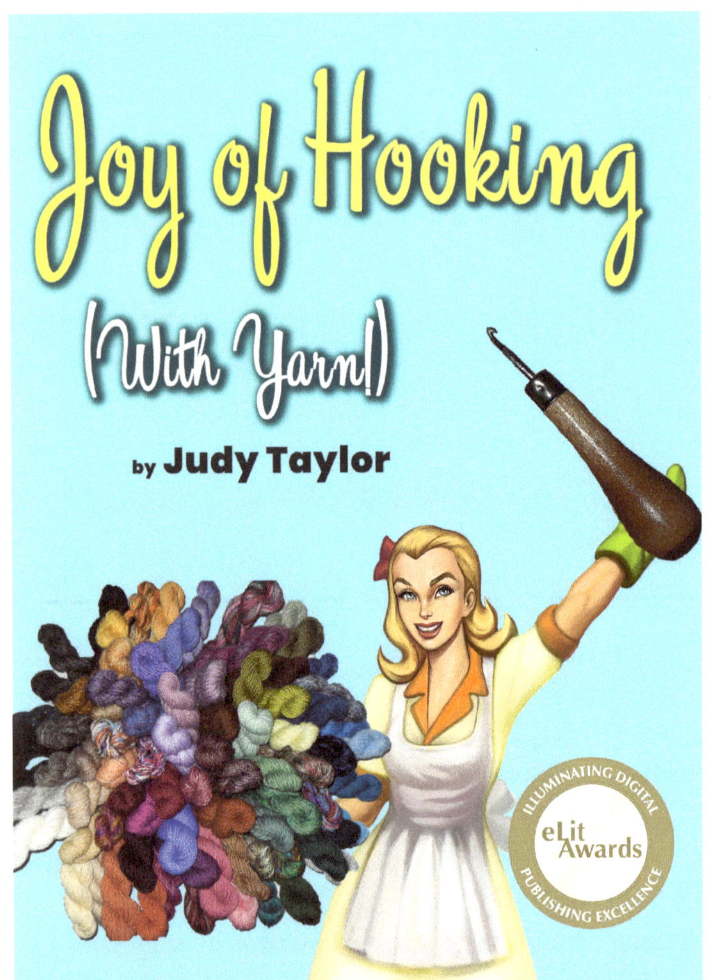

Joy of Hooking (With Yarn!)

This is the perfect beginner's book. You will learn all the basics to this delightful craft, including what yarns work best for rug hooking, which backing to choose, how to transfer your designs to the backing, step-by-step hooking instructions, cleaning and caring for your hooked treasures, and so much more. The book includes our award-winning DVD and 4 easy projects for you to practice your skills. With hundreds of photos from dozens of yarn-hookers, you will be inspired to create your own hand-hooked rugs with yarn.

$34.95

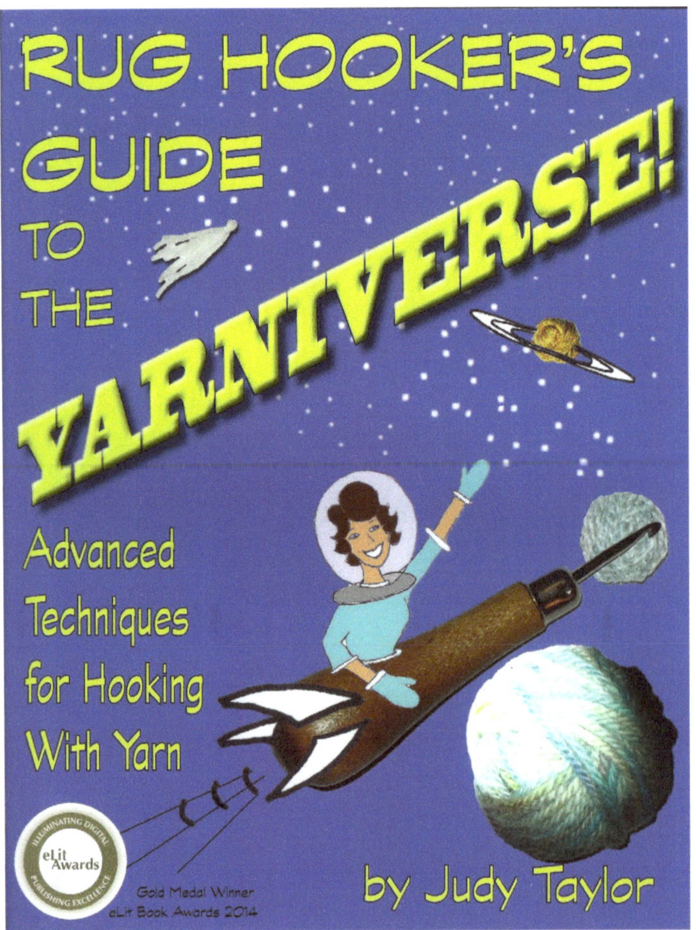

Rug Hooker's Guide to the YARNIVERSE!

This book takes you beyond the basics of hooking with yarn. You'll learn how to create realistic shading, how to hook primitive designs, incorporating fine detail in your rugs, the wonders of natural colors, how to repair old rugs, the magic of overdyeing, with dozens of templates for you to try your new found skills.

$24.95

To order these books, or to browse the supplies, patterns, kits and finished rugs, visit https://www.littlehouserugs.com

NOTES

CPSIA information can be obtained
at www.ICGtesting.com
Printed in the USA
BVHW021401151019
561108BV00001B/1/P

9780997671209